EU INTERNAL MARKET LAW

The College of Law ✕
of England and Wales

London • Sydney • Portland, Oregon

EU INTERNAL MARKET LAW

Second Edition

Gareth Davies

Lecturer in European Law
The University of Groningen, The Netherlands

Cavendish
Publishing
Limited

London • Sydney • Portland, Oregon

Second edition first published in Great Britain 2003 by
Cavendish Publishing Limited, The Glass House,
Wharton Street, London WC1X 9PX, United Kingdom
Telephone: + 44 (0)20 7278 8000   Facsimile: + 44 (0)20 7278 8080
Email: info@cavendishpublishing.com
Website: www.cavendishpublishing.com

Published in the United States by Cavendish Publishing
c/o International Specialized Book Services,
5824 NE Hassalo Street, Portland,
Oregon 97213-3644, USA

Published in Australia by Cavendish Publishing (Australia) Pty Ltd
45 Beach Street, Coogee, NSW 2034, Australia
Telephone: + 61 (2)9664 0909   Facsimile: + 61 (2)9664 5420
Email: info@cavendishpublishing.com.au
Website: www.cavendishpublishing.com.au

© Davies, Gareth	2003
First edition	2002
Second edition	2003

British Library Cataloguing in Publication Data
Davies, Gareth
European Union internal market law – 2nd ed
1 European Union 2 Foreign trade regulation – European Union countries
I Title 341.7'54

Library of Congress Cataloguing in Publication Data
Data available

ISBN 1-85941-878-3

1 3 5 7 9 10 8 6 4 2

Printed and bound in Great Britain

CONTENTS

Table of Cases   *ix*

Table of Treaty Articles   *xxiii*

Table of Community Acts and Secondary Legislation   *xxv*

1   INTRODUCTION   **1**

   1.1   Introduction to the internal market   1

   1.2   Note on terminology   2

   1.3   Note on Treaty numbering   3

2   THE FREE MOVEMENT OF GOODS: TAXES AND DUTIES   **5**

   2.1   Customs duties   5

   2.2   Discriminatory taxation   12

3   THE FREE MOVEMENT OF GOODS: QUANTITATIVE RESTRICTIONS   **19**

   3.1   What is a quantitative restriction?   19

   3.2   What is a measure?   19

   3.3   Public and private measures   20

   3.4   Article 28   20

   3.5   Article 29   37

4   THE FREE MOVEMENT OF PERSONS   **41**

   4.1   Workers   41

   4.2   Establishment   58

   4.3   Students   65

   4.4   Citizens   66

5   THE FREE MOVEMENT OF SERVICES   **75**

   5.1   What are services?   75

   5.2   The three service situations   79

   5.3   The particular problems of services   84

6	**THE FREE MOVEMENT OF CAPITAL**	**89**
6.1	The development of capital movement	89
6.2	The future of capital movement	92
6.3	Note on economic and monetary policy	94
7	**EXCEPTIONS TO FREE MOVEMENT**	**99**
7.1	The exception articles	99
7.2	Distinguishing Treaty exceptions from objective justifications	101
7.3	Interpretation of Treaty exceptions	102
7.4	The public service exception	115
8	**COMMON PRINCIPLES: DISCRIMINATION AND MARKET ACCESS**	**117**
8.1	Discrimination	117
8.2	Market access	127
8.3	Convergence: freedoms united?	130
8.4	Conclusion	133
9	**COMPETITION AND THE INTERNAL MARKET**	**135**
9.1	Competition law and free movement law	135
9.2	The influence of competition ideas	138
10	**THE PROCESS OF HARMONISATION**	**145**
10.1	What is harmonisation?	145
10.2	The old and new approaches to harmonisation	147
10.3	The legal base	150
10.4	The effect of harmonisation	153
10.5	The relationship between judicial and legislative harmonisation	154
10.6	Examples of harmonisation: recognition of qualifications	155
10.7	Examples of harmonisation: e-commerce	158

11 THE WHOLLY INTERNAL SITUATION   **163**

   11.1   Facts within the scope of community law   164

   11.2   Reverse discrimination and 'normal' discrimination   169

   11.3   Abstract questions   172

12 PRIVATE ACTORS   **175**

   12.1   Should private actors be bound?   175

   12.2   Applying free movement law to private actors   176

13 INTELLECTUAL PROPERTY   **185**

   13.1   What is intellectual property?   185

   13.2   IP rights in Europe   185

   13.3   IP rights and free movement   186

   13.4   Existence and exercise of rights   187

   13.5   Using IP rights   188

   13.6   Exhaustion of rights   189

   13.7   Copyright   193

   13.8   Note on economics   194

14 SOCIAL ISSUES OF INTERNAL MARKET LAW   **197**

   14.1   Human rights in the internal market   197

   14.2   Third country nationals in the internal market   205

   14.3   The internal market and the welfare state   210

Further Reading and Bibliography   217

Index   221

TABLE OF CASES

Well known cases are often referred to just by the name of one party, or by the subject matter of the case (eg German Beer). These short, user-friendly names have been used in the text. They will also have an official name under which they appear in the European Court Reports. Cases are listed below under their informal name, and when this is significantly different, under their official name as well.

To find the text of a case the most important piece of data is the case number, which enables the judgment and other documents to be found on CD-ROMs or the Europa website (www.europa.eu.int). Remember to use the C- or T- prefixes for Court of Justice or Court of First Instance judgments respectively only if they date from 1990 or later.

ASBL Vereniging van Vlaamse Reisbureaus v ASBL Sociale
    Dienst van de Plaatselijke en Gewestelijke
    Overheidsdiensten, Case 311/85 [1987] ECR 3801 180
Adoui and Cornuaille (Rezguia Adoui v Belgian State
    and City of Liège; Dominique Cornuaille v Belgian State),
    Joined Cases 115 and 116/81 [1982] ECR 1665 108
Alpine Investments BV v Minister van Financiën,
    Case C-384/93 [1995] ECR I-1141 .... 84–86, 129, 130
American Home Products (Centrafarm BV v American Home
    Products Corporation), Case 3/78 [1978] ECR 1823 192
Angonese v Cassa di Risparmio di Bolzano SpA,
    Case C-281/98 [2000] ECR I-4139 .... 180–82, 184
Antonissen v Commission of the European Communities and
    Council of the European Union,
    Case C-393/96 [1997] ECR I-0441 .... 45, 54
Apple and Pear Development Council v KJ Lewis Ltd and
    Others, Case 222/82 [1983] ECR 4083 177

Baumbast, Case C-413/99 [2002] ECR I-7091 .... 49, 71, 72
Belgium v Humbel, Case 263/86 [1988] ECR 5365 .... 77, 78, 84
Bernini v Minister van Onderwijs en Wetenschappen,
    Case C-3/90 [1992] ECR I-1071 43
Bettray v Staatssecretaris van Justitie,
    Case 344/87 [1989] ECR 1621 42
Bickel and Franz (Criminal proceedings against Horst Otto
    Bickel and Ulrich Franz), Case C-274/96 [1998] ECR I-763 .... 82, 120, 169, 180, 203, 206
Blaizot v University of Liège and Others,
    Case 24/86 [1988] ECR 379 66
Bonsignore v Oberstadtdirektor der Stadt Köln,
    Case 67/74 [1975] ECR 297 .... 100, 112

Bosman (Union Royale Belge des Sociétés de Football Association
    ASBL v Jean-Marc Bosman, Royal Club Liégeois SA v Jean-
    Marc Bosman and Others and Union des Associations
    Européennes de Football (UEFA) v Jean-Marc Bosman),
    Case C-415/93 [1995] ECR I-4921 .... 55, 57, 63, 94, 127, 128,
                                                                       130, 138, 178–80, 203
Bouchereau (Régina v Pierre Bouchereau),
    Case 30/77 [1977] ECR 1999 .... 100, 104, 105
Brown v Secretary of State for Scotland,
    Case 197/86 [1988] ECR 3205 55
Buy Irish (Commission of the European Communities
    v Ireland), Case 249/81 [1982] ECR 4005 .... 20, 177

Caisse d'Allocations Familiales de la Région Parisienne
    v Mr and Mrs Richard Meade,
    Case 238/83 [1984] ECR 2631 205
Campus Oil Limited and Others v Minister for Industry and
    Energy and Others, Case 72/83 [1984] ECR 2727 .... 110, 111
Carpenter v Secretary of State for the Home Dept,
    Case C-60/00 [2002] ECR I-6279.. 166
Cassis de Dijon (Rewe-Zentral AG
    v Bundesmonopolverwaltung für Branntwein),
    Case 120/78 [1979] ECR 649 .... 26, 28, 29, 31–35, 38, 125,
                                                                       126, 130, 140, 145, 146,
                                                                       148, 150, 154, 213
Centrafarm BV v American Home Products Corporation,
    Case 3/78 [1978] ECR 1823 192
Centrafarm BV et Adriaan de Peijper v Sterling Drug Inc,
    Case 15/74 [1974] ECR 1147 188
Centrafarm BV et Adriaan de Peijper v Winthrop BV,
    Case 16/74 [1974] ECR 1183 189
Centre Leclerc (Cullet and Chambre syndicate des separateurs
    automobiles et detaillants de produits petroliers
    v Centre Leclerc Saint-Ovens-de-Gemeville),
    Case C-231/83 [1985] ECR 305 104
Centre public d'aide sociale de Courcelles
    v Marie-Christine Lebon, Case 316/85 [1987] ECR 2811 .... 49, 50, 54
Chemial Farmaceutici SpA v DAF SpA,
    Case 140/79 [1981] ECR 0001 18
Clinique (Verband Sozialer Wettbewerb eV v Clinique
    Laboratoires SNC et Estée Lauder Cosmetics GmbH),
    Case C-315/92 [1994] ECR I-0317.. 31, 35

Coditel v Ciné Vog (Compagnie générale pour la diffusion de la
 télévision, Coditel, and Others v Ciné Vog Films and Others),
 Case 62/79 [1980] ECR 881 193
Co-Frutta (Cooperativa Co-Frutta Srl v Amministrazione
 delle finanze dello Stato), Case 193/85 [1987] ECR 2085 . . . . 8, 10
Commission v Belgium, Case 149/79 [1980] ECR 3881 115
Commission v Belgium (Walloon Waste),
 Case C-2/90 [1992] ECR I-4431 . . . . 110, 111
Commission v Belgium, Case C-503/99 [2002] ECR I-4809 92
Commission v Denmark (Danish Recycling),
 Case 302/86 [1988] ECR 4607 . . . . 31, 150
Commission v France, Case 168/78 [1980] ECR 347 . . . . 14, 15, 17
Commission v France, Case 21/84 [1985] ECR 1355 19
Commission v France, Case 307/84 [1986] ECR 1725 . . . . 115, 116
Commission v France (French Farmers),
 Case C-265/95 [1997] ECR I-6959. . . . . 103, 182, 184
Commission v France, Case C-483/99 [2002] ECR I-4781 92
Commission v Germany (German Beer),
 Case 178/84 [1987] ECR 1227 . . . . 30, 90
Commission v Germany, Case 18/87 [1988] ECR 5427 7
Commission v Germany, Case C-24/97 [1988] ECR I-2133. 47
Commission v Germany (Quality Products),
 Case C-325/00 [2002] ECR I-9977. . . . . 23, 171
Commission v Greece, Case C-198/89 [1991] ECR I-0727 79
Commission v Ireland (Sea Fisheries),
 Case 61/77 [1978] ECR 417 126
Commission v Ireland, Case 249/81 [1982] ECR 4005. . . . . 20, 177
Commission v Ireland (Irish Pipes),
 Case 45/87 [1988] ECR 4929 24
Commission v Ireland, Case C-151/96 [1997] ECR I-3327 60
Commission v Italy, Case 7/68 (Italian Art Case)
 [1968] ECR 423 . . . . 5, 6
Commission v Italy, Case 24/68 [1969] ECR 193 5
Commission v Italy, Case 184/85 [1987] ECR 2013 15
Commission v Italy, Case 225/85 [1987] ECR 2625. 116
Commission v Italy, Case 63/86 [1988] ECR 29 81
Commission v Netherlands, Case 89/76 [1977] ECR 1355 8
Commission v Portugal, Case C-367/98 [2002] ECR I-4731 92
Commission v UK (Wine and Beer),
 Case 170/78 [1983] ECR 2265 . . . . 14, 17

Commission v UK (Newcastle Disease),
Case 40/82 [1982] ECR 2793 103

Commission v UK (Origin Marking),
Case 207/83 [1985] ECR 1201 24

Commission v UK, Case 261/85 [1988] ECR 547 113

Compagnie générale pour la diffusion de la télévision,
Coditel, and Others v Ciné Vog Films and Others,
Case 62/79 [1980] ECR 881 193

Compassion in World Farming (R v Minister of Agriculture,
Fisheries and Food ex p Compassion in World
Farming Ltd), Case C-1/96 [1998] ECR I-1251;
[1998] All ER (EC) 302. 105

Conegate Limited v HM Customs and Excise,
Case 121/85 [1986] ECR 1007 107

Corsten, Case C-58/98 [2000] ECR I-7919 80

Cooperativa Co-Frutta Srl v Amministrazione
delle finanze dello Stato, Case 193/85 [1987] ECR 2085. . . . . 8, 10

Corsten Case C-58/98 . . . . 80, 86

Cowan v Trésor Public, Case 186/87 [1989] ECR 195 . . . . 82, 169, 203, 206

Criminal proceedings against Arthur Mathot,
Case 98/86 [1987] ECR 809 168

Criminal proceedings against Bernard Keck and Daniel
Mithouard, Joined Cases C-267/91
and C-268/91 [1993] ECR I-6097 . . . . 32, 34–37, 129, 130,
132, 163, 172

Criminal proceedings against Florus Aril
Wijsenbeek, Case C-378/97 [1999] ECR I-6207 . . . . 70, 71, 208, 210

Criminal proceedings against Frans-Nederlandse Maatschappij
voor Biologische Producten B, (Dutch Plant Checks),
Case 272/80 [1981] ECR 3277 114

Criminal proceedings against Gilbert Even et Office
National des Pensions pour Travailleurs Salaris
(ONPTS), Case 207/78 [1979] ECR 2019 53

Criminal proceedings against Herbert
Gilli and Paul Andres, Case 788/79 [1980] ECR 2071 31

Criminal proceedings against Jacques Pistre,
Joined Cases C-321–24/94 [1997] ECR I-2343 . . . . 155, 163, 170, 172, 173

Criminal proceedings against Jan van de Haar
and Kaveka de Meern BV, Joined Cases 177 and
178/82 [1984] ECR 1797 . . . . 24, 83, 137, 176

Criminal proceedings against Jean-Pierre Guimont,
Case C-448/98 [2000] ECR 173

Criminal proceedings against Lucas Emilio Sanz
de Lera, Raimundo Daz Jimnez and Figen Kapanoglu,
Joined Cases C-163/94, C-165/94 and
C-250/94 [1995] ECR I-4821 .... 90, 93, 94
Criminal proceedings against Martino Grado and Shahid Bashir,
Case C-291/96 [1997] ECR I-5531 83
Criminal proceedings against Sandoz BV,
Case 174/82 [1983] ECR 2445 106
Cristini v Société Nationale des Chemins de Fer Français,
Case 32/75 [1975] ECR 1085 53
Cullet and Chambre syndicate des separateurs
automobiles et detaillants de produits petroliers v
Centre Leclerc Saint-Ovens-de-Gemeville,
Case C-231/83 [1985] ECR 305 104

D v Council, Case C-122/99P [2001] ECR I-4319 51
D'Hoop, Case C-224/98 [2002] ECR I-6191 121
Danish Recycling, (Commission v Denmark),
Case 302/86 [1988] ECR 4607 .... 31, 150
Dansk Denkavit ApS v Danish Ministry of Agriculture,
Case 29/87 [1988] ECR 2965 9
Dansk Supermarked A/S v A/S Imerco,
Case 58/80 [1981] ECR 181 180
Dassonville (Procureur du Roi v Benoît and
Gustave Dassonville), Case 8/74
[1974] ECR 837 .... 21–23, 32–34
de Agostini (Konsumentombudsmannen v De Agostini
(Svenska) Frlag AB and TV-Shop i Sverige AB),
Joined Cases C-34/95, C-35/95 and C-36/95
[1997] ECR I-3843 .... 36, 84, 85
Decker v Caisse de Maladie des Employees Prives,
Case C-120/95 [1998] ECR I-1831 .... 203, 213, 214
Denkavit v France, Case 132/78 [1979] ECR 1923 9
Diamantarbeiters (Sociaal Fonds voor de Diamantarbeiders
v SA Ch Brachfeld & Sons and Chougal Diamond & Co),
Case 2/69 [1969] ECR 211 6
Diatta v Land Berlin, Case 267/83 [1985] ECR 567 49
Dutch Plant Checks (Criminal proceedings against
Frans-Nederlandse Maatschappij voor Biologische
Producten BV), Case 272/80 [1981] ECR 3277 114

ERT (Elliniki Radiophonia Tilorassi AE and Panellinia
    Omospondia Syllogon Prossopikou v Dimotiki Etairia
    Pliroforissis and Sotirios Kouvelas and Nicolaos
    Avdellas and Others), Case C-260/89 [1991] ECR I-2925. . . . . 114, 138, 200
Elliniki Radiophonia Tilorassi AE and Panellinia
    Omospondia Syllogon Prossopikou v Dimotiki Etairia
    Pliroforissis and Sotirios Kouvelas and Nicolaos
    Avdellas and Others (ERT),
    Case C-260/89 [1991] ECR I-2925. . . . . 114, 138, 200
Estée Lauder Cosmetics GmbH v Lancaster Group GmbH,
    Case C-220/98 [2000] ECR I-0117. 153
Even (Criminal proceedings against Gilbert Even et Office
    National des Pensions pour Travailleurs Salaris
    (ONPTS)), Case 207/78 [1979] ECR 2019 53

Familiapress (Vereinigte Familiapress Zeitungsverlags
    v Heinrich Bauer Verlag GmbH),
    Case C-368/95 [1997] ECR I-3689. 35
Feldain v Directeur des services fiscaux du departement
    du Haut-Rhin, Case 433/85 [1987] ECR 3521. 16
French Farmers, (Commission v France,)
    Case C-265/95 [1997] ECR I-6959. . . . . 103, 182, 184

Geraets-Smits v Stichting Ziekenfonds VGZ and
    HTM Peerbooms v Stichting CZ Groep
    Zorgverzekeringen, Case C-157/99. . . . . 78, 213
Gebhard v Consiglio dell'Ordine degli Avvocati e Procuratori
    di Milano, Case C-55/94 [1995] ECR I-4165 . . . . 64, 76, 101, 129–31, 133, 182
German Beer, (Commission v Germany),
    Case 178/84 [1987] ECR 1227 . . . . 30, 90
Germany v Parliament and Council (Tobacco Advertising
    Directive), Case C-376/98 [2000] ECR I-8419. . . . . 140, 153
Gilli and Andres (Criminal proceedings against Herbert
    Gilli and Paul Andres), Case 788/79 [1980] ECR 2071 31
Gourmet International (Konsumentombudsmannen (KO)
    v Gourmet International Products AB (GIP)),
    Case C-405/98 [2001] ECR. 37, 85, 130
Grado and Bashir (Criminal proceedings against Martino
    Grado and Shahid Bashir),
    Case C-291/96 [1997] ECR I-5531 83
Graf v Filzmoser Maschinenbau GmbH,
    Case C-190/98 [2000] ECR I-0493 . . . . 57, 128, 132, 137

Grant v South-West Trains Ltd,
    Case C-249/96 [1998] ECR I-0621 50

Gravier v City of Liège, Case 293/83 [1985] ECR 593 66

Groener v Minister for Education and the City of Dublin
    Vocational Educational Committee,
    Case 379/87 [1989] ECR 3967 52

Groenveld BV v Produktschap voor Vee en Vlees,
    Case 15/79 [1979] ECR 3409 .... 38, 39, 93

Grogan (The Society for the Protection of Unborn Children
    Ireland Ltd v Stephen Grogan and Others),
    Case C-159/90 [1991] ECR I-4685 .... 78, 84, 200, 201

Grzelczyk v Centre public d'aide sociale d'Ottignies-Louvain-
    la-Neuve, Case C-184/99 [2001] ECR I-6193 .... 66, 68, 121

Guimont (Criminal proceedings against Jean-Pierre Guimont),
    Case C-448/98 [[2000] ECR I-10663 173

Gullung v Conseil de l'Ordre des Avocats du Barreau de
    Colmar et de Saverne, Case 292/86 [1988] ECR 111 129

HM Customs and Excise v Gerhart Schindler
    and Jörg Schindler, Case C-275/92 [1994] ECR I-1039 85

Hauer v Land Rheinland-Pfalz, Case 44/79 [1979] ECR 3727 201

Heimdienst (Austrian Grocers) (Schutzverband gegen
    unlauteren Wettbewerb v TK-Heimdienst Sass GmbH),
    Case C-254/98 [2000] ECR I-151 .... 29, 36, 37

Henn and Darby (Regina v Maurice Donald Henn and John
    Frederick Ernest Darby), Case 34/79 [1979] ECR 3795 107

Heylens (Union nationale des entraneurs et cadres
    techniques professionnels du football (Unectef) v Georges
    Heylens and Others), Case 222/86 [1987] ECR 4097 62

Hoffman-La Roche v Centrafarm, Case 102/77 [1978] ECR 39 191

Humbel (Belgium v Humbel), Case 263/86 [1988] ECR 5365 .... 77, 78, 84

Humblot v Directeur des Services Fiscaux,
    Case 112/84 [1985] ECR 1367 16

Inzirillo v Caisse d'allocations familiales de l'arrondissement
    de Lyon, Case 63/76 [1976] ECR 2057 53

Irish Pipes (Commission of the European Communities
    v Ireland), Case 45/87 [1988] ECR 4929 24

Italian Art Case, (Commission v Italy), Case 7/68
    [1968] ECR 423 .... 5, 6

Johnny Walker v Ministeriet for Skatter og Afgifter,
Case 243/84 [1986] ECR 875 17

Kaur (R v Secretary of State for the Home Department ex p
Manjit Kaur), Case C-192/99 [2001] ECR I-1237 67
Keck and Mithouard (Criminal proceedings against Bernard
Keck and Daniel Mithouard), Joined Cases C-267/91
and C-268/91 [1993] ECR I-6097 . . . . 32, 34–37, 129, 130,
132, 163, 172
Kempf v Staatssecretaris van Justitie,
Case 139/85 [1986] ECR 1741 44
Klopp (Ordre des Avocats au Barreau de Paris
v Onno Klopp), Case 107/83 [1984] ECR 2971 . . . . 63, 64, 126
Knoors v Secretary of State for Economic Affairs,
Case 115/78 [1979] ECR 399 167–69
Kohll v Union des Caisses de Maladie,
Case C-158/96 [1998] ECR I-1931 . . . . 78, 84, 109, 128, 212–15
Konle v Republik Österreich,
Case C-302/97 [1999] ECR I-3099 . . . . 90, 91
Konstantinidis v Stadt Altensteig,
Case C-168/91 [1993] ECR I-1191 198
Konsumentombudsmannen v De Agostini
(Svenska) Frlag AB and TV-Shop i Sverige AB,
Joined Cases C-34/95, C-35/95 and C-36/95
[1997] ECR I-3843 . . . . 36, 84, 85
Konsumentombudsmannen (KO) v Gourmet International
Products AB (GIP), Case C-405/98 [2001] ECR 37, 85, 130
Kraus v Land Baden-Württemberg,
Case C-19/92 [1993] ECR I-1663 . . . . 64, 129, 131, 167
Kremzow v Republik Österreich,
Case C-299/95 [1997] ECR I-2629 . . . . 168, 203

La Reine v Vera Ann Saunders, Case 175/78 [1979] ECR 1129 164
Lair v Universität Hannover, Case 39/86 [1988] ECR 3161 54
Land Nordrhein-Westfalen v Kari Uecker and Vera Jacquet
v Land Nordrhein-Westfalen, Joined Cases C-64/96 and
C-65/96 [1997] ECR I-3171 . . . . 167, 169
Lawrie-Blum v Land Baden-Württemberg,
Case 66/85 [1986] ECR 2121 42
Lebon (Centre public d'aide sociale de Courcelles
v Marie-Christine Lebon), Case 316/85 [1987] ECR 2811 . . . . 49, 50, 54

Leclerc-Siplec (Société d'Importation Edouard Leclerc-Siplec
    v TF1 Publicité SA and M6 Publicité SA),
    Case C-412/93 [1995] ECR I-0179...129
Levin v Staatssecretaris van Justitie,
    Case 53/81 [1982] ECR 1035...43, 44, 55, 70, 77
Luisi and Carbone v Ministero del Tesoro,
    Case 286/82 [1984] ECR 377...81, 89, 206

MRAX, Case C-459/99 [2002] ECR I-6591...47
Martinez Sala v Freistaat Bayern,
    Case C-85/96 [1998] ECR I-2691 ....120, 168
Mathot (Criminal proceedings against Arthur Mathot),
    Case 98/86 [1987] ECR 809 168
Meeusen, Case C-337/97 [1999] ECR I-3289 60
Merck Sharp and Dohme v Paranova,
    Case C-443/99 [2002] ECR I-3703..192
Merck v Stephar, Case 187/80 [1981] ECR 2063 191
Michel S v Fonds National de Reclassement Social des
    Handicaps, Case 76/72 [1973] ECR 457 53
Morson and Jhanjan v State of the Netherlands,
    Joined Cases 35 and 36/82 [1982] ECR 3723 ....164, 167
Müller-Fauré v OZ Zorgverzekeringen and
    van Riet v ZAO Zorgverzekeringen,
    Case C-385/99, 13 May 2003..213

Newcastle Disease (Commission v UK),
    Case 40/82 [1982] ECR 2793...103

O'Flynn v Adjudication Officer,
    Case C-237/94 [1996] ECR I-2617 ....52, 54, 56, 124–26, 132
Olazabal (Ministre de l'Intérieur v Olazabal),
    Case C-100/01 [2002] ECR I-10981..109
Ordre des Avocats au Barreau de Paris
    v Onno Klopp, Case 107/83 [1984] ECR 2971 ....63, 64, 126
Origin Marking (Commission v UK),
    Case 207/83 [1985] ECR 1201 24
Outokumpu Oy, Case C-213/96 [1998] ECR I-1777 8

Pharmon BV v Hoechst AG, Case 19/84 [1985] ECR 2281 190
Pistre (Criminal proceedings against Jacques Pistre),
    Joined Cases C-321–24/94 [1997] ECR I-2343 ....155, 163, 170, 172, 173

Preussen Elektra v Schleswag, Case C-379/98 [2001] ECR 110, 111

Procureur du Roi v Benoît and Gustave Dassonville,
Case 8/74 [1974] ECR 837 . . . . 21–23, 32–34

Quality Products, (Commission v Germany),
Case C-325/00 . . . . 23, 171

R v Immigration Appeal Tribunal et Surinder Singh
ex p Secretary of State for Home Department,
Case C-370/90 [1992] ECR I-4265. . . . . 165, 166–69

R v Maurice Donald Henn and John Frederick Ernest Darby),
Case 34/79 [1979] ECR 3795 107

R v Minister of Agriculture, Fisheries and Food ex p Compassion
in World Farming Ltd, Case C-1/96 [1998] ECR I-1251;
[1998] All ER (EC) 302. 105

R v Royal Pharmaceutical Society of Great Britain
ex p Association of Pharmaceutical Importers and Others,
Joined Cases 266 and 267/87 [1989] ECR 1295. 178

R v Secretary of State for the Home Department ex p
Manjit Kaur, Case C-192/99 [2001] ECR I-1237 67

R v Thompson, Case 7/78 [1978] ECR 2247. 6

RI-SAN Srl v Comune di Ischia, Italia Lavoro SpA and Ischia
Ambiente SpA, Case C-108/98 [1999] ECR I-5219 164

Rau (Walter Rau Lebensmittelwerke v De Smedt PVBA),
Case 261/81 [1982] ECR 396 30

Reed (State of the Netherlands v Ann Florence Reed),
Case 59/85 [1986] ECR 1283 . . . . 50, 60

Régina v Pierre Bouchereau, Case 30/77 [1977] ECR 1999. . . . . 100, 104, 105

Rewe-Zentral AG v Bundesmonopolverwaltung für Branntwein,
Case 120/78 [1979] ECR 649 . . . . 26, 28, 29, 31–35, 38, 125,
126, 130, 140, 145, 146,
148, 150, 154, 213

Rezguia Adoui v Belgian State and City of Liège; Dominique
Cornuaille v Belgian State,
Joined Cases 115 and 116/81 [1982] ECR 1665. 108

Royal Pharmaceutical Society (R v Royal Pharmaceutical
Society of Great Britain ex p Association of
Pharmaceutical Importers and Others),
Joined Cases 266 and 267/87 [1989] ECR 1295. 178

Royer, Case 48/75 [1976] ECR 497 47

Rutili v Ministre de l'intérieur, Case 36/75 [1975] ECR 1219 . . . . 108, 109

Safir v Skattemyndigheten i Dalarnas Län, formerly
  Skattemyndigheten i Kopparbergs Län,
  Case C-118/96 [1998] ECR I-1897 90
Säger v Dennemeyer & Co Ltd,
  Case C-76/90 [1991] ECR I-4221 . . . . 84, 86
Sagulo, Gennaro Brenca et Addelmadjid Bakhouche,
  Case 8/77 [1977] ECR 1495 48
Sandoz (Criminal proceedings against Sandoz BV),
  Case 174/82 [1983] ECR 2445 106
Sanz de Lera (Criminal proceedings against Lucas Emilio Sanz
  de Lera, Raimundo Daz Jimnez and Figen Kapanoglu),
  Joined Cases C-163/94, C-165/94 and
  C-250/94 [1995] ECR I-4821 . . . . 90, 93, 94
Saunders (La Reine v Vera Ann Saunders),
  Case 175/78 [1979] ECR 1129 164
Schindler (HM Customs and Excise v Gerhart Schindler
  and Jrg Schindler), Case C-275/92 [1994] ECR I-1039 85
Scholz v Opera Universitaria di Cagliari and Cinzia Porcedda,
  Case C-419/92 [1994] ECR I-505 166
Schottle v Finanzamt de Freudenstadt,
  Case 20/76 [1977] ECR 247 13
Schutzverband gegen unlauteren Wettbewerb
  v TK-Heimdienst Sass GmbH,
  Case C-254/98 [2000] ECR I-151 . . . . 29, 36, 37
Scientology International, Case C-54/99 [2000] ECR I-1335. 113
Sea Fisheries (Commission of the European Communities
  v Ireland), Case 61/77 [1978] ECR 417 126
Semeraro Casa Uno v Sindaco del Comune di Erbusco,
  Case C-418–21/93 [1996] ECR I-2975. . . . . 35, 37
Silhouette International Schmied GmbH & Co KG
  v Hartlauer Handelsgesellschaft mbH,
  Case C-355/96 [1998] ECR I-4799. 193
Sociaal Fonds voor de Diamantarbeiders
  v SA Ch Brachfeld & Sons and Chougal Diamond & Co,
  Case 2/69 [1969] ECR 211 6
Société d'Importation Edouard Leclerc-Siplec
  v TF1 Publicité SA and M6 Publicité SA),
  Case C-412/93 [1995] ECR I-0179. 129
Society for the Protection of Unborn Children Ireland Ltd
  v Stephen Grogan and Other),
  Case C-159/90 [1991] ECR I-4685 . . . . 78, 84, 200, 201

State of the Netherlands v Ann Florence Reed,
   Case 59/85 [1986] ECR 1283 . . . . 50, 60

Steymann v Staatssecretaris van Justitie,
   Case 196/87 [1988] ECR 6159 44

Stoke County Council (Rochdale Borough Council
   v Stewart John Anders),
   Case C-306/88 [1993] 1 CMLR 426. 31

Stoke-on-Trent City Council v B & Q Ltd,
   Case C-169/91 [1992] ECR I-6635. 31

Surinder Singh (R v Immigration Appeal Tribunal et
   Surinder Singh ex p Secretary of State for Home
   Department), Case C-370/90 [1992] ECR I-4265 . . . . 165, 166–69

Svensson et Lena Gustavsson v Ministre du Logement et de
   l'Urbanisme, Case C-484/93 [1995] ECR I-3955 90

Thieffry v Conseil de l'Ordre des Avocats la Cour de Paris,
   Case 71/76 [1977] ECR 765 61

Tobacco Advertising Directive (Germany v Parliament and
   Council), Case C-376/98 [2000] ECR I-8419 . . . . 140, 153

Torfaen Borough Council against B & Q plc,
   Case 145/88 [1989] ECR 3851 31

Trummer, Case C-222/97 [1999] ECR I-1661 90

Uecker and Jacquet (Land Nordrhein-Westfalen v Kari
   Uecker and Vera Jacquet v Land Nordrhein-Westfalen),
   Joined Cases C-64/96 and C-65/96 [1997] ECR I-3171 . . . . 167, 169

Union nationale des entraneurs et cadres techniques
   professionnels du football (Unectef) v Georges
   Heylens and Others, Case 222/86 [1987] ECR 4097 62

Union Royale Belge des Sociétés de Football Association
   ASBL v Jean-Marc Bosman, Royal Club Liégeois SA
   v Jean-Marc Bosman and Others and Union des Associations
   Européennes de Football (UEFA) v Jean-Marc Bosman,
   Case C-415/93 [1995] ECR I-4921 . . . . 55, 57, 63, 94, 127, 128,
   130, 138, 178–80, 203

van Binsbergen v Bestuur van de Bedrijfsvereniging voor de
   Metaalnijverheid, Case 33/74 [1974] ECR 1299. 80

van de Haar (Criminal proceedings against Jan van de Haar
   and Kaveka de Meern BV), Joined Cases 177 and
   178/82 [1984] ECR 1797 . . . . 24, 83, 137, 176

Van Duyn v Home Office, Case 41/74 [1974] ECR 1337 . . . . 102, 107, 108

Verband Sozialer Wettbewerb eV v Clinique Laboratoires
SNC et Estée Lauder Cosmetics GmbH,
Case C-315/92 [1994] ECR I-0317 . . . . 31, 35
Vereinigte Familiapress Zeitungsverlags v Heinrich Bauer
Verlag GmbH, Case C-368/95 [1997] ECR I-3689 35
Vlaamse Reisbureaus (ASBL Vereniging van Vlaamse
Reisbureaus v ASBL Sociale Dienst van de
Plaatselijke en Gewestelijke Overheidsdiensten),
Case 311/85 [1987] ECR 3801 180
Vlassopoulou v Ministerium für Justiz, Bundes- und
Europaangelegenheiten Baden-Württemberg,
Case 340/89 [1991] ECR 2357 . . . . 62, 64

Walloon Waste (Commission of the European Communities
v Kingdom of Belgium), Case C-2/90 [1992] ECR I-4431 . . . . 110, 111
Walrave and Koch v Association Union Cycliste
Internationale, Koninklijke Nederlandsche Wielren
Unie et Federación Española Ciclismo,
Case 36/74 [1974] ECR 1405 178–81
Walter Rau Lebensmittelwerke v De Smedt PVBA,
Case 261/81 [1982] ECR 396 30
Watson and Belmann, Case 118/75 [1976] ECR 1185 47
Webb, Case 279/80 [1981] ECR 3305 80
Werner v Finanzamt Aachen-Innenstadt,
Case C-112/91 [1993] ECR I-0429 168
Wijsenbeek (Criminal proceedings against Florus Aril
Wijsenbeek), Case C-378/97 [1999] ECR I-6207 . . . . 70, 71, 208, 210
Wine and Beer, (Commission v UK),
Case 170/78 [1983] ECR 2265 . . . . 14, 17
Wirth v Landeshauptstadt Hannover,
Case C-109/92 [1993] ECR I-6447 . . . . 78, 84, 212

X and Y v the Netherlands (1985) 8 EHRR 235 203

TABLE OF TREATY ARTICLES

EC Treaty 3, 5, 19, 28, 41, 47, 53,
66, 72, 76, 79–84, 91, 94, 95, 99–104,
109, 110, 113, 114, 117, 119, 121, 128,
131, 132, 135, 139, 140, 145, 152,
163–65, 167, 168, 175–84,
188, 200–04, 206–08,
211, 215
Title IV 209
Art 2 146
Art 3 146
Art 3(c)...179
Art 3(1)(g)......................................136
Art 10 ....145, 183
Art 12 ....41, 66, 68, 73, 82, 83, 117–21,
175, 178, 179, 181, 207, 209
Art 13 51
Art 14....................................1, 71, 137, 208–10
Art 15 161
Art 16 ....214, 215
Art 17 ....66, 118–21, 167, 168, 207
Art 17(2).................................68, 118, 120
Art 18 ....68–73, 118–21, 133,
169, 209, 210
Art 18(1)...71
Art 19 68
Art 20 68
Art 21 68
Art 22 68
Art 25................................5–8, 10–12, 18, 19
Art 28......................19–29, 31–36, 38, 39, 75,
99, 104, 107, 110, 111, 117, 125,
129, 130, 168, 171, 172, 175,
177, 178, 180, 181,
183–88, 193, 205
Art 29 ....19, 20, 37–39, 99
Art 30......................................8, 24, 28, 37, 38, 99,
103, 104, 107, 111, 114, 151,
173, 180, 185, 187–89,
193, 194
Art 39................41, 45, 47, 52, 55–57, 60, 72,
100, 108, 115, 117–21, 125, 126,
128, 151, 164, 166, 175, 178,
179, 181, 182, 184,
198, 205
Art 39(2)......................................205
Art 39(3) 100, 109
Art 39(4)......................................100

EC Treaty (cont)—
Art 40 ....151, 155
Art 43......................56, 58–61, 63–65, 76, 117,
120, 124, 167, 175,
181, 198, 205
Art 44 151
Art 45 100
Art 46...................................83, 84, 100, 108
Art 47....................................62, 151, 155, 159
Arts 45–48 100
Art 48 ....54, 56
Art 49 ....75–81, 84, 85, 117, 120,
166, 178, 179, 181, 186,
198, 206, 212
Art 50....................................75, 77, 79, 179
Art 52 ....151, 179
Art 53 179
Art 54 ....117, 124
Art 55 ....100, 155, 159
Arts 56–60 89
Art 56 89–94
Art 57 89
Art 58 ....89, 101
Art 58(1)(b)...................................101
Art 60 ....76, 78
Art 62 209
Art 63(4)...209
Art 67 209
Art 81 ....135, 137
Art 82 ....135, 137, 215
Art 86 ....136, 215
Art 90 ....8–19, 136
Art 90(1), (2)..................................12
Art 93 151
Art 94....................................137, 146, 151–53
Art 95 ....151–53, 159
Art 95(2), (4), (5)...........................151
Arts 98–115......................................94
Arts 98–104......................................94
Art 103 95
Art 105 97
Art 108 97
Art 141 181
Art 149 65
Art 150 65
Art 234 64
Art 251 159

EC Treaty (cont)—
    Art 295..91, 186–88, 194
    Art 296...99, 100
    Art 296(1)(b)..100
    Art 308...152

Treaty on European Union
    (Treaty of Amsterdam)
    Title IV 209
    Title VI...135, 136, 209
    Art 6 ....201, 208, 209

COMMUNITY ACTS AND SECONDARY LEGISLATION

Charter of Fundamental
  Rights.............................197, 201, 202

European Convention on the Protection
  of Human Rights and Fundamental
  Freedoms 1951 ....51, 198–201, 203
  Art 10...114

Kyoto Agreement.......................111

Schengen Agreement 70, 205, 207–09

White Paper on a 'new approach'
  to harmonisation
  COM(85)310, 14 June 1985...............148, 149

DIRECTIVES

Directive 64/221 .... 100, 104, 105
  Art 3 ....100, 112

Directive 68/360 .... 45–48, 59
  Arts 3–8................................46
  Art 8 47

Directive 73/148 .... 47, 59, 60, 206
  Art 1(b) 206

Directive 77/249........................59

Directive 89/48 .... 59, 155–57
  Art 4 156
  Art 4(a)......................................156

Directive 89/49.....................59, 157

Directive 89/104.......................186

Directive 90/364.................. 69, 70, 72
  Art 1 70

Directive 90/365.......................69

Directive 92/51 .... 59, 155, 156

Directive 93/96.....................65, 69
  Art 1 66
  Art 3 65

Directive 93/98........................186

Directive 99/93........................160

Directive 2000/31 158–62
  Art 1 162
  Art 1(1)......................................159
  Art 2 159
  Art 3 159
  Art 4 159
  Art 5 159
  Art 6 159
  Art 7 159
  Art 8 159
  Arts 9–11......................................160
  Art 9 ....160, 161
  Art 9(1)......................................160
  Art 10 160
  Art 11......................................160
  Arts 12–15 160
  Art 15......................................161

Directive 2000/43/EC.................. 202

Directive 2000/78/EC.................. 202

Proposed Directive on
  Citizenship COM(2001) 257
  23 May 2001 70

REGULATIONS

Regulation 1612/68 .... 45, 46, 48, 50, 55,
                          59, 60, 70, 121, 164,
                          168, 181, 205
  Art 1 48
  Art 3 ....48, 49, 51
  Art 3(1)......................................51, 52
  Arts 4, 5......................................48
  Art 7......................................48, 49, 51, 52, 54, 175
  Art 7(2)......................................53, 54
  Art 7(4)......................................48, 49
  Art 8 48
  Art 10 ....48, 50
  Art 11......................................48, 59
  Art 12 48

Regulation 40/94......................186

Regulation 6/2002.....................186

CHAPTER 1

INTRODUCTION

This book aims to provide a guide to the law governing the internal market for undergraduates and those on Masters courses. Its primary aim is to give a clear presentation of the essentials, but it is also hoped that it provides a conceptual framework for more in-depth thought and reading. For clarity and simplicity of use there are few footnotes, but at the end there are suggestions for further reading. There a selection of articles from journals, and some books, can be found. They have been chosen to complement each other and this book, providing differing views of the issues raised and discussed in the text.

It is intended that the book alone should provide enough information for introductory courses, or for revision. A student with a good knowledge of this law should be able to pass most internal market law exams. For those on more demanding or higher level courses, or who are more ambitious, the combination of the book and the further reading should provide in-depth knowledge of all the core internal market subjects, and an introduction to some of the related areas.

Of course, all students will also benefit from reading judgments and opinions. They are often quoted here, sometimes extensively, but getting to know the most important judgments in full will still be helpful in understanding the law.

A knowledge of basic Community law concepts is assumed – things like direct effect and supremacy – as well as some idea of what the European Union is. However no detailed knowledge of any other areas of Community law is needed to use this book.

1.1 INTRODUCTION TO THE INTERNAL MARKET

Article 14 EC Treaty states that the European Community shall establish an internal market. This will be 'an area without internal frontiers, in which the free movement of goods, persons, services and capital is ensured in accordance with the provisions of this Treaty'.

It is hoped that this will achieve two main ends. One is to increase prosperity in the member states of the European Union. The other is to bind those states more closely to each other, and move towards the 'ever-closer union of the peoples of Europe' which is mentioned in the preamble to the Treaty.

The process of building the internal market began with its economic side. Goods, workers, self-employed people, services and capital are all things that contribute to the economy (they are sometimes called economic factors). Treaty articles providing for their free movement between member states were the first part of the internal market to come into force, and remain central to it. Indeed, the European Court of Justice has taken to calling the free movement of these things 'fundamental freedoms'.

These economic articles identify and prohibit the different kinds of national acts and rules which might inhibit free movement. Some of these are obvious, others less so. The articles themselves are short and straightforward, but their interpretation by the Court has been creative and purposive, sometimes radical. They dominate the legal framework of the internal market.

However, the framework of the market is not just economic. Free movement has been extended even to citizens of member states that are not economically active. Just because they are European Union citizens, a term explained in Chapter 4, they now have a right to move freely throughout the EU. This right is in its early stages, and perhaps not quite complete, but it is well on its way.

Moreover, in the future we may expect that frontiers will even be removed for people within the EU who are not EU citizens. Third country tourists, or workers, or refugees, may also acquire the chance to move freely from member state to member state. This may take some time, but the ultimate goal is that frontiers in Europe will be no more than signboards by the road.

The first section of this book, Chapters 2 to 8, deals with the basic law of free movement, introducing the Treaty articles, the major secondary legislation, and the way they have been interpreted by the Court. It also identifies the common themes underlying the different freedoms.

Chapters 9 and 10 then look at harmonisation. It is easy for a student to think that contentious caselaw and judgments are what European law is all about, but the harmonisation process, led by the European Commission, is at least as important. It is the legislative motor of the internal market. Underpinning it – the conceptual motor – is the philosophy of free markets and competition. Therefore Chapter 9 gives a brief explanation of the ideas and role of competition, before the next chapter looks at their application in the legal processes of harmonisation, using some recent examples.

Chapters 11 to 13 then look at some more sophisticated legal issues in free movement law. Chapters 11 and 12 explore its boundaries: does it extend to non-governmental bodies, and to situations within one state? Chapter 13 considers the position of intellectual property. Any discussion of this topic must be incomplete, partly because of the vastness of the subject matter, and partly because so many other areas of law, notably competition law, are involved. However, it is too important to ignore, and a student must have some idea of the particular problems raised.

Finally, Chapter 14 looks at social issues. Does the law of free movement reflect basic 'European' values, by protecting the rights of EU citizens and of third country nationals present here? Or does it rather undermine those values, by attacking European welfare states?

1.2 NOTE ON TERMINOLOGY

The articles regulating the free movement of economic factors are often referred to in this book as 'economic articles', to distinguish them from those concerned with non-economic persons, such as EU citizens.

The (economic and non-economic) articles directly governing free movement are often called the 'free movement articles' to distinguish them from those concerned with, say, harmonisation, or competition.

The words 'Community' and 'European Union', or 'EU', are used fairly interchangeably. There is still a difference; the EU contains the Community, which contains the institutions; but it matters less and less. In any case, the law made by the Community institutions, pursuant to the European Community Treaty, is the law that applies throughout the EU, so it is EU law, as well as being Community law. In the text I have tended to say 'Community law' but talk about the 'EU' when the broader thing is being referred to. I just think it sounds nice that way.

In the context of the Treaties, the single market, the common market, and the internal market are the same thing. To my ear a common market emphasises the components of which it is made – the member states. It is clearly a shared thing. A single market only makes sense when contrasted with multiple markets – so it also highlights the division of Europe. An internal market, by contrast, seems to emphasise the wholeness and unity of what is being created, and so perhaps reflects best the purpose of it all.

1.3 NOTE ON TREATY NUMBERING

Revision of the Treaties has resulted in the Treaty articles changing their numbers several times over the years. This can be confusing. For example, an old judgment will mention Art 36, meaning what is now Art 30. If it mentions Art 30, it will be referring to what is now Art 28. In the text, current (post-Amsterdam and Nice) numbering is used. Old numbers have been left in judgments but the new ones have been inserted in square brackets.

CHAPTER 2

THE FREE MOVEMENT OF GOODS: TAXES AND DUTIES

There are three kinds of obstacle to the inter-state movement of goods that are recognised by the EC Treaty. These are customs duties, the presence of discriminatory taxation, and quantitative restrictions on imports and exports. Each of these is dealt with in separate Treaty articles, and requires its own explanation, although the first two are closely related.

2.1 CUSTOMS DUTIES

Article 25 EC says that *'customs duties on imports and exports and charges having equivalent effect shall be prohibited between member states. This prohibition shall also apply to customs duties of a fiscal nature'*. This article is directly effective.

2.1.1 What are customs duties and charges having equivalent effect?

A customs duty is strictly a tax on border crossing – rather like a toll that must be paid by each item, or kilo, or pounds-worth of goods, according to the particular rules. However it is not necessary to worry about this too much. The article has been partially explained by the Court in a way that removes such technicalities:

> ... any pecuniary charge, however small and whatever its designation and mode of application, which is imposed unilaterally on domestic or foreign goods by reason of the fact that they cross a frontier, and which is not a customs duty in the strict sense, constitutes a charge having equivalent effect.[1]

This means that the name and the precise way the money is collected don't matter. Even if it isn't called a customs duty, and it isn't collected by customs authorities, if the member state imposes a charge on goods just because they cross a frontier, this is caught by Art 25.

2.1.2 What are goods?

This raises the question 'what are goods?'. The answer seems to be that they are any objects that can be valued in money. The Italian government imposed a charge on works of art leaving the country, and said that such artistic objects should not be considered as goods.[2] They were priceless, beyond mere monetary value, and anyway not the same thing as commercial or consumer goods. The Court responded very simply:

> ... by goods ... there must be understood products which can be valued in money and which are capable, as such, of forming the basis of commercial transactions.

---

1   *Commission v Italy* Case 24/68.
2   *Commission v Italy* Case 7/68.

Thus, however vulgar it might be, since the works of art were obviously the sort of things that could be bought and sold, and therefore somebody thought it was possible to value them, they should be treated as goods. This suggests that almost any physical thing will be 'goods'.

There may be some exceptions, or at least subtleties. In one case it was said that money which was still legal tender was not goods.[3] Therefore a charge on the import or export of money was not caught by Art 25. This may seem sensible insofar as it is quite difficult conceptually to deal with the idea of buying and selling money (foreign exchange dealing apart), but in fact the decision was made because such charges were better dealt with under the rules of free movement of capital. Also, in the case of certain types of goods, such as weapons, or drugs, there are special Treaty rules which apply, and so one cannot simply use Art 25.

2.1.3 Does the purpose of the charge make a difference?

The article says that the charge must be levied '*by reason of the fact*' that the goods cross a frontier. It is tempting to think that, therefore, if the charge was levied for some other reason – such as a tax on bananas that went to a fund that helped sick ex-banana workers – it would escape. This would not be right. The purpose of the member state is completely irrelevant.

Some cases have made this very clear. In the *Italian Art* case, the levy collected was used by the Italian government to pay for monitoring and protecting Italian art treasures. The state claimed that this was not a customs duty, or a charge having equivalent effect, because it wasn't really any kind of tax, and it wasn't adding noticeably to the budget, and in fact it was helping the art market in some ways.[4]

These arguments were not wrong, they were just beside the point. The point is that any charge which is imposed adds to the cost of the goods and therefore creates the same effect as if it was called a true customs duty. The reasons behind it, and even the fact that, in the long run or the wider context, it may do a lot of good things, are simply to be ignored.

This was confirmed in a well known case in which Belgium imposed a tax on the importation of diamonds, which went to a social fund for diamond workers.[5] This time the state argued that the money was for a legitimate purpose, that the money raised was not going to the government, and that this was not an attempt to protect native production. Therefore it should not be considered equivalent to a customs duty, and should not be caught by Art 25. Again, its protests were dismissed.

Therefore in an Art 25 situation one should simply focus on the presence of the charge, and not be distracted by arguments about its aims and effects.

---

3   *R v Thompson* Case 7/78.
4   See note 2 above.
5   *Diamantarbeiters* Case 2/69.

2.1.4   Are there any exceptions?

There are no exceptions to Art 25. If a charge is caught, it is prohibited. However, there are some situations where what looks like a charge having equivalent effect turns out not to be one at all. These fall into two categories: payment for a service, and where the charge is really part of a system of internal taxation.

2.1.5   Payment for a service

At a border crossing a carrier of goods may receive various services directly related to the goods. He may store his goods in a warehouse for a while, or have them repackaged, or have them undergo some kind of treatment, or be inspected for quality or the presence of bugs or disease. If he chooses freely to receive these services, then his payment for them, even though it is at the border, is not *'by reason of the fact'* that he crossed the border, but *'by reason of the fact'* that he received the service. The action that incurred the obligation to pay was not the frontier crossing, it was accepting the service. It is not therefore an Art 25 matter. This is obviously sensible.

However, if the member state makes services (in this case usually inspections) obligatory then the fee will be caught by Art 25. The reality is that at the border the carrier must then pay a charge, whether he wants to or not. The fact that the member state then insists his goods are treated in some way, and claims that the charge is for this, does not excuse it. A payment is only to be considered as for a service if that service is voluntarily received. This also seems sensible. The purpose and effect of the inspections is, as you would expect from the discussion of the purpose of charges above, not relevant.

Slightly more surprising is an exception to this second situation. If the service is compulsory not as a result of national law, but as a result of Community law, then, subject to conditions, the member state may claim payment. Note that this is only if the service – again almost always in practice an inspection – is compulsory. If Community law merely allows a state to make the inspections, the state may not charge, and if it does it will be caught by Art 25.

The conditions under which a member state may charge for these 'mandatory inspections' or other processes that Community law requires at the border were set out in a case concerning cattle entering Germany.[6] A European directive required certain compulsory inspections on transports of live animals, for the protection of the welfare of the animals. The German government conducted these inspections, and charged the carrier. The Court said:

> ... such fees may not be classified as charges having an effect equivalent to a customs duty if the following conditions are satisfied:
>
> a   they do not exceed the actual cost of the inspections in connection with which they are charged;
>
> b   the inspections in question are obligatory and uniform for all the products concerned in the Community;

6   *Commission v Germany* Case 18/87.

c   they are prescribed by Community law in the general interest of the Community;

d   they promote the free movement of goods, in particular by neutralizing obstacles which could arise from unilateral measures of inspection adopted in accordance with Art 36 [now 30] of the Treaty.

This statement is fairly clear, and remains the law, but there are several things to note about it. One is that because the cost of inspections may vary from country to country because of, for example, differences in wage costs of inspectors, the legal charge will also vary. Another is that the second requirement is that the inspections be uniform across the Community. Therefore if Community law insisted that cattle leaving the UK, France and Germany be inspected, because of an outbreak of some disease there, while cattle leaving other countries were not required to be, these inspections could not carry a charge. Thirdly, it is interesting that the Court's justification for its approach, implicit in the last two conditions, is that the inspections are for the general good of the Community and the particular market. These are precisely the kind of arguments that it rejects when they are made by states trying to justify a charge. We see here how the Community has a monopoly on policy decisions concerning inter-state trade.

A final addendum to this category are inspections (or other services) carried out pursuant to an obligation in international law. If an international agreement *to which all the member states are parties* requires some form of inspection, then the Court has accepted that it is legitimate to charge a fee proportional to the cost and not exceeding it.[7]

2.1.6   An apparent charge, that is in fact internal taxation

Within a member state it is acceptable for the government to impose taxation on goods or the sale of goods. Thus we have VAT on most things that are sold, and some kinds of goods may also be subject to particular taxations – for example, there might be an environmental tax on cars, or high rates of tax on tobacco or alcohol. These taxes usually pursue some particular policy objective, such as discouraging harmful activities, or passing the costs of pollution on to the polluter. Some of these objectives may be compatible with Community law, while others may not be, or may be dubious – such as a tax that went to help fund domestic industry, or a tax aimed at preventing the use of national resources. Whether or not these taxes are acceptable is something mainly considered under Art 90 of the EC Treaty. However, before coming to that it is necessary to know how to decide whether a sum of money collected on imports or exports should be considered as a tax that is to be considered under Art 90, or a charge under Art 25. These two articles are mutually exclusive, so the money always falls under one or the other, never both.[8] The difference is important, because the consequences are not the same. Art 25 is much stricter than Art 90.

The rule is that if the money collected is part of *'a general system of internal dues applied systematically to categories of products in accordance with objective criteria irrespective of the origin of the products',*[9] then it is taxation, to be considered under Art 90. If it does not fall within that definition, it may be an Art 25 charge.

7   *Commission v Netherlands* Case 89/76.
8   *Outokumpu Oy* Case C-213/96.
9   *Co-Frutta* Case 193/85.

Applying this is usually not too difficult. For tax purposes the rule in Europe is that a sale of goods is normally located geographically at the place of the buyer, not the seller. Thus if a buyer buys from a domestic producer, or from an importer, for domestic tax purposes these transactions are equivalent. Then, if the member state has a tax on sales of such products it may impose it on both these sales.

The major difference is in methods of collection. It is convenient to collect most sales taxes via the seller, who records his sales and passes on a percentage to the authorities. However, if the seller is abroad, this is obviously practically difficult. Therefore, it may be convenient to collect sales tax on imports either from the buyer, or the importer. Thus, sometimes, for convenience, member states may well demand money at the border from importers, who might then claim a customs duty was being imposed.

However, if in fact the member state has a tax system in which the sale of types of good is taxed according to various criteria, then when that tax is demanded from goods being commercially imported, even if at the border, this will just be a part of that internal tax system, and so not a duty, but an Art 90 matter. Of course, if the import is not part of a commercial transaction but for personal use, no tax may be collected, unless, exceptionally, there is a tax on ownership.

Problems just arise in a few situations, where it may seem that a so called tax is disguising what is really a customs duty. These situations are when there is a levy on domestic producers, when no equivalent domestic products are produced, and when tax is refunded.

2.1.7 The levy on domestic producers

In Denmark those supplying animal feed were subject to government checks on the safety and quality of the feed.[10] The cost of these checks was recouped by imposing a levy on all suppliers. Domestically, this levy was imposed on the producers. However for feed imported from abroad, the levy was imposed on the importers.

One way of looking at this is to say that although both these payments had the same name, and originated in the same law, in reality they were different things. The first was a tax on producers. However, foreign producers would obviously not be subject to this. Therefore, in 'revenge' Denmark could be seen as imposing a levy on imports, to balance out the domestic tax, and protect national producers. Thus, an argument could be made that this was a customs duty.

However, on the facts this was wrong; the levy was imposed on those initially introducing animal feed onto the Danish market – on the first Danish sale, as it were. This was because it was at this level that it was necessary to have the safety checks. Importers and producers were both 'first sellers' and therefore comparable, and so the levy on importers could be seen as part of an internal taxation system applied only according to objective criteria. It was an Art 90 matter.

This is made very clear by contrast with another case, apparently involving the French arm of the same company, Denkavit.[11] This time it concerned meat imports to

---

10   *Dansk Denkavit* Case 29/87.
11   *Denkavit v France* Case 132/78.

France. French slaughterhouses had to pay a levy on the animals they processed, calculated on a per kilogram basis. Importers had to pay the same amount per kilogram of meat they imported. Was this a customs duty, or part of the tax system? The French authorities said tax, arguing that the slaughterhouse levy was an equivalent domestic charge. However, they lost. The Court said that in order for this to be seen as internal taxation, the two charges must be applied 'in accordance with the same criteria to domestic products and imported products alike'. The basis for levying the domestic tax in this case was slaughter, not sale. Applying that to importers would not justify a charge – since they did not slaughter in France. Thus, the comparability the Court demanded did not exist.

Another way of putting this, using the language that the Court used in the case, is to say that the 'chargeable event' was not the same for the imports and domestic goods, or that the charges were not applied at the same 'marketing stage'. These are all ways of making essentially the same point; unlike in the Danish case, there was not one rule for both imports and domestic products. Therefore the two charges, even though of the same amount, were not to be seen as part of the same tax system. Therefore, there was a customs duty.

Nor was it enough to say, as the French government did, that the charge on imports was intended to 'compensate' for the domestic tax. That is really just an admission that this was indeed a protectionist customs duty! As the Court said, if the desire to balance domestic taxes was enough to justify imposing charges on imports, then the customs duty prohibition would be meaningless.

2.1.8   When no equivalent domestic goods are produced

This situation has most famously arisen in the context of bananas. Italy imposed taxes on 19 products destined for human consumption. All these taxes were expressed to be identically applicable to imports and domestic production, and the level of the tax was fixed by objective criteria to do with the product, and nothing to do with its geographical origin. So far so good. However, one of the products was bananas, but there are no bananas produced in Italy, or at least so few that they could be ignored. Therefore in practice the tax only applied to imports.

The question was then raised – shouldn't this be seen as an Art 25 charge, albeit perhaps a disguised one? In fact the Court found that it was not; it accepted the authenticity of the overall system, and so found that the mere absence of domestic production did not automatically discredit the tax:

> [E]ven a charge which is borne by a product imported from another member state, when there is no identical or similar domestic product, does not constitute a charge having equivalent effect but internal taxation within the meaning of Art 95 [now 90] if it relates to a general system of internal taxation applied systematically to categories of products in accordance with objective criteria irrespective of the origin of the products.[12]

---

12   *Co-Frutta*, see note 9 above.

The advantage of this perhaps surprising decision is that otherwise member states would not be able to impose taxes on anything they did not produce, since Art 25 would outlaw them. This might undermine legitimate policy aims such as the protection of the environment or the punishment of self-indulgence. Nevertheless, one should not assume that the Court would always come to the same decision. If it looked as if the charge was really not an integral part of a coherent system, but an add-on aimed at imports, it would certainly find it fell under Art 25.

2.1.9 Refunds of taxes

Sometimes member states assign the money from a particular tax to a particular fund, which is then used in a particular way. For example, domestic apple growers and apple importers might pay a levy each year which goes to a fund called the 'national apple fund'. Perhaps this would promote research and marketing relevant to apples, and in certain years would perhaps even refund some of its income to the contributors, if, for example, average apple prices had been low.

The problem arises if the benefits from this fund go disproportionately to national contributors. This can easily happen – national producers and sellers are likely to be far more involved in a such a national body than importers are, and may be better placed to benefit from its research and marketing activities. Then although the apparent tax is equal, the refunds, or the benefits resulting from the fund's activities, make the real contributions of the domestic producers lower. In short, they get something for their money, while importers do not.

In this situation the Court asks three questions:

i   Is the refund or fund activity for the sole benefit of domestic producers (that is, only the national apple growers)?

ii Does the benefit go only to the taxed product, and not, for example, to other domestic products as well (that is, not to other fruit producers)?

iii Does the value of the benefit entirely equal the value of the tax paid (that is, is the value of the apple producers' contributions equal to the value of the marketing and research help they get)?

If the answers to all three questions are positive, then the charge falls under Art 25. There is a complete cancelling out of the domestic producers' contributions by the benefits they receive. In reality they pay nothing. Therefore only importers pay, and that is a customs duty.

Otherwise the system falls under Art 90. There may still be a partial cancelling out of the national contributions. The value of the benefit received by the domestic taxed product may then be set off against the tax paid, making their real contribution less, and no doubt resulting in a finding of discriminatory taxation.

It is important to note here that if the money or benefits received by the national producers do not come from the tax revenues they produced, but from general state funds, then this does not negate the tax, and should not be taken into account. The proper way to complain about the refunds or benefits here would be via the rules on state aids.

2.1.10 Fiscal duties

Finally it is necessary to say a word about the last sentence of Art 25. This states that the article also applies to *'customs duties of a fiscal nature'*. This reflects the fact that customs duties were often levied primarily to protect domestic industry by keeping out imports, rather than to raise revenue. If they were levied to raise revenue, they might be called duties of a fiscal nature, 'fiscal' being to do with tax. The sentence serves merely to pre-emptively rebut the argument from member states that their duties are different, because they are not protectionist, but revenue-raising, and so should be allowed. As we have seen, the purpose of the duty is irrelevant, and so this argument would fail anyway. The second sentence is almost entirely unimportant today, and may be safely ignored.

2.2 DISCRIMINATORY TAXATION

The most important tax provision in the goods section of the EC Treaty is Art 90, which deals with what is commonly called discriminatory taxation. The article says:

> No member state shall impose, directly or indirectly, on the products of other member states any internal taxation of any kind in excess of that imposed directly or indirectly on similar domestic products.
>
> Furthermore, no member state shall impose on the products of other member states any internal taxation of such a nature as to afford indirect protection to other products.

The two paragraphs are quite often referred to as 90(1) and 90(2), although they are not in fact numbered in the Treaty. Here they will just be called the first and second paragraphs. They are both directly effective.

2.2.1   The first paragraph

The essential point of this paragraph is quite clear – that tax should be the same for domestic and foreign products. However, of course, there are certain aspects that need a little more consideration. These are now dealt with.

2.2.2   What is a product?

This seems a ridiculously pedantic question, except that in its interpretation of Art 25 the Court has tended to use the word 'goods'. Thus one might wonder if there is intended to be some difference between 'goods' and 'products'. The answer is that there does not seem to be.

2.2.3   What about third country imports coming via another member state?

If, say, American goods are imported into Germany, and then sent to France, would they count as *'the products of other member states'* for the purposes of applying the article to

French taxes? The answer is yes. They do come from another member state. Their distant history is not relevant to the movement over the Franco-German border.

2.2.4   What is internal taxation?

There are many ways in which member states may impose a charge on goods. It may be linked to their value, or weight, or quantity, or the way they are made or what they contain. It may be imposed on their sale, or use, or production, or even transport. Sometimes it will be called a tax, but at other times it will be called a levy, a charge, a contribution, a fee, a surcharge, or many other colourful names. For the purpose of Art 90 these may all be forms of taxation, provided they are the compulsory payment of money and they are not something else – such as payment for a voluntary service, or a customs duty. The term *'internal taxation'* is interpreted widely and non-technically. The word *'internal'* does not appear to play any particular role.

2.2.5   'Directly or indirectly'

These words qualify the way the tax is imposed. They make it clear that indirect imposition is also to be counted. The indirect imposition of a tax may be something like that which occurred in *Schottle*.[13] In this case there was a German system for the taxation of road transport of goods. To simplify it somewhat, long journeys were taxed, but short ones were not. If a truck came over the border from another country though, the authorities did not know how far it had come. The rule adopted was to treat it as if it was on a long journey, even if it only had a further kilometre to go inside Germany. All cross-border journeys were 'long'.

This clearly meant that a truck coming fifty kilometres from Austria was taxed more highly than a truck coming from a German town the same distance away. One journey was called 'short', and not taxed, while the other was. However, it could be said that the discriminatory taxation was on the transport, and not actually on the goods, and strictly this is so.

Nevertheless, the Court found that Art 90 was infringed. It said that different transport conditions could cause an obstacle to the movement of goods, and so Art 90 should apply. The logic must be that the extra costs would in the end be part of the price of the goods, and so they were the ultimate bearers of the tax.

2.2.6   'Similar domestic products'

By far the most important and difficult question arising out of the first paragraph is the precise meaning of the phrase 'similar domestic products'. This paragraph only applies to products that are similar to each other, so if an importer complains, under this paragraph, that domestic products are more lightly taxed, it is a perfect defence to show that they are not similar to those he imports. The idea therefore has to be well defined.

---

13   *Schottle* Case 20/76.

The defining phrase used by the Court is that similar products *'have similar characteristics and meet the same needs from the point of view of consumers'*.[14] Thus there are two aspects to similarity – the views of consumers, often called consumer preference, and the objective characteristics of the product: what it's made of, what it does, what it tastes like, and so on.

However, the obvious problem with the definition is that it also relies on an idea of similarity, and so is circular. Why is this?

The problem may be explained as follows: since the important function of Art 90 is to ensure an equal opportunity on the domestic market for foreign and domestic goods, the obvious basis for similarity would be consumer preference. The important thing for an importer is that his goods are taxed no more highly than the domestic alternatives. He does not necessarily care whether the goods are made in the same way or of the same thing, but if domestic goods are possible alternatives from the consumer's point of view, then he wants equal taxation conditions. Thus, in defining similarity, one might expect that the law would take an approach similar to that in competition law, and try to find out which goods consumers consider as possible alternatives to the imported ones. These would then be classified as 'similar'. Apples might be similar to oranges then, even though they are physically very different, since a consumer who finds oranges too expensive might well turn to apples, but a pair of scissors would not be similar to a pair of wire cutters, even though their physical characteristics are remarkably alike.

However, the danger of doing this is that sometimes it is not so clear what the alternative products are – is beer an alternative to wine? For some people, yes, for others, not – and the attitudes that determine this are themselves influenced by price, and so by tax. Thus in the UK it may be that most people would not turn to wine (which is imported) if beer (which is not) was taxed more heavily, so one might think these are not similar. But is their reluctance to change precisely because wine has always been highly taxed and so expensive, and so they have never built up a taste for it? If so, one should not 'fix' that advantage by saying the two are not alternatives. On the contrary, perhaps, potentially, they are. This is what the Court meant when it said in a rather complicated phrase that *'the tax policy of a member state must not therefore crystallise given consumer habits so as to consolidate an advantage acquired by national industries concerned to respond to them'*.[15]

Since the Court does not wish to rely only on consumer preference, it also looks to some extent at the 'objective' characteristics of the products. This is really an attempt to assess their potential for future competition. However, it is very difficult to devise any kind of formula for doing this methodically. Some things are physically remarkably similar, yet should not be called similar for the purposes of the article – the scissors and the wire cutters again. The Court therefore focuses on what it considers the relevant characteristics, and it does so in a flexible and pragmatic way. The aim is really to use a degree of common sense to decide which things are similar. This approach means that the Court probably does not want to go beyond simply saying that similar products have similar characteristics. To enter the topic too deeply would be to tie itself in linguistic and logical knots.

---

14 *Commission v France* Case 168/78.
15 *Commission v UK* Case 170/78.

Sometimes there are still difficult situations. In one case the Court had to answer the apparently impossible question of whether bananas were similar to other fruit. In the end it decided they were not, because, unlike apples or pears or oranges, they were not thirst quenching, were particularly good for babies, and had different 'organoleptic' properties. The result may, in the context of the case, be sensible, but the judgment comes dangerously close to the ridiculous, and shows the problems in assessing similarity.[16]

2.2.7   The second paragraph

The second paragraph of Art 90 is not very unlike the first, with a notably similar general thrust, but different and more general wording. It prohibits taxation on imported products where this will protect other products. The idea behind this is that if imports are taxed more highly, this makes them more expensive relative to the domestic products, and the domestic products will therefore gain a market advantage, and may be said to be 'protected'.

The phrase 'other products', in theory, goes beyond 'domestic products'. It is possible to imagine a scenario where high taxes on imports from one country had the effect of protecting imports from another country. However, this has not been the situation which has arisen in practice. Invariably the products claimed to be protected were domestic.

The issue which always arises in consideration of the second paragraph is how to distinguish it from the first. The excess taxation of the first paragraph is also protective, and one would further think that if a product is protected by a discriminatory tax on another product, then they must be similar in some ways. In short, the two paragraphs seem to do much the same thing, and indeed, as will be discussed below, there is a tendency of the Court not to distinguish clearly between them. However, sometimes it does indicate a specific role for the second paragraph, and this should be explained first.

It has been outlined in the quotation below:

> The function of the second paragraph of Art 95 [now 90] is to cover, in addition [to the first paragraph], all forms of indirect tax protection in the case of products which, without being similar within the meaning of the first paragraph, are nevertheless in competition, even partial, indirect or potential, with certain products of the importing country.

> [I]t is sufficient for the imported product to be in competition with the protected domestic production by reason of one or several economic uses to which it may be put, even though the condition of similarity for the purposes of the first paragraph of Art 95 [now 90] is not fulfilled.[17]

The Court said further on in the same case:

> Whilst the criterion indicated in the first paragraph of Art 95 [now 90] consists in the comparison of the tax burdens ... the second paragraph of that article is based upon a more general criterion, in other words the protective nature of the system of internal taxation.

---

16   *Commission v Italy* Case 184/85.
17   *Commission v France*, see note 14 above.

Thus the second paragraph is essentially a broadening of the first. It goes somewhat further, and catches products with a more distant market relationship, and less in common, but which would still benefit from price increases to the other.

It is also a slightly weaker paragraph than the first. If two products are similar, any discriminatory taxation is prohibited. There is no need to explore the effects of this. On the other hand, it is arguable that the second paragraph actually demands some kind of empirical investigation. Even if the products are in competition, and even if they are taxed differently, is there actually 'protection'? It may be that a *de minimis* tax difference simply has no effect. Would you be influenced in your choice of television by a difference in price of one euro? Thus, theoretically, the second paragraph can tolerate some difference in the amount of tax imposed.

This could be important. Products that are not similar, but just have some competitive relationship, may well be different enough to fall under different tax rules. For example, fizzy drinks and fruit juices might not be similar, but might come within the second paragraph, yet might be taxed quite differently for perfectly sensible reasons – they are very different in important ways, such as how healthy they are. To require identical amounts of tax on any products that might be to some extent in competition, even if they have important differences, would be an impossible demand. Thus the second paragraph reflects this, with its more flexible wording.

However, the differences between the paragraphs have not emerged as clearly from the cases as one might expect. This is as a result of what has been called 'globalisation'.

2.2.8 Globalisation

This is the term used to describe the common practice of the Court of considering Art 90 as if it was not divided in two. Faced with a factual situation it asks whether the taxes applied are *'discriminatory or protective'* and answers that question in a general way, without distinguishing between the two. The overall Art 90 rule, as understood by the Court, then seems to be that taxation must be levied according to objective criteria related to the products, so that any difference between the tax on an import and a domestic product can be traced to these real differences, and not to discrimination or protectionism. Moreover, even if there is an objective basis for different tax levels, if the effect is that imports tend to be in the higher class, the tax differences probably need to be proportionate. This is what emerges from the cases discussed below.

While on the one hand this approach can be criticised as imprecise, and damaging to the individual character of each paragraph, it is also practical and easy, and avoids the drawing of impossible distinctions, while allowing a focus on the substantive issues. In fact, the majority of the most important Art 90 cases have been decided in this way. Some of these deserve a brief examination.

In the *Humblot*[18] case, and its follow-up, *Feldain*,[19] a French tax on cars was in issue. The tax increased with the car's power rating. Above a certain power rating there was a 'special tax' which was almost five times as high as the tax on cars below this rating. It

---

18   *Humblot* Case 112/84.
19   *Feldain* Case 433/85.

just so happened that no cars were made in France which exceeded this power rating, and so the exceptionally high tax caught only imported cars.

The Court found that this was clearly discriminatory and protective. The idea of a progressive tax might be acceptable, but the sudden leap in tax was not justified by any objective considerations, and since it only caught imports must therefore be seen as contrary to Art 90. Had there been some good reason why cars above this power rating should have such a special tax – because there was some dramatic increase in their pollution output, for example – the situation might have been different. The objective difference in characteristics might have made them dissimilar, and non-comparable. However, there was no such difference and therefore, there was discrimination.

This is a good example of what is often called indirect discrimination. The tax system was not based explicitly on the origin of the cars, but in practice domestic cars and imports were taxed differently, without any objective basis for this.

Another set of important cases are the drinks cases. In most countries alcohol is relatively highly taxed, but the levels vary according to the drink. The question therefore arises whether different types of drinks are in competition with each other. As discussed above, this issue is partly about consumer preference, but also requires the Court to think beyond this. The matter is complicated by the different tastes and traditions in each country.

In a case against the United Kingdom, it was found that beer and wine could not generally be compared, but cheap wine and beer could, and here the higher tax on wine had a protective effect on the domestic beer production. It marked wine as a 'luxury product', making people less likely to buy it as an alternative to beer.[20]

In a case against France, a spirits tax was under consideration.[21] Spirits made from grapes were taxed at a lower rate than spirits made from grains. France is, of course, a producer of brandy – made from grapes – but not of vodka or whisky – made from grains. The French government contested that these two categories were not comparable. The first were digestives, drunk after a meal, while the second were aperitifs, drunk before. Therefore they were not similar, and there was no protective effect. The Court decided not to decide about similarity, since it was sure that there was at least some competition between the two types of drink, and so at least the second paragraph was infringed.

Most importantly, in a case against Denmark, the Court had to consider a situation where there was a significant domestic production of both the higher and lower taxed drinks.[22] Spirits were taxed highly, and wine at a lower rate. Scotch whisky producers complained, saying that fruit wine made in Denmark was being protected. The Danish retorted that most of the – highly taxed – spirits consumed in Denmark were also made in Denmark. Therefore they could hardly be accused of protectionism.

The Court accepted this. It said that where a system distinguishes between products on the basis of objective criteria, and a significant proportion of domestic production falls in each tax category, it is not contrary to Art 90. In some ways this is a strange ruling; the

---

20 *Commission v UK*, see note 15 above.
21 *Commission v France*, see note 14 above.
22 *Johnny Walker* Case 243/84.

protective effect on the fruit wine is not affected by the fact that Denmark makes lots of highly taxed aquavit. The Court's logic seems elusive. However, as a general principle, the fact that a lot of domestic production is as highly taxed as imports is good evidence that the tax system is intended to reflect legitimate policy aims, and not to discriminate against imports. In the light of this the Court will of course be more sympathetic to it.

2.2.9 Justification

This last point raises a final issue: supposing there are different tax rates on two products, that do provide for a protective effect on the domestic production, but there is also a very good reason for the different tax rates; does the existence of this justification make any difference? Reading Art 90 one might think that the answer would be negative. It does not mention justifications for taxation differences, but merely prohibits them. However, some of the caselaw suggests that the Court is more flexible.

In *Chemial Farmaceutici SpA v DAF SpA*,[23] Italy taxed synthetic alcohol at a much higher rate than that produced by natural fermentation, even though the final products of the two processes were identical, indistinguishable in fact. Italy produced only natural alcohol. Foreign synthetic alcohol producers complained that this was contrary to Art 90, but the Court rejected this. There were good reasons for encouraging natural alcohol production rather than the synthetic version. Thus *'the system of taxation pursues an objective of legitimate industrial policy'*. Moreover, *'although the rate of tax prescribed for synthetic alcohol results in restraining the importation of synthetic alcohol originating in other member states, it has an equivalent economic effect in the national territory in that it also hampers the establishment of profitable production of the same product by Italian industry'*.

Now a process of manufacture could perhaps be seen as part of the 'characteristics' of a product, and so one can see that maybe the two kinds of alcohol were not similar, in the meaning of the first paragraph. However, it is very hard to see that there was not a protective effect within the second paragraph. They were clearly in direct and complete competition, but the natural alcohol was favoured by lower tax. Thus, although there was no direct nationality discrimination, in practice the domestic production was protected. Neither the policy aims, nor the stifling of any embryonic Italian synthetic alcohol industry, would seem to affect this.

Therefore the Court must be understood as consciously introducing the possibility of justification of a protective effect into the second paragraph. This may be explained by the fact that without this possibility member states would not be able to tax more highly any product which they did not produce – a similar situation to that of the bananas under Art 25, discussed above. There would be a circularity; a member state might introduce a high tax rate on an environmentally damaging product which was produced domestically, and succeed in replacing it on the national market with a more friendly one, but would then be no longer able to continue its policy. In order to avoid this kind of destructive interference with government, if the Court is satisfied that different tax rates really are justified by objective considerations, it may find that no protective effect exists. Put another way, perhaps it is saying that the real protection is not of the national product, but of the beneficial one, and this is acceptable.

---

23   *Chemial* Case 140/79.

CHAPTER 3

THE FREE MOVEMENT OF GOODS: QUANTITATIVE RESTRICTIONS

Article 28 EC says that *'quantitative restrictions on imports, and all measures having equivalent effect, shall be prohibited between member states'*.

Article 29 EC says that *'quantitative restrictions on exports, and all measures having equivalent effect, shall be prohibited between member states'*.

Although the wording of the two is very similar, they have been interpreted differently, and so need to be dealt with separately. However, the meanings of the terms 'quantitative restriction' and 'measure' are the same in each article. These can therefore be dealt with as preliminaries.

3.1 WHAT IS A QUANTITATIVE RESTRICTION?

Quantitative restrictions are those which limit imports or exports to a particular quantity. Thus a rule that only 10,000 cars per year may be imported, or that only 10% of national coal production may be exported, would be a quantitative restriction. A total ban on imports or exports is also caught.

Contrast this with Arts 25 and 90. They concerned themselves with measures which imposed duties or taxes on imports or exports. In practice such imposition will also reduce the total amount of cross-border movement, but it does not set any particular limit to the total quantity. It merely asks a price.

3.2 WHAT IS A MEASURE?

A measure is a catch-all word covering the various types of rule and act which may contravene Arts 28 or 29. The types of act or thing that may be a 'measure' include a law of any kind, an internal regulation, or even a mere practice.

The first case includes, in theory, judicial acts – the decisions of judges. Thus, if a judge applied the EC Treaty wrongly, in a way that restricted imports, this would in itself be a violation of Art 28, attributable to the member state. However, in those circumstances a simple appeal and a reference to the Court would probably be a more sensible course of action than a new lawsuit on the basis of the judge's 'violation'.

The second case covers administrative rules and regulations which govern the behaviour of authorities but may not technically be laws. They are still measures.

The last case covers the situation where an authority behaves in a way affecting trade, but it is not possible to point to a particular rule or regulation governing this. In this situation, it has been said that the practice should have enough regularity and generality that it looks rule-like[1] in order to be a measure. Thus a true one-off act – a particular

---

1   *Commission v France* Case 21/84.

decision without a basis in any law, rule or practice – may not be one. A decision by a civil servant to refuse all tenders from foreign companies for a particular supply contract, that was not part of any general practice, might therefore escape.

However, if the act was really without normative basis, it would probably be contrary to national procedure – civil servants are not usually allowed to indulge their whims. In that case national law would be sufficient to overturn the decision. On the other hand, if there was a true discretion then the legal basis of this discretion could be seen as the measure, and we would be back within one of the first two cases. It could then be argued that the rules giving discretion to discriminate were measures contrary to Art 28.

The last case also covers situations such as that in *Buy Irish*.[2] The Irish government had set up a body to promote Irish goods, and it was being claimed that this was contrary to Art 28. One proposed defence was that the body provided publicity and moral support to Irish producers, but did not lay down any binding rules or have a decision-making function. It was merely a marketing body. Therefore neither its creation, nor its actions, could be described as 'measures'.

The Court rejected this because:

> ... regardless of the means used to implement it, the campaign is a reflection of the Irish government's considered intention to substitute domestic products for imported products on the Irish market, and thereby to check the flow of imports from other member states.

This shows a broad approach to the idea of a measure. The Court does not want substantive anti-movement behaviour to escape on technical grounds.

3.3 PUBLIC AND PRIVATE MEASURES

Articles 28 and 29 do not say who the measures must be by. Here, a measure has been described as if it was something done by the state. This is usually true. 'Measures' within the articles are usually acts of the government, or any public authority or body, or agent thereof. However, that is not the whole truth. As discussed in Chapter 12, some measures of private bodies are also included. It is useful to bear this in mind.

3.4 ARTICLE 28

Article 28 is the most important article in the free movement of goods, and has been the basis of some of the most significant and creative jurisprudence of the Court of Justice. This jurisprudence has revolved around the idea of the measure having equivalent effect.

Quantitative restrictions are now very rare, and when they do occur they are extremely obvious. There is therefore very little to know about them. However, the article also prohibits measures which have an equivalent effect to quantitative restrictions. These are often referred to as MEEs. They are measures which do not explicitly set limits to imports, but in practice do have the effect of restricting the import of goods. Thus, the same result is achieved as if an explicit quantitative restriction existed.

---

2   *Buy Irish* Case 249/81.

An easy example might be a rule that importers had to apply for a licence to import, and where the processing and issuing of these was slow and inefficient. There would be no explicit quantitative restriction on imports, but the problems caused for importers would certainly cause a reduction in actual imports. Therefore the measure would be an MEE.

The prohibition of MEEs is an example of the purposiveness of Community law, and its emphasis on substance over form. The point is to ensure goods move freely, and member states will not be allowed to escape this obligation by legalistic arguments about whether a rule is truly a quantitative restriction or not. It is the effect that matters, not the form. This emphasis on effect has also led to free movement law being called 'effects-based'.

However, a concentration on effects requires the Court to be realistic. It must consider the real-world effects of a measure. This is not always easy. What kind of rule does have the same effect as a quantitative restriction? How far do we go? For example, if a member state raises taxes, this may lead to a drop in individual incomes. This may reduce consumer spending, and so reduce the volume of imports. In that sense, it could be argued that the measure is an MEE. Does this mean that Art 28 prohibits tax increases? Politics, common sense, and a knowledge of the caselaw will all show that in fact it does not, but any explanation of the article will have to show why not. What are the limits of Art 28? Potentially it seems to go very far indeed. Where and why do we draw our line? This is the central issue of Art 28. A discussion of it always begins with *Dassonville*.[3]

3.4.1 *Dassonville*

In *Dassonville* a Belgian rule came under scrutiny. It required that spirits imported and sold as Scotch whisky had to be accompanied by an official document from the government of the country of origin – which would be the UK government – certifying that they were indeed what they claimed. On the one hand, this rule could be defended as protecting the Belgian consumer from fake whisky. On the other hand, it blocked importers from buying Scotch in France, where it was cheap, and selling it in Belgium. In practice it was impossible to obtain the certificate they needed this way. They could still buy directly from the manufacturers in Scotland, and get a certificate, but then they would have to pay a higher price for the whisky. This arose because the manufacturers sold at different prices to different countries, according to what the market could bear. They sold cheap to France because they were trying to break into the market.

The Court has no tolerance at all for rules that tend to divide the internal market into national units. The Belgian rule did precisely this, entirely preventing exports from France to Belgium. It was a perfect example of an MEE. The Court gave what has now become the classic definition:

> ... all trading rules enacted by member states which are capable of hindering, directly or indirectly, actually or potentially, Intra-Community trade are to be considered as measures having an effect equivalent to quantitative restrictions.

---

3   *Dassonville* Case 8/74.

The first thing to note about this is that it is strikingly, almost insanely, broad. Not only are indirect hindrances included, but so are potential ones. Although the Court does limit itself to trading rules – so this formula would not apply to tax increases – it is hard to think of any rule to do with commerce which could not be said, arguably, to potentially hinder trade in some indirect way.

Therefore, although the phrase is highly quotable, and often quoted, and nice as a nutshell of what Art 28 is all about, it is not much practical use. It needs both explanation and refinement. The caselaw since largely performs this function. If, as has been said, all philosophy since the Greeks is merely footnotes to Plato, then goods law is not much more than footnotes to *Dassonville*.

3.4.2 The 'rule of reason'

The first refinement actually came in *Dassonville* itself. In the paragraph after the quotation above, the Court said:

> ... in the absence of a Community system guaranteeing for consumers the authenticity of a product's designation of origin, if a member state takes measures to prevent unfair practices in this connection, it is however subject to the condition that these measures should be reasonable and that the means of proof required should not act as a hindrance to trade between member states ...

The Court is saying here that measures to protect consumers, such as the Belgian rule in question, are only acceptable to Art 28 if they are reasonable, and the demands they make are not a hindrance to trade. These two conditions could be seen as cumulative – thus a rule must be reasonable *and* it must be no hindrance. In this case the paragraph adds nothing to what we know, since a rule that is not a hindrance is clearly not a problem.

However, another reading of the paragraph, which was adopted by many commentators, was that the conditions were really one condition – the second one was a restatement of the first in another form. Thus, the sentence really said 'these measures should be reasonable, that is, they should not be a hindrance to trade'. From this it was inferred that 'reasonable' measures would not be a hindrance to trade, and so would not be contrary to Art 28.

This tortuous and far from obvious reasoning can be justified on two grounds. First, the idea that reasonable trading rules are not contrary to Art 28 is attractive, and restricts the apparent broadness of that article which we have already discussed. Secondly, there is a precedent for such an idea in American competition law.

According to American antitrust law, as they call it, contracts 'in restraint of trade' are illegal. This is intended to preserve competition from cartels and other restrictive agreements. However, in one sense all contracts are in restraint of trade. If I promise to sell you my car, I cannot sell it to someone else. My trading options are restricted by the contract.

Therefore, when this law was passed, the US Supreme Court was faced with the apparent outlawing of all contracts and the consequent catastrophic destruction of US commerce. To prevent this, it acted decisively. It judged that contracts that were 'reasonable' were not 'in restraint of trade'. Thus normal business could continue as usual, and only 'unreasonable' contracts – such as between members of a cartel – would be illegal under the rule.

Many European commentators saw a parallel to this in *Dassonville*. Having apparently included all trading rules in a desperately wide formula, perhaps the Court was then qualifying this by saying that reasonable ones would not be understood as being hindrances to trade. Article 28 would therefore catch only unreasonable trading rules.

It was not possible to know whether this was correct from *Dassonville* itself, because the Court went on to say that the Belgian rule was contrary to Art 28. It was really only possible for direct importers from the country of origin to satisfy it. Thus it was a case of 'arbitrary discrimination or a disguised restriction on trade' and so presumably both a hindrance and unreasonable.

However, later developments would show that the rule of reason idea was largely correct, and reasonable trading rules do escape the article. However, to understand what is a reasonable trading rule it is necessary to take a broader view, and look at all the kinds of measures which may violate Art 28.

These can be grouped into three categories: discriminatory measures, indistinctly applicable measures, and selling arrangements. The position of each of these categories in the law is different.

This is not at first sight an obvious scheme, but it is fairly conventional in the UK and some other countries, and it does follow the language of the Court, and, as will become clear, in fact it covers all the situations that are likely to arise. It should not be understood to be a rigid gospel though – it is simply a way of arriving at the right answer for a given situation. However, one could also do this by different categorisations, and different rules for each category, and lawyers in some European countries would not recognise this particular approach. It does work though, and one has to make sense somehow, so it will do.

3.4.3 Discriminatory measures

The precise meaning of the term 'discrimination' in free movement law is not simple, and the Court's use of it is vague and sometimes contradictory. This can be a problem, and is discussed in more detail in Chapter 8. However, in the free movement of goods, restrictions which discriminate on grounds of nationality are usually easy to identify. They are measures that apply only to imports or differently from the way they do to national products. The origin of the product is made the basis of its legal treatment.

Thus quantitative restrictions are discriminatory. A rule that 'no imports of X from Y' clearly does not apply to domestic products, only to imports from Y.

Also, many MEEs are discriminatory. For example, a rule like that in *Dassonville*, that all imports must have a certificate of authenticity, imposes a requirement on foreign goods that domestic goods do not have to meet. Alternatively, there may be a benefit that is only available to domestic goods. In the *German Quality Products* case,[4] a mark bearing this phrase (approximately, in German) was reserved by law to German products of various types which could show they complied with various quality standards. The Court found the measure contrary to Art 28. Although it did not even apply to imports, it

---

4   *Commission v Germany* Case C-325/00.

was discrimination, and therefore an MEE, because it created a marketing advantage that was exclusively available to national goods.

Some discriminatory MEEs are not quite so clear. For example, in the *Origin Marking*[5] case the UK government required that some goods had to be marked with their country of origin if they were to be sold in the UK. They said that this was not discriminatory – the rule applied equally to domestic and imported goods.

However, the Court took the view that the rule did not really apply equally. It said:

> The requirements relating to the indication of origin of goods are applicable without distinction to domestic and imported products only in form because, by their very nature, they are intended to enable the consumer to distinguish between those two categories of products, which may thus prompt him to give his preference to national products.

Thus a mark saying 'France' was not equivalent to one saying 'England' in the eyes of the consumer, and so the rule in fact imposed different requirements on foreign and imported goods. The Court is looking much more at substance, and effect, than at form.

This is also true of the *Irish Pipes*[6] case. An Irish local authority insisted that tenders for a pipe contract be based on pipes certified as complying with Irish standards. The only authority certifying this was in Dublin. In practice, then, a foreign supplier, even offering pipes just as good, even meeting the Irish specification, would not be able to bid, since it would not have the certification.

The Court found this to be contrary to Art 28, and said the matter could have been avoided just by asking for Irish Standard 'or equivalent'. This would have allowed foreign pipe suppliers with pipes of equivalent specification to bid. It can be understood from this that by not allowing equivalent specifications, the council was *in reality* saying 'Irish pipes only', and so was discriminating on grounds of nationality.

Discriminatory restrictions on the free movement of goods are always contrary to Art 28. If they are to be allowed to stand it can only be because they satisfy one of the exceptional requirements of Art 30, discussed in Chapter 7. However, this situation is rare. Such restrictions are an offence against the basic principles of the internal market, and so the Court takes a very hard line.

It might be thought that discrimination alone would not be enough to infringe Art 28. It should also be necessary to show some actual effect – following the wording of the article. Thus an example of discrimination that was too trivial to make any practical difference would not be caught.

There are two responses to this. One is the practical one that if somebody has gone to the trouble to take the matter to court then there is probably some significance to the discrimination. The cost and trouble of legal action will filter out the genuinely unimportant case.

A more legal response is that in any case there appears to be no *de minimis* rule in free movement law. In the *Van de Haar*[7] case the Court said that Art 28 does not distinguish between rules according to the size of their effect. Any possible effect, however small, on

---

5   *Origin Marking* Case 207/83.
6   *Irish Pipes* Case 45/87.
7   *Van de Haar* Joined Cases 177 and 178/82.

inter-state trade is sufficient to make a measure an MEE. This statement must be understood subject to other caselaw; as we will see, the Court has declared that some types of measure have no effect at all. However, if the measure is of a type which may have an effect, the size of that effect will not be an issue.

3.4.4 Indistinctly applicable measures

The second type of measure which may infringe Art 28 is the 'indistinctly applicable' measure. This disastrous phrase may be the result of the translation problems that come with a multi-lingual legal system. There is much to be said for not using it, since what little meaning it may bear in normal English has only a weak relation to the function it performs in the law. The measures it describes are not 'indistinctly applicable' in a normal English sense. However, the phrase seems to have become standard in both the reports of cases and academic writing and textbooks, so it will be used. It should be seen merely as a label, not a meaningful description.

Indistinctly applicable measures in the goods context are rules to do with the production or marketing of goods that apply without distinction to both foreign and domestic goods. This is an enormous category; it covers rules such as safety specifications for electrical goods, and consumer protection rules to do with labelling and information, as well as rules about product descriptions, and packaging or transport rules that are intended to protect the environment. These are all measures which affect the making and marketing of the goods, and which typically apply to all goods on the national territory irrespective of their origin. Thus if the law says that all pizza packaging must be recyclable, the importer of pizzas, and so ultimately the foreign producer, will have to take this into account as much as the domestic producer.

The problem is that the foreign producer probably structures all his manufacturing processes to his national market. He may make his pizzas in plastic packs because that is how Spanish people like them, for example. If he has to change to cardboard to sell to Germany this involves extra costs. By contrast, the German producer will be geared up for the German market, where he probably sells most of his pizzas, and so cardboard will be his basic packaging. He may have a problem if he wants to export to Spain if, for example, cardboard packaging is prohibited there. Therefore, although in both countries the rules are non-discriminatory in the sense that they make no distinction on the basis of the origin of the pizza, the effect is that the internal market will tend to be divided into national units, and there will be less trade in pizzas between Germany and Spain. This may be overcome – if the Spanish producer is confident he will make the extra investment in new packaging processes and perhaps break into Germany. However, he may also decide it is not worth the risk. Therefore there will be some drag on trade.

This obstacle effect is sometimes summed up in the idea of a 'dual burden'. The idea is that complying with regulation is a burden on all business activities, which imposes costs and tends to reduce trade. A national producer selling in his home market only has to comply with one lot of regulations – the home ones. However, the potential exporter – our Spaniard – has to comply with both his home regulations, and his export market regulations. This compliance with two sets of regulations is the 'dual burden' – an extra burden by comparison with the domestic producer. This may be seen as a disadvantage, and an inhibition to export.

Although this sort of obstacle to free movement is of great practical importance – indeed, for the business person, differing national regulations are probably the greatest single practical obstacle to selling abroad – for a long time it was thought that it was not contrary to Art 28 because there was no discrimination involved. Member states were not trying to exclude imports, but merely to regulate markets in the interests of their population, which was surely the right and duty of a national government. As long as an importer was free to import if he complied with national regulation, there was no Art 28 issue. Why should importers not have to comply? Should a member state have to structure its regulation to satisfy foreign producers?

3.4.5   *Cassis de Dijon*

In the end the answers to these questions were made clear in *Cassis de Dijon*.[8] In this case a complaint was made about a German rule that fruit liqueurs had to contain a certain minimum amount of alcohol – around 30%. It was the view of the German government that this rule protected the consumer, by ensuring that he got a certain minimum alcohol level. Otherwise he might be tempted by a cheaper liqueur, only to discover later that it was weak. This was particularly so since alcohol was the most expensive part of a fruit liqueur. Thus by cutting the alcohol levels producers could undercut their competitors in price. This was also considered unfair competition.

The complaint was from French producers of cassis – a blackcurrant liqueur. Cassis is a traditional French drink, but it is typically weaker there than in Germany – and contains less than the minimum alcohol level. Thus French producers could not export to Germany without remaking their production process, with the costs that involves. When the Court considered this case, it first set out some fairly general principles:

> ... in the absence of common rules relating to the production and marketing of alcohol ... it is for the member states to regulate all matters relating to the production and marketing of alcohol and alcoholic beverages on their own territory.

> Obstacles to movement within the Community resulting from disparities between the national laws relating to the marketing of the products in question must be accepted in so far as those provisions may be recognized as being necessary in order to satisfy mandatory requirements relating in particular to the effectiveness of fiscal supervision, the protection of public health, the fairness of commercial transactions and the defence of the consumer.

The Court is saying that if there is no harmonisation in the area – on which see Chapter 10 – in principle it remains for member states to regulate these kinds of production and marketing matters. However, it is also saying that where these regulations cause an obstacle to movement they will only be accepted – by Art 28 – *insofar* as they may be justified by some good reason. This is the meaning of the rather obscure second paragraph.

The phrase 'mandatory requirements' is another unfortunate example of Court-speak, but is now being replaced in most writing, and some more recent judgments, by phrases using the idea of 'objective justification'. This is what is done in the remainder of this text.

---

8   *Cassis de Dijon* Case 120/78.

Thus the test for whether an indistinctly applicable measure is acceptable is whether it can be 'objectively justified'. This is what the Court intended to say.

This idea will be discussed extensively below, but first it is useful to see how the Court applied its principles in the particular case. It considered the German government's arguments, and dismissed them fairly easily, pointing out that all its worries could be met by requiring clear labelling. If the alcohol content was clearly displayed on the label the consumer would be protected, and the effect on inter-state trade of such a requirement would be much less, if any, than the minimum alcohol rule.

The point was, although the Court did not put it this openly, that perhaps French producers already displayed the alcohol content, and even if they didn't, the costs of amending labels were clearly less than those of amending alcohol content. They then said:

> ... it is clear from the foregoing that the requirements relating to the minimum alcohol content of alcoholic beverages do not serve a purpose which is in the general interest and such as to take precedence over the requirements of the free movement of goods, which constitutes one of the fundamental rules of the Community.

> In practice, the principal effect of requirements of this nature is to promote alcoholic beverages having a high alcohol content by excluding from the national market products of other member states which do not answer that description.

> It therefore appears that the unilateral requirement imposed by the rules of a member state of a minimum alcohol content for the purposes of the sale of alcoholic beverages constitutes an obstacle to trade which is incompatible with the provisions of Art 30 [now 28] of the Treaty.

> There is therefore no valid reason why, provided that they have been lawfully produced and marketed in one of the member states, alcoholic beverages should not be introduced into any other member state; the sale of such products may not be subject to a legal prohibition on the marketing of beverages with an alcohol content lower than the limit set by the national rules.

This is a concise and clear statement of why the alcohol requirement was an MEE, and why it should not be allowed. It is, as will be seen by comparison with other cases discussed below, a typical indistinctly applicable measure offending against Art 28.

One of the most important points is in the last paragraph – the statement that goods lawfully produced and marketed in one member state should be able to enter and go on sale in any other member state. This is of course a basic internal market idea, but it is often referred to as the principle of mutual recognition. The idea is that all member states in the Community have essentially adequate regulation, and so if a product complies with the regulation of one state, it should be accepted by others – they should recognise that compliance, and be satisfied by it. This in turn relies on another idea – mutual trust – which is not always present. However, the Court is not going to admit or encourage this lack of confidence in foreign product rules. That in itself might be divisive. There is more than a small element of fiction in Community law.

The only concession the Court does make is the one we have seen above – of allowing regulations that are objectively justified and proportionate to remain. It now becomes necessary to examine the scope of this concession.

3.4.6   Objective justification: some theory

In the first quotation from *Cassis* the Court said that indistinctly applicable rules would not be contrary to Art 28 where they could be objectively justified in certain ways, and it listed some examples – in order to protect public health, or to protect the consumer, for example. It has since become clear that these examples were not exhaustive – the list is open. In principle, any good enough reason may serve as an objective justification.

This is the realisation of the *Dassonville* rule of reason idea. Although the rule in *Cassis* was in fact not reasonable/justifiable it was beyond doubt after that case that if it had been, it would have been allowed. In fact the use of the rule of reason analogy is not ideal, and in some ways misleading. In the US ordinary reasonable contracts were allowed, not grudgingly, but because they were the very stuff of trade. They were not a hindrance to trade that had to be accepted, but necessary to it. By contrast, in *Cassis* the Court said that obstacles resulting from national regulatory differences had to be 'accepted' if they were justifiable. It did not find them desirable, or positive; it was merely that it acknowledged that they were too important to simply sweep away. They nevertheless remained negative – obstacles – in the internal market context.

There are two important outcomes from this. One is that where the Court finds a justifiable indistinctly applicable rule, and therefore allows it to stand, it follows that there may be an obstacle to trade that cannot be removed judicially, and so the Commission may begin looking at possibilities of harmonisation. It may seek to issue a directive or regulation standardising national rules so that the obstacle is removed. This is discussed in Chapter 10.

The other outcome is that it seems that *Cassis* may be a fine example of judicial legislation. If the Court had said that justified rules were not obstacles at all, therefore not MEEs, while one might have been able to argue with this factually, it would be staying within the Treaty in allowing them to remain. Article 28 only requires MEEs to be removed.

However, it seemed to say that the rules were still obstacles, and therefore it would seem to follow that they were MEEs. In that case, in inventing the idea of objective justifications that allow the rules to remain, it was inventing an exception to Art 28. There are already exceptions to this article in Art 30, which are discussed in Chapter 7, but these, as will be seen, are a quite different matter. The objective justifications seem to be new, judicially invented exceptions – judicial derogation from the EC Treaty.

On the one hand, the Court is so purposive in its approach to the law, and the objective justification idea seems in some ways to be a practical and sensible one that perhaps it is over pedantic to be too worried about just another example of loose, but functional, European Court of Justice jurisprudence. On the other hand, some academics and lawyers found it outrageous that the Court should take it upon itself to rewrite the Treaty. Others still maintain that a justified indistinctly applicable rule is not contrary to Art 28.

Thus there are two debates, both rather academic – did the Court rewrite the Treaty, and was it right to? – but probably more important than these for most people is the question of what objective justification has been found to mean in the cases.

3.4.7 Objective justification: interpretation in practice

The Court said in *Cassis* that an indistinctly applicable measure escapes Art 28 only 'insofar as it is necessary' to satisfy the objectively justifiable requirement in question. Thus it is only insofar as it is necessary to protect the consumer, or the stability of financial markets, or whatever, that the measure is allowed. Insofar as it goes beyond the necessary, it is no longer justifiable and is condemned.

This is using the idea of proportionality, alongside that of justification. The way it is commonly stated is that a measure must pursue a justified aim *and* be proportionate to be allowed. Thus one should first look at the broad aim, and decide if it is a reasonable one, and then one should ask whether the measure is proportionate to that aim. There are a few things to say about both these points.

Whether the aim pursued is justifiable is essentially a common sense matter. Is it a legitimate policy aim for a government to pursue? This is usually not the point on which a rule falls or stands, although it is worth remembering that aims which are contrary to the purposes of the internal market, such as protecting national habits or tastes, although they can sometimes be presented in a way which makes them look quite reasonable, are less likely to be considered justifiable by the Court, for obvious reasons. For example, in a recent Austrian case the aim of preserving local businesses in a very remote area was not accepted as justified.[9]

Proportionality is originally a concept from German law, where it is quite scientifically composed of a number of different elements. For a measure to be proportionate it must be effective towards the end that it aims at (that is, it must to some extent *work*), it must go no further than is necessary to achieve this (so a sensible aim can't be used as a cover for rules that aren't necessary to achieve it), and it must be, confusingly, proportionate. This last – 'small p' proportionality – is therefore just one part of overall – 'big P' – proportionality. Small p proportionality means that the measure must be in proportion to what it aims to achieve. A reasonable but not incredibly important aim would not justify a massively burdensome rule, even if that rule did achieve the aim very effectively, and was necessary to achieve it.

Fortunately for non-German lawyers, the Court does not use the concept this precisely. It takes a fairly global view, usually concentrating on whether a measure goes beyond what is necessary to achieve its aims. It will only examine effectiveness and small p proportionality if there is an obvious need to.

Thus in *Cassis* the aim – protecting the consumer – was justified, but the measure – banning low alcohol liqueurs – was disproportionate. While it did achieve its end, it went beyond that and also made intra-Community trade unnecessarily difficult. Labelling could protect the consumer adequately, while not causing the same difficulties. It was a more efficient, less burdensome solution.

Justification and proportionality have now been applied in a large number of Art 28 cases. A few examples of some of the most famous and important show their extent.

---

9 *Heimdienst (Austrian Grocers)* Case C-254/98.

One of the more amusing is the case of *Rau*.[10] A Belgian decree stated that all margarine had to be sold in cube-shaped packs. A foreign supplier of cone-shaped packs of margarine complained. The Belgian government said that the rule was necessary so that consumers could tell butter and margarine apart, and thus not make unfortunate mistakes. It said that cuboid margarine was 'rooted' in the habits of Belgians.

The Court admitted the desirability of not confusing the Belgian population, but said that:

> If a member state has a choice between various measures to attain the same objective it should choose the means which least restricts the free movement of goods.

And then it said that consumers could be protected just as well by labelling.

Here there is a clear choice between protecting the population through paternalistic and authoritarian rules, or by providing them with information to make their own decisions (labels). Although this choice is not always as simple as in this case – see the section on Market Access in Chapter 8 for more – the replacement of the first approach, which it may be said is the traditional Continental European one, with the second, is a very strong theme in the indistinctly applicable caselaw. Endless restrictive national product regulations have been wearily swept aside with the comment that labels could protect the consumer just as well. The Court has much more faith in the ability of consumers to make informed decisions than do the member states.

Another, highly controversial, example of this is the *German Beer* case.[11] As beer lovers will know, German beer enjoys an excellent reputation, largely because of ancient beer purity laws providing that only beer made only of hops, barley, yeast and water may be sold in Germany. No other ingredient may be added. This meant that cheap foreign beers, in which flavour has been replaced by various chemicals, could not be imported to Germany. Beer manufacturers complained.

As well as arguing that the rule protected the consumer, and also public health – because Germans drank so much beer it was particularly important that it was pure – the German government also very creatively argued that 'Bier' in German meant the pure version. A drink with chemicals in it simply was not 'Bier' in German eyes and so could not be marketed as such. The issue was thus not just one of consumer protection, but of language itself.

The Court rejected the health and language arguments, and to the consumer one its response was again that consumers could be protected by labels. If beer was made according to the purity laws it could declare this on the label. Impure beer could not. The consumer could then choose.

One important point about this is that the Court did not object to the continued regulation of German producers. Thus it is still compulsory for beer made in Germany to comply with the purity laws. However, beer from outside Germany that does not comply may not be kept out.

---

10   *Rau* Case 261/81.
11   *German Beer* Case 178/84.

Other examples of rules that have been found not to be justified and proportionate are an Italian rule that only vinegar made from wine could be sold as vinegar[12] – importers of apple vinegar from Germany complained – and a German ban on Clinique cosmetics on the ground that they would confuse consumers into thinking they were medical products (Klinik is German for hospital).[13]

An example of a rule that was accepted as justified and proportionate, at least in part, is in the *Danish Recycling* case.[14] A Danish law provided that sellers of soft drinks had to have a system for return and recycling of the containers. In order to make this practical it also provided that all but a very small proportion of the drinks sold had to be in one of a number of approved container types. By limiting the number of types of container on the market it hoped to make recycling easier. Both rules were based on environmental considerations.

Foreign soft drinks producers complained that this meant that they could not sell their drinks in Denmark, because they did not use the approved containers, and it was expensive to change to them. Moreover, if they were trying to break into the market they might have only low sales, and for a small market player it was very expensive to ensure a recycling scheme. Thus this rule was also an obstacle to free movement.

The Court allowed the compulsory recycling, but not the approved containers. It said that the protection of the environment was a legitimate aim, and re-using containers a legitimate part of this. In order to achieve this, compulsory recycling was indispensable, and did not go further than necessary. Therefore it was not contrary to Art 28.

However, the approved container scheme did go further than necessary, since a scheme for returning non-approved containers would also achieve the overall end of re-use and environmental protection. The scheme might be a little less efficient if there were non-standard containers, but foreign drinks in such containers were only a small part of the overall market, and so this point was not enough to outweigh the problems caused to importers. Therefore they should be allowed to import in non-approved containers provided they arranged for return and re-use.

This is a good example of very pragmatic and facts-based reasoning by the Court, achieving a compromise between legitimate views on both sides. The decision was received with considerable dismay in Denmark though, where the environment is often considered more important than a single European market.

3.4.8 Selling arrangements/socio-economic rules

Cassis was a very powerful deregulatory case – it enabled the Court to overrule a broad range of national regulations in the cause of openness. However, a feeling gradually grew that it was possible to go too far. This was particularly prompted by a number of Sunday Trading cases in the UK.[15] At that time shops were not allowed to open on Sundays, and a number of importers complained that this was reducing overall sales, and therefore

---

12 *Gilli and Andres* Case 788/79.
13 *Clinique* Case C-315/92.
14 *Danish Recycling* Case 302/86.
15 Eg, *Torfaen* Case 145/88; *Stoke-on-Trent City Council* Case C-169/91.

overall imports, and was therefore an MEE, and contrary to Art 28. Sunday trading rules were largely implemented by local authorities in the UK, and several of them referred questions about this to the Court.

These do look like trading rules within *Dassonville*, but not obviously rules to do with production or marketing in the *Cassis* sense. Nevertheless the Court analysed them as indistinctly applicable rules – since there was no unequal application anywhere – and seemed to suggest that while they were obstacles they must be accepted because they were justified and proportionate. It was for each member state to choose its own Sunday trading rules.

In one sense this was a relief for those who thought that Art 28 should not be used to interfere with this kind of social issue. The Court had accepted that opening restrictions could be justified. However, in another sense it was a shock. Why should the rules need to be justified? Why should regulation of what was a social, even for many people religious, matter have to comply with trade laws?

From another perspective, that of the Court, its approach meant that it could expect a growing caseload. Rules to do with opening hours, perhaps employment of shop assistants, maybe planning permission for building stores, why not road maintenance and public transport, might all be challenged under Art 28 and the member states would have to show they were justified and proportionate to save them. Things seemed potentially out of control.

Control was reasserted in the *Keck* case.[16] This set the limits to Art 28 which still stand.

3.4.9 *Keck*

Messieurs Keck and Mithouard sold coffee in France at below the price they had paid for it. They did this in order to build up market share. Later they would probably raise the price to a normal level. This sort of initial discount is a fairly standard marketing technique. However, it is illegal in France, and they were prosecuted. In their defence they claimed that the rule was contrary to Art 28, because it was an obstacle to the free movement of goods. It made it harder to break into a new market, and therefore restricted intra-Community trade.

Contrary to the Sunday Trading cases, and a number of other similar cases which had been before the Court in previous years, the Court decided to draw a line. It is worth setting out several paragraphs of the judgment, because they are very clear, and also important:

11 By virtue of Art 30 [now 28], quantitative restrictions on imports and all measures having equivalent effect are prohibited between member states. The Court has consistently held that any measure which is capable of directly or indirectly, actually or potentially, hindering intra-Community trade constitutes a measure having equivalent effect to a quantitative restriction.

12 National legislation imposing a general prohibition on resale at a loss is not designed to regulate trade in goods between member states.

---

16 *Keck* Case C-267/91.

13 Such legislation may, admittedly, restrict the volume of sales, and hence the volume of sales of products from other member states, in so far as it deprives traders of a method of sales promotion. But the question remains whether such a possibility is sufficient to characterize the legislation in question as a measure having equivalent effect to a quantitative restriction on imports.

14 In view of the increasing tendency of traders to invoke Art 30 [now 28] of the Treaty as a means of challenging any rules whose effect is to limit their commercial freedom even where such rules are not aimed at products from other member states, the Court considers it necessary to re-examine and clarify its case-law on this matter.

15 It is established by the case-law beginning with 'Cassis de Dijon' that, in the absence of harmonization of legislation, obstacles to free movement of goods which are the consequence of applying, to goods coming from other member states where they are lawfully manufactured and marketed, rules that lay down requirements to be met by such goods (such as those relating to designation, form, size, weight, composition, presentation, labelling, packaging) constitute measures of equivalent effect prohibited by Art 30 [now 28]. This is so even if those rules apply without distinction to all products unless their application can be justified by a public-interest objective taking precedence over the free movement of goods.

16 By contrast, contrary to what has previously been decided, the application to products from other member states of national provisions restricting or prohibiting certain selling arrangements is not such as to hinder directly or indirectly, actually or potentially, trade between member states within the meaning of the *Dassonville* judgment, so long as those provisions apply to all relevant traders operating within the national territory and so long as they affect in the same manner, in law and in fact, the marketing of domestic products and of those from other member states.

17 Provided that those conditions are fulfilled, the application of such rules to the sale of products from another member state meeting the requirements laid down by that state is not by nature such as to prevent their access to the market or to impede access any more than it impedes the access of domestic products. Such rules therefore fall outside the scope of Art 30 [now 28] of the Treaty.

18 Accordingly, the reply to be given to the national court is that Art 30 [now 28] of the EEC Treaty is to be interpreted as not applying to legislation of a member state imposing a general prohibition on resale at a loss.

The Court here reaffirms *Dassonville* (para 11), and *Cassis* (para 15), and then accepts that the rule in question may well reduce overall inter-state trade (para 13). One would imagine that it would follow from this that it would be caught by Art 28. However, the Court then makes an entirely policy-led, pragmatic decision to limit Art 28, acknowledging that this may be contrary to some of its earlier cases (paras 14 and 16). It says that rules governing selling arrangements, by contrast with indistinctly applicable rules governing production and marketing, are not generally MEEs (para 16).

It justifies this on two grounds. First, it says that such rules are not designed to regulate inter-state trade (para 12). 'Designed' here looks like another way of saying 'intended'. In an effects-based law this ought to be irrelevant. The Court's comment is therefore odd. Secondly, it says that such rules do not prevent market access, or at least no more for imports than for national goods (para 17). Therefore, they are not MEEs.

The implication of the second point seems to be that Art 28 only applies to rules that have a greater effect on foreign goods than national ones – rules with what is generally called a 'disparate impact'. This does indeed support the exclusion from Art 28 of rules governing selling arrangements such as that in *Keck*, or in the Sunday Trading cases. Whereas a foreign producer may have a greater burden than a national one in complying with product rules – the dual burden argument above – he only has to sell his goods once. If a shop is closed on Sunday it may well affect him, but no more than it would affect a national supplier. There is nothing differential.

This limiting of Art 28 to rules of disparate impact, and consequent excluding of selling arrangements, is the key point of *Keck*, and one of obvious importance. It is also a point which has been greatly discussed and criticised. Most of these criticisms centre on policy matters, which are discussed in Chapter 8. Here it will be enough to explain in more detail how *Keck* fits into the rest of goods law, and what exactly its effects are.

3.4.10 *Keck* in context

Since the Court suggests that it is overruling some of its previous judgments, it makes sense to briefly test *Keck* for consistency with the rest of Art 28 law, beginning with the article itself.

Therefore the first question is: does the article suggest that only rules with a disparate impact are MEEs? Probably yes; a quantitative restriction of course affects foreign goods more than domestic ones. Therefore it would seem to follow that a measure that is equivalent to one ought to do so also.

A second test might be against *Dassonville*. Here it is not really consistent. *Dassonville* simply says that all hindrances are caught. *Keck* is clearly a retreat from this. However, as we have seen, *Dassonville* is a statement of philosophy, not a piece of practical interpretation. It is a light to run towards, not to see by. Therefore, perhaps it would be misguided to expect it also to be implemented.

Thirdly, *Keck* may be tested against *Cassis*. Here it does seem to fit. For the reasons just above, indistinctly applicable product rules do have a greater effect on importers, and the Court did make this part of the reasoning, in that case, and in subsequent indistinctly applicable caselaw. This supports the proposition that disparate impact is central to the idea of an MEE.

On balance, it seems fair to say that *Keck* is not a radical departure from the important previous principles. It does form part of a reasonably consistent approach to the law. It was in fact the Sunday Trading cases that were the aberration, in extending *Cassis*-type principles to non-*Cassis* situations – those not involving product rules.

3.4.11 What is a selling arrangement?

Selling arrangements, in the sense that the Court uses the phrase, are, fairly obviously, measures which govern how goods are sold. They are sometimes called 'socio-economic' measures, meaning that although they are economic rules, to do with business, a large part of their purpose is usually social – for example opening hours, and perhaps (arguably) minimum wages for shop staff. The most important thing for the lawyer to know about selling arrangements is how to distinguish them from indistinctly applicable product rules. This determines whether they come within or without Art 28.

Here the question to ask is whether the rule in question requires the product or its packaging to be changed before it may be sold.[17] If it does, it is a *Cassis* product rule. If it does not, it may be a selling arrangement. So, in *Cassis* itself, in order to comply with the German rule the French manufacturers would have had to have added more alcohol. Similarly, in *Clinique*, because the product packaging bore the brand name, a physical change would also have had to have been made to comply.

On the other hand, in *Keck*, the coffee and its packaging were of no importance. It was the manner of sale that mattered, just as in the Sunday Trading cases. Advertising, the licensing of certain kinds of shops, or the restriction of certain goods – such as alcohol or sex goods – to certain kinds of shops, would all be selling arrangements.

A difficult area might come where rules that were selling arrangements only applied to certain kinds of product. For example, supposing Germany had an advertising ban on impure beer. It might be said this was a selling arrangement, but one could also say that in order to advertise one had to change one's product, and so the rule was a product rule. In fact, in this kind of situation the rule probably is a selling arrangement, because the product can be sold as it is – just not advertised. This may seem odd, because such a ban would look like protectionism, which is clearly contrary to the internal market. The answer would probably lie in the *Keck* proviso, which is now discussed.

3.4.12 The *Keck* proviso

There are limits to the restriction in *Keck*. Selling arrangements are excluded from Art 28, but only *'so long as they affect in the same manner, in law and in fact, the marketing of domestic products and of those from other member states'*. If this is not true, then one has to treat the rule in the same way as if it was a product rule: first ask if it is discriminatory, and if so, prohibited. Then, if it is applied equally to national and foreign goods (but merely has a difference in effect in fact) ask if it is justified and proportionate.

Therefore a rule that only national goods could be sold in supermarkets would clearly be back within Art 28, and prohibited as a discriminatory rule. A rule that only local goods could be sold in local Sunday markets might be found to be discriminatory also, because underlying it was a distinction between foreign and native, but it might also be found to be non-discriminatory (see Chapter 8 for more on this), even though it kept away foreign goods, because the underlying principle was, for example, a legitimate environmental one to do with goods transport on Sundays, and not to do with national origin. In this latter case the Court would then ask if the rule was justified and proportionate.

In practice, the *Keck* proviso has been of very limited use. A number of creative attempts have been made to use it, but with little success. One of the more unusual attempts was in the case of *Semeraro*.[18] Italian rules prohibited big out-of-town shopping centres from opening on Sundays, while small urban stores were allowed to. It was argued that this did not affect foreign and domestic goods equally in fact, because the big

---

17 *Familiapress* Case C-368/95.
18 *Semeraro* Cases C-418–21/93.

stores sold a much higher proportion of foreign goods. Thus, effectively, national goods could be sold for more time each week than foreign ones.

The argument was backed up with statistics, but the Court did not give a meaningful answer to it. It just reiterated that selling arrangements were outside Art 28. It may well have been fearful that once it began to listen to this type of statistical argument it would be very difficult to draw lines, and the limiting effect of *Keck* would be undone. No doubt if one is creative enough almost any rule can be shown to have differential effects. Perhaps sex shops sell a higher proportion of foreign goods than the average of other shops. Would this then mean that licensing sex shops but not other shops is back within Art 28? The Court simply does not want this kind of thing to happen. *Keck* is a formalistic drawing of a line, sacrificing the finer points of philosophy to practicality.

A slightly more successful attempt to use the proviso occurred in *de Agostini*.[19] Here a manufacturer of toys complained that he was unable to break into the Swedish market because there was a ban on advertising aimed at children. The Court did not exclude the possibility that there might be an unequal effect on foreign and domestic producers (presumably because domestic producers were already established and so had less need of advertising) but left the decision to the national court.

However, the most significant change in the Court's generally reluctant attitude to the proviso has occurred in two recent cases. One was *Heimdienst*.[20] In remote parts of Austria many villages are served by travelling grocers and other tradespeople. They sell their goods from vans, and thus people in a community too small or distant to support an ordinary shop can still buy basic goods nearby. However, a rule required that in order to travel around selling in a particular administrative district, a tradesperson must have a permanent establishment in that district. The aim of the rule was to ensure the stability of supply in these areas, which might be vulnerable to having these supplies cut off if they depended upon the whim of firms based further away.

However, it meant German salesmen, even though they might be based just across the border, and not far away, could not compete in Austria. They argued this was contrary to Art 28. In reply, the Austrian government pointed out that Austrian salesmen from more distant areas were also affected. The rule was not based on nationality.

The first thing to note is that the rule is clearly a selling arrangement, and so *prima facie* outside the article. The judgment then continues the argument:

> However, it does not affect in the same manner the marketing of domestic products and that of products from other member states.

> Such legislation imposes an obligation on bakers, butchers and grocers who already have a permanent establishment in another member state and who wish to sell their goods on rounds in a particular administrative district such as an Austrian Verwaltungsbezirk to set up or purchase another permanent establishment in that administrative district or in an adjacent municipality, whilst local economic operators already meet the requirement as to a permanent establishment. Consequently, in order for goods from other member states to enjoy the same access to the market of the member state of importation as domestic goods, they have to bear additional costs.

19 *de Agostini* Case C-34–36/95.
20 *Heimdienst* Case C-254/98.

That conclusion is not affected by the fact that, in each part of the national territory, the legislation affects both the sale of products from other parts of the national territory and the sale of products imported from other member states. For a national measure to be categorised as discriminatory or protective for the purposes of the rules on the free movement of goods, it is not necessary for it to have the effect of favouring national products as a whole or of placing only imported products at a disadvantage and not national products.

Therefore, because the rule was discriminatory it could not benefit from *Keck*.

In *Gourmet International*,[21] a Swedish ban on alcohol advertising came into question. Importers of whisky and wine claimed that this inhibited their entry to the Swedish market.

Although this was a selling arrangement, the Court concluded that it did not apply equally to domestic and imported goods. First, because the consumption of alcohol was influenced by custom and tradition, national products had less need of advertising than imported ones. They could rely on cultural inertia. On the other hand, importers needed to change attitudes to get people to try new drinks.

Secondly, certain types of advertising were not prohibited, notably 'advertorial'. These are advertisements written with the editors of a magazine, in a style that makes them look like content more than advertising. The Court noted that 'for cultural reasons' domestic producers were likely to have more access to this kind of advertising, perhaps because they were in a better position to have good relationships with publishers and editors of national magazines.

As a result, once again, there was discrimination, although the Court also found that this could be justified by use of Art 30.

What is significant about this case is that the differences between the effects on national and imported goods, although important to the complainant, are very amorphous and vague, yet the Court still takes them into account. It acknowledges practical and cultural realities, rather than just legal form. It therefore goes further than *Heimdienst*, where the discrimination was clearer, the role of the national frontier playing a more visible role in the relevant rules.

Together these cases show that the proviso may be used, and how it would work. They also show that a rigid or explicit difference between national and foreign goods is not necessary. It is enough that a pattern is there. However, *Semeraro* and other cases show that in the past the Court has not been quick to find such a pattern. It is too early to tell whether *Austrian Grocers* and *Gourmet* indicate a definite change in approach. It may simply be that the factual situation in those cases was particularly convincing.

3.5 ARTICLE 29

Article 29 is a much more timid beast than its cousin. It raises its head less often and has a somewhat quieter roar. Member states usually have very little interest in restricting exports.

---

21 *Gourmet International* Case C-405/98.

One theoretical situation where Art 29 might be relevant is where a member state wishes to protect some vital natural resource, such as coal or oil, from going abroad. However, this arises only in time of crisis, and not only have there been few of these in recent years, but in such crises member states would be justified in relying on the public policy exceptions to be found in Art 30 (see Chapter 7).

It is also possible to imagine that member states might wish to restrict exports in order to concentrate national goods on the national market, and thus ensure that the national market was dominated by a national producer. Thus if UK Coal Inc cannot sell coal abroad, it may well follow that because it has to sell all of its coal in the UK it ends up dominating the UK coal market, which a government might find politically desirable. However, this is also not a situation which is likely to occur often, and may well even seem a little far-fetched.

Moreover, restrictions on exports can be seen as less of an attack on the internal market than those on imports. They seem to harm primarily nationals, and so perhaps are an internal affair. One might therefore expect the Court to be less active in attacking them. The leading case, *Groenveld*,[22] shows that this is the case in one sense, but also shows that the two articles cannot really be compared. Their similar form hides fundamental differences.

Groenveld concerned a ban on the presence of horsemeat in Dutch meat processing plants. This was not from national ethical or taste reasons, but because various lands where horsemeat was banned were important export markets for the Netherlands. They trusted Dutch meat not to be contaminated because they knew that Dutch plants were horsemeat-free, and the Dutch government wished to preserve this situation. There was no ban on the sale of horsemeat in the Netherlands. Thus foreign horsemeat could be imported and sold, but there was no domestic competition.

Some Dutch processors wished to sell horsemeat, and protested that the ban was an Art 29 MEE. Although the rule was equally applicable to goods to be sold at home and abroad, it was a product rule, and in fact restricted cross-border trade, and therefore had to be justified and proportionate, by analogy with *Cassis*.

This argument failed, because it is a simplistic reading of the Art 28 law. As we have seen above, the reason why equally applicable rules that in fact restrict trade can be Art 28 MEEs is because they impose an extra burden on importers – the dual-burden idea again. The Court dealt with this dual burden situation by expressing a preference for country of origin regulation; thus it said that the importing state could only apply its own rules if they were justified and proportionate. Thus the indistinctly applicable caselaw can be summed up as solving the problem of regulatory differences by giving the country of origin freedom to regulate, and restricting the freedom of the country of destination to do so. This was, as discussed above, justified using the idea of mutual recognition. It clearly also has practical advantages. It is easier for the member state where the factory is situated to regulate it than for the member state where the goods are sent to do so.

Applying this broader philosophy to Art 29 it remains the case that it should be for the Dutch government to regulate its meat plants, provided it is not doing so in a way that creates different burdens for exports and non-exports. Here it was not doing so – the

---

22 *Groenveld* Case 15/79.

ban was general. There was absolutely no difference between the position of a Dutch producer who wished to sell at home and one who wished to export.

The temptation is to argue that the proper comparison is between national products and foreign imports. Then one can say there is a difference in treatment. Foreign producers may sell in the Netherlands, but in practice not domestic ones. However, the article is about exports. Therefore the comparison would have to be of exports with imports – yet this seems to make no sense; they are goods for a different market. It is bizarre to compare the position of goods that are not even in competition. To be meaningful one would have to compare national goods not intended for exports – the horsemeat the *Groenveld* would have liked to sell at home – with imports. Yet while there is a difference here, it is very difficult to see what it has to do with Art 29!

Thus the Court made it quite clear that it did not consider the Dutch regulations to be contrary to Art 29. It said:

> ... a national measure ... is not incompatible with Art 34 [now 29] of the Treaty if it does not discriminate between products intended for export and those marketed within the member state in question.

Thus, on one level there is a discrepancy between Art 28 and Art 29. The latter only catches unequally applicable rules. However, this is because the ideas which underlie the treatment of equally applicable restrictions in Art 28 do not translate to exports. (Note that it is often said that Art 29 only applies to discriminatory rules, where Art 28 goes beyond that. This is contentious; it depends what one means by discrimination – see Chapter 8 for a full discussion of this.)

CHAPTER 4

THE FREE MOVEMENT OF PERSONS

The law of the free movement of persons is layered. At the bottom is a mass of secondary legislation dealing with the specific issues relevant to the different kinds of person moving around Europe, and spelling out their rights. Most of this may soon be replaced by a single, global, directive (this is discussed under 'citizenship') but for the moment it remains.

Above this are specific articles in the EC Treaty for each category of person. The secondary legislation must come within its article – it is merely a detailing of what the article says more generally, and it cannot extend the scope of the article. The article is the authority for the legislation. This means that secondary legislation is always conditional, to be overturned and removed if it is found to in fact be in conflict with the basic principles of the Treaty article. However, the article may go beyond the secondary legislation. Thus the articles remain important, even where secondary legislation exists.

Top of the pile is Art 12 EC, which is a general prohibition on discrimination, applying to all areas of the Treaty. It is not formally superior to other Treaty articles, but it is more general, and it serves as a reference point, helping to establish a uniform and Treaty-wide applicable principle of discrimination. In this way it irons out many of the differences between categories. Most of the law seems to be just application of the non-discrimination principle. This often makes one wonder whether all the detailed rules actually perform any function any more.

The answer is that in practice they do; they are the practical day-to-day tools that the Court and lawyers use to decide what the general principles of law mean in particular situations. There is also a general principle in many European legal systems that where a specific law and a more general one both exist, one should turn to the specific first – the *lex specialis* rule. Therefore, even if the secondary legislation adds no conceptual content to the law, it is necessary to know it.

In this chapter the aim is first to introduce the specific secondary legislation and Treaty articles dealing with different categories of person. The application of Art 12 is also considered to a certain extent. Full discussion of the application of Art 12 is found in Chapter 8.

4.1 WORKERS

The free movement of workers is governed primarily by Art 39 EC. This states that:

1   Freedom of movement for workers shall be secured within the Community.

2   Such freedom of movement shall entail the abolition of any discrimination based on nationality between workers of the member states as regards employment, remuneration and other conditions of work and employment.

3   It shall entail the right, subject to limitations justified on grounds of public policy, public security or public health:

    (a) to accept offers of employment actually made;

    (b) to move freely within the territory of member states for this purpose;

    (c) to stay in a member state for the purpose of employment in accordance with the provisions governing the employment of nationals of that state laid down by law, regulation or administrative action;

    (d) to remain in the territory of a member state after having been employed in that state, subject to conditions which shall be embodied in implementing regulations to be drawn up by the Commission.

    4   The provisions of this article shall not apply to employment in the public service.

The exceptions to movement found in paras 3 and 4 are dealt with in Chapter 7.

Although there are some quite specific examples of what free movement of workers requires, in paras 2 and 3, there is also a very general statement in para 1. Thus we cannot assume that paras 2 and 3 describe the whole extent of free movement of workers, and in fact they do not. Paragraph 1 is sufficiently vague to allow a very broad development of free movement by the Court, and this is what has occurred.

The first question to consider is 'who is a worker?'. Which people are covered by this article? Then one may ask 'what are their rights?'.

4.1.1 Who is a worker?

4.1.1.1 Who decides?

The word 'worker', or its equivalent in other languages, may be used in different ways in different countries. Issues of translation, social practice and law might make a difference to how judges and people would understand it. However, the term as it appears in the Treaty is a term of Community law, and therefore has a Community-wide meaning to be interpreted by the Court. National judges may not interpret in the light of national systems. They must accept this Community interpretation. The Court has what Advocate-General Mancini has called a 'hermeneutic monopoly'.

4.1.1.2 What is work?

The Court has said '*the essential feature of an employment relationship ... is that for a certain period of time a person performs services for and under the direction of another person in return for which he receives remuneration*'.[1]

This is not enough though. It seems as if the work must also be of value to someone other than the would-be worker. In *Bettray*[2] the Court considered a programme where drug addicts were rehabilitated through being provided with work. The jobs were specially created and supervised, and the idea was to gradually train people back into normal employment. The Court decided this did not count as work, and the participants were not workers. The people were not chosen for their ability to do the job; rather the jobs were created for the people. Moreover, the whole programme existed only to provide jobs for the participants, not to perform any other useful function.

---

1   *Lawrie-Blum* Case 66/85.
2   *Bettray* Case 344/87.

The judgment can be criticised, because such programmes do have a value to society, and perform a social function. They do not exist only for the workers. However, the Court was not prepared to think this broadly.

This is by contrast with its approach to trainees, who it generally does accept as workers, even though their immediate activities may be of benefit primarily to themselves. They are within the context of a relationship with their employer in which the employer clearly does think they have some value, at least in the longer term; he gave them a job. The fact that, for example, they have low productivity is not necessarily a problem, although it might be if they were completely useless.[3] The phrase used by the Court is that activities must be 'genuine and effective' in order to be work.[4]

4.1.1.3 How much work do you have to do, and how much do you have to earn?

Ms Levin, who was British, was a part-time chambermaid in Amsterdam. The Dutch government said she was not a worker. There were three arguments:

1 She had got her job only in order to get a residence permit, which was a sort of abuse of the free movement rules.

2 She worked part-time.

3 She earned less than the social assistance level in the Netherlands. This means that the level of income at which the state provided financial help to people was higher than her salary. Moreover, it was not that she was especially frugal – she was only able to live because she had income from other (non-work) sources.

Sneaky people doing just a little work and not earning enough to live off were not real workers, said the Dutch State.

The Court rejected this decisively.[5] First, it said that her motives for working were quite irrelevant, and should not be considered. It is not possible, nor important to the law, to know why people are motivated to work.

Secondly, it said that part-time work could be work, provided that it amounted to *'genuine and effective activities, to the exclusion of activities on such a small scale as to be marginal and ancillary'*. Where precisely this cut-off line would come is difficult, but it is clearly at a low level of work. People working around eight hours per week are commonly considered workers in many member states. There is no established line though, and it is a question of fact, for the national judge, whether the work comes within the definition above.

Thirdly, it said that the amount that was earned was not necessarily of importance either. Provided that there was 'genuine economic activity', it did not matter that the worker had income from other sources. In particular, the social assistance level of the state in question could not be set as a sort of minimum qualifying wage, because this would make the position different in different countries, and a worker must be a Community-wide concept.

---

3   *Bernini* Case C-3/90.
4   Eg, *Levin* Case 53/81.
5   *Levin*.

On both the second and third points the Court justified its answers by saying that the point of the free movement of workers was, amongst other things, to raise the standard of living of people in the Community:

> Since part-time employment, although it may provide an income lower than what is considered to be the minimum required for subsistence, constitutes for a large number of persons an effective means of improving their living conditions, the effectiveness of Community law would be impaired and the achievement of the objectives of the Treaty would be jeopardised if the enjoyment of rights conferred by the principle of freedom of movement for workers were reserved solely to persons engaged in full-time employment and earning, as a result, a wage at least equivalent to the guaranteed minimum wage in the sector under consideration.

Part-time work helps people get on in life, and that is part of the purpose of the Treaty. Therefore it is included as work.

Kempf[6] went further even than this. It came about because workers are entitled to equal treatment with nationals within the national social security and benefits systems. Ms Kempf earned less than the social assistance level from her twelve hours of piano teaching each week, and claimed benefits as a result. Ms Levin had not actually claimed benefits, because of her private income. In *Kempf* the Dutch government said that a person who relied on the state in order to live could not be called a worker. The Court said they could. The tests for a worker were the same as outlined in *Levin* and it made no difference whether any extra income came from personal or public funds.

This can be justified by the same arguments as in *Levin*, but it has the negative effect of giving member states a motive to make their social security systems more restrictive or less generous. It becomes in their interests to link benefits to a period of past employment, or to make them conditional upon seeking full-time work, in order to prevent people moving to the country with the intention of claiming financial support.

4.1.1.4 Work formalities

Not everyone has a contract. Not everyone gets paid in money. Are they still workers? The question came up in *Steymann*,[7] where a member of a religious community claimed he was a worker. Within the community everyone had responsibilities and tasks, and in return their material needs were met; they received food and shelter and so on. Mr Steymann was responsible for the community's plumbing.

Despite the lack of a formal legal employment relationship, the Court found that these activities could be work. The work was of genuine economic value to the community, and the food and shelter could be seen as payment.

Mr Steymann's case was helped by the fact that the community survived by providing services to the outside world – including running a discotheque and a laundry. Thus his activities did have a genuine economic context. If the community had been one that was entirely self-sufficient, or lived from donations, even though he might have worked hard in a real sense, he might not have been found to be a worker in the Treaty

---

6   *Kempf* Case 139/85.
7   *Steymann* Case 196/87.

sense. The requirement that an economic element be present in work, a providing of value to the wider world, is a recurring theme in the cases.

4.1.1.5 Work seekers

Freedom of movement for workers will be limited to those who do the sort of jobs that are advertised abroad or on the internet, which in practice will tend to mean the elite, unless there is also a freedom to go and look for work.

The Court confirmed that this is the case in *Antonissen*.[8] It said that Art 39 entailed such a right, and a work seeker had the same right not to be deported as a worker – he could be deported only if one of the exceptions in para 3 of the article could be relied upon.

This right did not last forever though. It lasted for however long was a reasonable time for a person to find out the work situation in his host state, find offers of employment, and find a job. The Court did not say how long this was, and there will be no fixed time for all cases, since it is something that may depend upon the circumstances of the case. However, it did think that after six months the time would probably have run out, unless the person could actually show that they were still looking for work and had a genuine chance of finding it.

This case has tended to be interpreted by administrative authorities as saying that, unusual situations aside, work seekers are entitled to six months' residence before they may be deported. This is simplistic, but not a bad rule of thumb.

In practice, today, deportation is almost unknown in such circumstances, since the openness of borders, as well as the extension of rights of movement and residence to non-economic actors, discussed under citizenship, means that almost anyone can go anywhere and stay there. However, not everyone has the same rights when they are there, and, as we will see, while a work seeker does not have all the rights of a worker, he may have some of them, and so the status of work seeker may not be quite irrelevant.

4.1.2   What rights do workers have?

The two most important pieces of secondary legislation for workers are Directive 68/360, and Regulation 1612/68. The first deals with formalities, such as residence permits, and the second is an expansion of the substantive principles of Art 39, setting out the rights of a migrant worker. As well as these two pieces of legislation and the caselaw interpreting them, there are also cases based on the general principles of Art 39. In particular, there has been important caselaw on the scope of the idea of free movement, setting out the limits of Art 39, and many cases concerning the principle of non-discrimination found in the article.

There is also other specialised legislation, concerning matters such as transferability of social security benefits and pensions, which while of great practical importance is a whole area of law in itself, far too detailed and complex to address here.

---

8   *Antonissen* Case C-393/96.

4.1.2.1 Directive 68/360

This Directive sets out the formalities that member states may require before they allow a foreign EU worker to enter their territory, live there, and work there. It is generally a clear and straightforward Directive, and most of what one needs to know can be gathered just by reading it. Nevertheless, a brief survey of some of the most important points follows:

> No document other than a passport (or EU ID card) may be requested at the border (Art 3). Some member states used to ask foreigners to produce their residence permits when they returned from visits abroad.

> If a worker produces a passport (or EU ID card) and a document showing he has a job – and a letter is enough, no formal contract is required – he must (subject only to the public policy, etc, considerations – see Chapter 7) be given a residence permit valid for five years. If the job is for less than three months, no permit is necessary, although the authorities would have the right to ask the worker to report his presence, and to produce a document showing he has a job. If the job is for between three and 12 months, the worker can get a temporary residence permit, for the length of the job. Once issued, these permits remains valid even if the worker stops working. These rules are found in Arts 4, 6, 7 and 8.

> It is not necessary to wait for the permit before starting work. Work may be begun immediately, without waiting for the completion of formalities (Art 5).

> The worker's family may get residence permits of the same length as the worker's. As well as ID they have to produce documents from the state they have come from to show their relationship. Who precisely counts as 'family' is considered under Regulation 1612/68.

> If the worker continues working in the host state, she is of course entitled to renewals of her residence permit, as are her family (Art 6).

There are more details in the Directive, but these are the main points. It is worth noting that there is no mention of *work* permits. For member state nationals within the Community such things no longer exist.

Although the requirements of the Directive are fairly light, in some cases even complying with these formalities has been burdensome and difficult. Both the time and effort involved in dealing with a slow bureaucracy, plus the hostility and arrogance sometimes experienced from front-line civil servants administering these rules, have been a disincentive to complying with the formalities. Moreover, since the member states have almost no discretion in issuing permits they have become a rather empty formality. This is even more so since the openness of borders now means that the idea of keeping track of people within the Community, while attractive to the more old-fashioned sort of government, is a lost cause. One may well ask what the point of these formalities is, and the answer is probably just that they serve as a comforter to neurotic administrations that have traditionally enjoyed a high degree of power over individuals in their lands.

Putting these things together, what happens is that many people simply do not bother to get their permits, and short-term workers do not bother to report to the authorities. The future of the state is not threatened by this, but its dignity may be, and there have been a number of cases where member states have attempted to punish migrants for non-compliance. They have answered the question 'do these formalities have any bite?'. The broad answer has been 'not much'.

In *Royer*,[9] a French worker in Belgium failed to get his permit, and was ultimately expelled from the country for this, and barred from re-entry. He went to the Court. The Court said that permits were merely evidence of the right of residence; they did not grant it. The right was granted by the Treaty. That meant that whether or not a person has a residence permit, he does have a right to reside. The residence right, in short, is not one granted by the state when it issues the permit, as the Belgian government had claimed, but one granted by the Community to all migrant workers. As a result Mr Royer could not be expelled. The argument that his failure to comply with the laws showed he was a threat to public policy was also rejected. The Court implicitly accepted that failure to comply with 68/360 was not a serious matter.

This principle that rights stem from the Treaty, and not from formalities, is one that has recurred in a number of different Treaty situations and is very important. It shows the substantive emphasis of Community law, and the reluctance of the Court to subordinate grand ideas to procedural requirements. It attacks bureaucratic culture, in which formalities are often a condition precedent for the exercise of rights, but this does not seem to trouble the Court at all.

In *Watson and Belmann*[10] the Italian government attempted to prosecute an Italian national and his British *au pair* for failing to report her presence to the authorities within three days of her arrival. They faced the possibility of months in prison, deportation for her, and a large fine. The Court said that while the requirement to report was acceptable, following Art 8 of 68/360, provided the time allowed was reasonable, the state was limited in the punishments it could impose for failure. First, it lacked the power to deport Ms Watson, for the same reasons as in *Royer*. Secondly, any fine or imprisonment had to be proportional to the gravity of the offence or it would be an obstacle to free movement, contrary to Art 39.

The Court seemed to suggest that proportionality in this context would mean a punishment on a similar scale to that given to nationals who fail to comply with other formalities, not related to foreign workers. This approach has since been confirmed.[11] Thus actions following failure to comply with 68/360 should be on a similar scale to actions following failure by a national to register with a local council, or to register to vote, or to obtain a new identity card, for example.

Since in practice this sort of administrative offence is often unpunished in many member states, the power to the states to punish violators of the Directive is also limited. Moreover, the proportionality requirement should be understood, it is suggested, as meaning that high fines, or imprisonment, would almost certainly be contrary to Community law.

A similar approach is taken to the family's rights to a residence permit under Directive 68/360 (and the equivalent Directive, 73/148, for established persons). This came to the fore in *MRAX*.[12] Belgian laws provided that a third-country national spouse of an economic migrant would not be issued with a residence permit, and would even be

---

9 *Royer* Case 48/75.
10 *Watson and Belmann* Case 118/75.
11 *Commission v Germany* Case C-24/97.
12 *MRAX* Case C-459/99.

deported, if that spouse could not produce a valid identity document, or if they had entered the country illegally – that is, before they had Treaty derived rights. This might seem a reasonable approach, but the Court rejected it. So long as the partner could prove their identity somehow, and so long as they could prove they were married to the economic migrant, they had a substantive right to residence, and to the permit, which could not be refused for reasons of national law.

Finally, in *Sagulo*,[13] the Court stated that a member state could not require any extra formalities to be completed, other than those in the Directive. The German government issued a 68/360 permit, but also required foreign workers to complete forms for another kind of permit. The fact that they might get it automatically would be irrelevant. No other formalities could be required.

4.1.2.2 Regulation 1612/68

Regulation 1612/68 is also reader friendly. It sets out the right of a member state national to work in another member state, and their right to bring their family. Some detail is provided on these things, so, again, an overview of the provisions will be useful:

> A national of a member state has the right to work in another member state on the same terms and conditions as a native [Arts 1 and 7].

> She will also have the same social and tax advantages, and access to education and retraining, as a native [Art 7], and the same access to housing [Art 8].

> Any national laws which contradict this, or restrict the access of foreigners or their ability to apply for jobs, or which impose different medical or other criteria on them, shall be invalid [Arts 3, 4 and 5].

> Any clause of an agreement relating to employment, whether an individual one, or a collective one, that authorises discriminatory conditions, shall be invalid [Art 7.4].

> The worker's spouse, and children under 21, and dependent children older than this, and dependent parents or grandparents (or great-grandparents, and so on!), may come and 'install themselves' with the worker, provided she has housing for them. Any other dependent relatives may have their entry 'facilitated' [Art 10].

> The worker's children shall have access to education on the same terms as nationals, and the member state shall do its best to facilitate this [Art 12].

> The worker's spouse, children under 21, and dependent children older than this, shall have the right to work in the member state [Art 11].

The last three points above, concerning the worker's family, are effective irrespective of the nationality of the family members. Spouses and dependants who are not citizens of member states can equally benefit from Arts 10, 11, and 12. This has caused some interesting problems of reverse discrimination in countries where nationals did not have the right to bring their foreign family members, which are discussed in Chapter 11.

Article 7.4, on collective agreements, should be noted. In many member states employment conditions are negotiated by trade unions, or organisations of trade unions, with organisations of employers. Collective agreements are therefore of great importance

---

13   *Sagulo* Case 8/77.

to almost all workers in these countries. Article 7.4 ensures that discrimination cannot creep in through the actions of these (often private) parties.

However, the aspects of the regulation which have caused most discussion are the situation of workers' families, and the scope of the non-discrimination terms in Art 3 and in Art 7. These are considered in turn.

4.1.2.3 Workers' families

One question is precisely which family members are allowed to come and join the worker. Is there any difference between those dependent family members whose entry is to be 'facilitated' and the others who have a right to install themselves? It looks as if a difference is intended, but since a member state has a power to admit who it wants, it is hard to see that it can be said to be facilitating entry if it does anything other than admitting the person. Thus, in practice, the right to entry may extend to all dependent relatives. Alternatively, member states may just have some lower level duty to the non-immediate relatives; for example, not to impose unduly difficult conditions for their admittance.

A second important question concerns the nature of the family members' rights. It is clear that they are derivative. This means that they exist so long as the worker has worker status, and are to be seen as an adjunct to her rights. Several results flow from this. One is that family members do not necessarily have the same rights as a worker, even though they may be allowed to work. In fact the Court has said in *Lebon*[14] that their employment rights are only to equal access to employment, not to equal social and tax advantages. Of course, if the family members are EU citizens they will have their own worker rights.

Another consequence arises in cases of divorce or separation. This could lead to the partner's loss of residence and work rights, which could be a rule of great cruelty, and also place extreme power in the worker's hands. By abandoning the relationship she would be able to ensure her partner's expulsion from a land where he may have lived and worked for many years. This was dealt with in the case of *Diatta*,[15] where in fact it was the non-EU partner who ended the relationship, and went to live elsewhere in Germany. The Court said that although the spouse's right of residence was derivative, as long as there was no completed divorce the right remained. Moreover, it did not require that the partners lived together, or even in the same area of the country. Thus it seems that as long as a couple remain formally undivorced, the spouse retains his rights.

A similar philosophy, but even more purposive, seems to underlie *Baumbast*.[16] This case concerned two families. In each one the man was a migrant worker in the UK, who had brought his wife and children to live with him. In both cases, the wife and children were not EU citizens. In both cases, there was a divorce, and the primary carer after the divorce was the wife. In one family, the man subsequently ceased to be a worker, while in the other he did not. The question arose of the children and their mothers' legal position.

The Court found that the children, in both cases, had a right to residence in order to continue their education. It made no difference at all whether their parents had divorced,

---

14 *Lebon* Case 316/85.
15 *Diatta* Case 267/83.
16 *Baumbast* Case C-413/99.

and whether one of them was still a worker. The Court said that otherwise there would be the risk of disruption to children's education in such circumstances, which would itself be a deterrent to movement in the first place. They must be allowed to stay and finish school.

Even more than this, the Court then found that since the children had a right to residence, such a right must also be found for their mothers, as primary carers. Clearly, it was incompatible with the children's right to exclude the parent caring for them.

This is quite a radical judgment, particularly considering that the nationality of the children and mothers was found to be completely irrelevant. It seems to suggest that although family rights may be initially parasitic on the worker, once the family is established it acquires a certain legal independence.

A third effect of the derivative nature of the rights is in the notion of dependency. Dependent relatives receive rights precisely because any benefit to them is perceived to be a benefit to the worker. Thus, in asking who is a dependant, which is a question of fact, not law, the national judge should take into account whether a benefit to that person would still be a benefit to the worker.[17] If it would, this shows that there is dependency. Thus if a grant to a 25-year-old child will in fact relieve the parent worker from payment, there is dependency.

4.1.2.4 Gay marriage

A final note may be made on homosexual marriages, which may present interesting legal problems. Gay marriage is now possible in the Netherlands, and may be introduced in some other member states. How will the Court deal with this? Will gay spouses be spouses according to Regulation 1612/68?

The Court's general approach to such sensitive issues is to follow the prevailing social consensus. Moreover, it has said in *Reed*,[18] in considering the meaning of 'spouse' in Art 10 of the Regulation, that it must consider the consensus across the whole Community, since 'spouse' must have a Community meaning. It concluded there that unmarried partners were not equivalent to spouses in the public perception, and has concluded in another case that homosexual partners are not equivalent to heterosexual ones.[19]

There are two possible situations. One is where a worker in a state where homosexual marriage is legal wishes to bring in her same-sex partner. Another is where a worker in a state where it is not legal wishes to bring in her partner to whom she was married legally in another state. In the first case it initially seems there would be no problem – if the state accepts homosexual marriage it is likely to accept homosexual spouses from other countries. The problem might be where the partner is not married, because the country of origin does not allow homosexual marriage.

Here the case of *Reed* is useful again. A British worker was able to bring his unmarried partner to the Netherlands even though she was not in fact his spouse – the Court was not prepared to extend the term to unmarried partners – using the principle of non-discrimination. This followed from Dutch national law which allowed unmarried partners equality with married ones in certain situations. As a result Dutch nationals

---

17 *Lebon*, note 14 above.
18 *Reed* Case 59/85.
19 *Grant* Case C-249/96.

could bring their unmarried partners to the Netherlands from abroad. Therefore this privilege had to be extended to foreign workers. It was an Art 7 social advantage, on which see below for more.

Translating this to the homosexual case, if the host member state recognised unmarried homosexual partners of its own nationals they would have to admit unmarried homosexual partners of migrant workers. Otherwise they would not have to. Even if they recognised unmarried heterosexual partners neither the European Convention on Human Rights nor the Treaty require that heterosexual and homosexual partners be treated the same. Article 13 EC does empower the Council to act to prohibit such discrimination on the grounds of sexual orientation, but it has not yet done this.

In the second situation, the relevant principle would be that of mutual recognition. If a couple have a legally valid marriage from a member state, other member states should recognise this. It is for each member state to determine who it marries, just as it determines who are its nationals. This view is supported by the case of D.[20] Community staff regulations granted various benefits to married employees and their spouses. An employee working at the Council (so probably in Brussels) whose partnership with his male partner had been registered in Sweden claimed these benefits too. In rejecting his case the Court built its argument around the fact that while registered partnerships were increasingly common they were not seen by member states as the same as marriage, had a different legal status, and therefore could not be seen as equivalent to marriage in the Community staff context. However, a consequence of this reasoning is that if the couple had actually been married, then the argument would crumble, and presumably the Community would have had to accept that marriage as equivalent to a heterosexual one. Applying this to other member states would suggest that they might too have to accept foreign homosexual marriages as authentic.

However, this may be naïve. Admission of the couple as worker and spouse would seem to require that they be treated equally to married national couples generally, in matters such as housing, tax, and administrative procedures. This might demand significant adaption of national law, and moreover might undermine that state's own refusal to allow homosexual marriage. The politics of forcing this on conservative southern or eastern member states could be just too frightening for the Court. It would either deny mutual recognition, or it would allow the member state to use a public morality exception to opt out. Alternatively, perhaps, it would require the partner's admission, but not internal recognition of the marriage.

One can also imagine interesting problems to do with differences in the age at which marriage is legal in different member states. Perhaps fortunately these do not seem to have arisen.

4.1.2.5 Article 3 of Regulation 1612/68

Article 3 prohibits a number of specific practices which will tend to exclude foreigners from the national labour market. However, its most important section is probably the most general: s 3(1), second paragraph, which provides that laws, regulations or administrative practices shall be invalid *'where, though applicable irrespective of nationality,*

---

20 *D v Council* Case C-122/99P

their exclusive or principal aim or effect is to keep nationals of other member states away from the employment offered'.

This is an expression of non-discrimination, applied to access to employment, that goes beyond direct, explicit discrimination, to what is sometimes called covert, or indirect discrimination. An example of this is *O'Flynn*,[21] considered below in the section on Art 7. Although *O'Flynn* is an Art 7 case, the principles of non-discrimination that it expounds are quite general, and it shows that where a measure concerning access to employment is not directly discriminatory but tends to keep away foreigners, the Court will ask whether it is justified and proportionate, and if it is not it will find it contrary to Art 3(1).

One particular situation of great relevance to migrant workers is the language requirement. This of course benefits natives, but is often perfectly sensible. In case the Court should get carried away and begin forcing employers to employ people with whom they could not communicate, the third paragraph of Art 3(1) provides that the quotation above *'shall not apply to conditions relating to linguistic knowledge required by reason of the post to be filled'.*

Thus if it is necessary for a job that the person speak a particular language, that requirement should not be considered contrary to para 2.

Of course, para 3 is not really needed, since if the language requirement was necessary the Court would inevitably find it justified and proportionate anyway. The paragraph is a reflection of the sensitivity of language as a political issue, and the desire of states that it be beyond argument that legitimate language requirements could remain.

This is also seen in the most famous case on language, *Groener*.[22] Ms Groener was a Dutch art teacher who applied for a job in Ireland and was refused because she did not speak Irish. The teaching, however, was to be entirely in English, which she did speak. One would think therefore that the requirement would not be seen as 'required by reason of the post to be filled'.

The Court did not take this view. It noted that it was quite legitimate to have a policy of protection and promotion of the national language. In the context of such a policy, teaching and education would obviously be important. Therefore, to ask that teachers speak the language was legitimate.

This case involved not just language, but also education and teaching qualifications. Together they make a politically powerful mix. It is hardly surprising that the Court chose to take a tactful approach and interpret Art 3(1) very broadly. The phrase 'requirements of the post' was, in essence, understood to embrace requirements of wider policy, since that policy was of great importance to the member states.

4.1.2.6 Article 7 of Regulation 1612/68

Article 7 of the Regulation has turned out to be one of the most useful clauses for the migrant worker. The first paragraph is very important – it prohibits discrimination in matters relating to employment – but does not really add to what is obvious from Art 39. In that sense it is not interesting. The second paragraph, however, is a much more creative

---

21 *O'Flynn* Case C-237/94.
22 *Groener* Case 379/87.

interpretation of the Treaty article. It provides that workers 'shall enjoy the same social and tax advantages as national workers'.

The power of this paragraph is in the ambiguity of the phrase 'social advantages'. By meaning nothing, it means everything. Initially it was thought by most people, including the Court, that it covered only benefits to do with employment.[23] Things like housing, training or transport benefits for workers might be social advantages.

However, this has gradually been abandoned. In *Cristini*[24] the Court had to consider a French allowance for reduced train fares for large families. It was refused to the widow of a migrant worker because of her nationality. The application had been made by the worker himself before his death, and was clearly of benefit to him, so the only question was whether it was a social advantage under Art 7(2). The Court said:

> ... in view of the equality of treatment which the provision seeks to achieve, the substantive area of application must be delineated so as to include all social and tax advantages, whether or not attached to the contract of employment, such as reductions in fares for large families.

Since there is no connection with employment required here, it seems that the only criterion for being a social advantage is that it must be of some benefit, and received by nationals. Moreover, it is clear that it can be of indirect benefit. In *Inzirillo*[25] the disabled son of a worker was entitled to a benefit because he was dependent and so helping him was a social advantage to the worker. The son had no personal right to help, but the worker's rights extended to his family. Essentially, a worker has the right that her family receive benefits, so long as they are also of benefit to her.

Although social advantages tend to be in the form of payments or reductions of some kind or another, it is not necessary that they be so. Elevation on a waiting list for some public service, for example, could also be a social advantage. One wonders, then, what is not a social advantage. Is there any benefit to which a worker is not entitled? Broadly, no.

The strange case of *Even*[26] is a rare exception to this. Belgian recipients of war pensions (from any allied nation) received certain financial advantages which foreign recipients of identical war pensions did not. Mr Even was French, and complained. The Court said that this advantage was not a social advantage because it was not granted *by reason primarily of his status of worker or resident on the national territory*.

The Court is saying that Belgians who received a war pension in fact received it because they had fought in the war, not just because they were workers or residents. However, Mr Even had also fought in the war. The difference must be that as a Frenchman Mr Even was assumed to have fought 'for' France, while a Belgian, in whichever army he may have fought, was to be assumed to have fought 'for' Belgium. Thus the pension was a sort of payment for services rendered, and since Mr Even had not rendered his services to Belgium, he had not earned it. This is a strange ruling, with a slight smell of nationalism. However, it may be useful in indicating that there are limits to Art 7(2).

---

23 *Michel S* Case 76/72.
24 *Cristini* Case 32/75.
25 *Inzirillo* Case 63/76.
26 *Even* Case 207/78.

All the above cases have concerned examples of direct discrimination. The nationality of the worker was relevant to his treatment. However, Art 7(2) encompasses a broader notion of discrimination than this. In *O'Flynn*[27] a contribution to the funeral expenses of workers was conditional upon burial in the United Kingdom. Mr O'Flynn's son wished to bury him in his native Ireland. The Court said that:

> The Court has consistently held that the equal treatment rule laid down in Art 48 of the Treaty and in Art 7 of Regulation No 1612/68 prohibits not only overt discrimination by reason of nationality but also all covert forms of discrimination which, by the application of other distinguishing criteria, lead in fact to the same result.
>
> Accordingly, conditions imposed by national law must be regarded as indirectly discriminatory where, although applicable irrespective of nationality, they affect essentially migrant workers or the great majority of those affected are migrant workers, where they are indistinctly applicable but can more easily be satisfied by national workers than by migrant workers or where there is a risk that they may operate to the particular detriment of migrant workers.
>
> It is otherwise only if those provisions are justified by objective considerations independent of the nationality of the workers concerned, and if they are proportionate to the legitimate aim pursued by the national law.
>
> It follows from all the foregoing caselaw that, unless objectively justified and proportionate to its aim, a provision of national law must be regarded as indirectly discriminatory if it is intrinsically liable to affect migrant workers more than national workers and if there is a consequent risk that it will place the former at a particular disadvantage.
>
> It is not necessary in this respect to find that the provision in question does in practice affect a substantially higher proportion of migrant workers. It is sufficient that it is liable to have such an effect. Further, the reasons why a migrant worker chooses to make use of his freedom of movement within the Community are not to be taken into account in assessing whether a national provision is discriminatory. The possibility of exercising so fundamental a freedom as the freedom of movement of persons cannot be limited by such considerations, which are purely subjective.

Thus, if a provision of national law concerning a social advantage will tend to be more favourable to nationals than to migrants, one must ask whether it is justified and proportionate. If it is not, it is an example of indirect discrimination and illegal.

4.1.2.7 Semi-workers

Work seekers, and those who have stopped working, either involuntarily or voluntarily, enter a sort of twilight land of semi-worker status. It is quite clear from a number of cases[28] that they do have some of the rights of a worker, but not necessarily all. It is necessary to take a purposive view to understand their situation. The rights that are necessary for them to find work or retrain, they will have.

Moreover the Court is prepared to be progressive on this. In *Lair*[29] it found that a degree in romance (Latin-based) languages was part of the development of the career of

---

27   See note 21 above.
28   *Lebon*, note 14 above; *Antonissen*, note 8 above; *Lair* Case 39/86.
29   Case 39/86.

an ex-bank worker, and she could use the worker's right to social advantages to get a grant for this. In the modern world people changed their careers, extended their education, and interrupted periods of work with periods of learning. Since Ms Lair had been working and was doing something which would give her a useful qualification (a degree) she retained her worker status to the extent necessary.

However, had she gone to meditate in a convent, she might well not have done so. Also, even while studying for her degree she would not have had all the benefits that she had as a working worker – only those that ex-working native students also had. Social advantages do not extend *beyond* non-discrimination.

In a similar but different case, the case of *Brown*,[30] work as a stagiaire for eight months prior to going to university was not enough to earn a grant, because the work had only been done as university preparation. The work was conditional upon the further study. While accepting that he was a worker, the Court denied some of Mr Brown's worker's rights, since his work was only 'ancillary' to his study; he had only been able to become a worker because he had the place at university.

If it is seen as looking at Mr Brown's motives, this case is not compatible with *Levin*. It should therefore probably be seen as setting out a narrow principle confined to its own facts. The judgment reflects the desire of the states not to have to pay grants to every foreigner who came and did a few months' work. It serves to show that there are no black-and-white lines to be drawn in this area.

4.1.2.8 Using Art 39

Usually the secondary legislation and its interpretation leads one to an answer in cases involving workers. However, while the Regulation cannot go beyond the article, Art 39 can and does extend beyond the ideas that have been embodied in secondary legislation. In particular, whereas most of the Regulations and Directives are little more than detailing of what non-discrimination means in particular situations, the first paragraph of Art 39 goes beyond this. It calls for free movement of workers to be secured.

Thus in some situations it is useful to appeal directly to the article. Mr Bosman did this in the case named after him.[31] The case concerned the rules governing football transfers, which are laid down by international football associations and apply in all European, and many other, countries. Mr Bosman was signed to Liège, a Belgian team, but wished to move to Dunquerque, a French one. Under the transfer rules Liège were able to block this transfer. Essentially Mr Bosman was their prisoner. He could not go and work as a footballer anywhere else unless they let him, even though they were not in fact playing him in their own team at the time.

Mr Bosman claimed that the rules were an obstacle to the free movement of workers, contrary to Art 39, and therefore illegal. The Court agreed. It said:

> ... nationals of member states have in particular the right, which they derive directly from the Treaty, to leave their country of origin to enter the territory of another member state and reside there in order there to pursue an economic activity.

---

30 *Brown* Case 197/86.
31 *Bosman* Case C-415/93.

Provisions which preclude or deter a national of a member state from leaving his country of origin in order to exercise his right to freedom of movement therefore constitute an obstacle to that freedom even if they apply without regard to the nationality of the workers concerned.

The Court has also stated that even though the Treaty provisions relating to freedom of establishment are directed mainly to ensuring that foreign nationals and companies are treated in the host member state in the same way as nationals of that state, they also prohibit the member state of origin from hindering the establishment in another member state of one of its nationals or of a company incorporated under its legislation which comes within the definition contained in Art 58 [now 48]. The rights guaranteed by Art 52 [now 43] *et seq* of the Treaty would be rendered meaningless if the member state of origin could prohibit undertakings from leaving in order to establish themselves in another member state. The same considerations apply, in relation to Art 48 [now 39] of the Treaty, with regard to rules which impede the freedom of movement of nationals of one member state wishing to engage in gainful employment in another member state.

... [the transfer] rules are likely to restrict the freedom of movement of players who wish to pursue their activity in another member state by preventing or deterring them from leaving the clubs to which they belong even after the expiry of their contracts of employment with those clubs.

... Consequently, the transfer rules constitute an obstacle to freedom of movement for workers prohibited in principle by Art 48 [now 39] of the Treaty. It could only be otherwise if those rules pursued a legitimate aim compatible with the Treaty and were justified by pressing reasons of public interest. But even if that were so, application of those rules would still have to be such as to ensure achievement of the aim in question and not go beyond what is necessary for that purpose.

The Court begins here by saying that even rules that apply without reference to nationality can be contrary to the free movement of workers. It then makes a comparison with the rules on establishment, and says that although most of the time the problem is with treatment by the host state, restrictions on movement from the state of origin are also caught by the Treaty. It then concludes that the transfer rules will stop players going abroad, and so are an obstacle to movement, and illegal. They could only escape if they pursued a legitimate aim and were proportionate.

The significance of this case is that it does not concern discrimination of any kind. When the Court said the rules applied irrespective of nationality it was not saying quite enough. In *O'Flynn* there was also no mention of the worker's nationality in the rules, but there was still indirect discrimination, because foreigners tended to come off worse than nationals. However, here that is not the case. The transfer rules are just as likely to block a Belgian from moving from one Belgian club to another Belgian club as they are to block him from moving abroad. Nor are they more likely to block a Frenchman from moving within Belgium than a Belgian. There is absolutely no element of discriminatory effect. There is simply a system that makes all movement very difficult.

The question that this case opens up is 'where do we stop?'. Once we escape from the cage of discrimination into the high pastures of mere obstacles, it is hard to see any fences ahead. What about rules on selling houses? If a member state makes the sale and purchase of housing expensive or cumbersome will this not also be an obstacle to movement? What about public transport? Or if we think that the rules must have something directly to do with employment – which is not something supported by analogy with the caselaw on social advantages – then what about employment protection? Making it difficult to sack people not only arguably reduces overall employment, but it certainly makes people less likely to move jobs, and so reduces vacancies, and makes it harder to get a first job. Is that not an obstacle to the free movement of workers?

Of course, rules such as these might be saved by being justified and proportionate, or even by public policy exceptions if necessary, but should they really be assessed under trade law? Is Art 39 the right place to consider employment policy?

To some extent all these questions remain open, but the worst fears have been laid to rest in the case of *Graf*.[32] This concerned a benefit which Austrian workers received if they were made redundant or sacked. They did not get it if they resigned voluntarily.

Mr Graf said that this discrepancy was contrary to Art 39. It provided a disincentive for workers to leave their jobs to go and work abroad, and an incentive to sit around and wait to be sacked or laid off. Thus it was an obstacle to movement.

This argument may seem far-fetched but it succeeded in some Austrian courts, by analogy with *Bosman* (see note 31). Once again there was no element of discrimination, but an obstacle. However, when the case came before the Court of Justice it drew a line. It reaffirmed *Bosman*, saying:

> Second, it is clear from the Court's caselaw, in particular from the judgment in *Bosman*, cited above, that Art 48 [now 39] of the Treaty prohibits not only all discrimination, direct or indirect, based on nationality but also national rules which are applicable irrespective of the nationality of the workers concerned but impede their freedom of movement.

But it then went on to say that in order to be an obstacle to movement rules must affect access of workers to the labour market, whereas these did not:

> Legislation of the kind at issue in the main proceedings is not such as to preclude or deter a worker from ending his contract of employment in order to take a job with another employer, because the entitlement to compensation on termination of employment is not dependent on the worker's choosing whether or not to stay with his current employer but on a future and hypothetical event, namely the subsequent termination of his contract without such termination being at his own initiative or attributable to him.

> Such an event is too uncertain and indirect a possibility for legislation to be capable of being regarded as liable to hinder freedom of movement for workers where it does not attach to termination of a contract of employment by the worker himself the same consequence as it attaches to termination which was not at his initiative or is not attributable to him.

The reasoning is not entirely transparent, since a hypothetical occurrence may still condition behaviour, but the important part is the beginning of the second paragraph. The effect of the rule was just too 'uncertain and indirect' to be an obstacle contrary to Art 39. While this may be a loose formula it is clearly a useful one, that can exclude all the wilder and more imaginative claims.

---

32   *Graf* Case C-190/98.

4.2 ESTABLISHMENT

Article 43 EC says that:

> ... restrictions on the freedom of establishment of nationals of a member state in the territory of another member state shall be prohibited. Such prohibition shall also apply to restrictions on the setting up of agencies, branches or subsidiaries by nationals of any member state established in the territory of any member state.

> Freedom of establishment shall include the right to take up and pursue activities as self employed persons and to set up and manage undertakings ... under the conditions laid down for its own nationals by the law of the country where such establishment is effected, subject to the provisions of the Chapter relating to capital.

'Establishment' is the term used when a self-employed person, or a company, bases their professional or commercial activities somewhere, or sets up a secondary office (this is usually called 'secondary establishment').

Therefore, Art 43 says that self-employed people, or companies, who are nationals of a member state, should be able to base themselves, or open a secondary office, in any other member state. Having done this, they should also be able to open a secondary office in their state of origin. Thus the Frenchman based in London must also be allowed by Art 43 to open a branch office in Paris.

Any restrictions on these things are prohibited. This applies to both restrictions from the state of origin or the host state, although the latter is usually more important. Further, the migrant people or companies should be treated the same as nationals. This is subject only to the rules on capital.

To deal with the last point first: this establishes a hierarchy, so that where a restriction on free movement of capital is still allowed, the rules on establishment should not be used to undermine this. This was very important once, when capital movement was still subject to many controls, but now that capital is largely liberalised – on which see Chapter 6 – it is less so. This is not to deny that there are still many issues where capital and establishment overlap – for example, rules that regulate banks and insurance companies and pensions will also tend to make it difficult for companies to move – and where both have to be taken into account. These are discussed to some extent in Chapter 6. However, they are relatively technical areas, and moreover they tend to have greater significance for companies than for persons. Although people may well be deterred from moving by problems in transferring pensions or capital, the deterrent is in general less than it will be for a company, where financial and regulatory factors are inevitably of the highest importance.

Therefore, in the consideration below, the emphasis will be on the establishment of persons, and the details of the application of Art 43 to companies, and the interaction with the rules on capital, will not be considered. A dedicated book is the best place for these topics.

4.2.1 The rights of established people

As with workers, there is secondary legislation on establishment, but also caselaw that is based on Art 43 itself, and develops the idea of a restriction on the freedom of establishment. As will be seen, the issues that have dominated this have been the recognition of qualifications and the regulation of professions. In both of these areas national practices have traditionally been very restrictive and insular, and the Court has responded to this with creative and far-reaching caselaw.

4.2.1.1 The secondary legislation

Directive 73/148 does for established people (natural people only) what 68/360 does for workers. It limits the formal requirements that may be applied to the established person and her family, and establishes their basic right to movement and residence. The requirements are essentially the same as for workers, and the caselaw discussed in the section on 68/360 can all be applied by analogy to established people.

The Directive also regulates the families of self-employed people in a manner analogous to Regulation 1612/68. (The families of service providers and recipients are in fact also covered. Service providers and recipients are discussed in Chapter 5.) Restrictions on movement and residence of their spouse, children under 21, dependent older children, and ascending dependants are abolished, and once again other dependants have their entry 'facilitated'. By Art 11 of Regulation 1612/68 the spouse and children of self-employed people also have the right to take up employment in the host state – this article, exceptionally, applies to both workers and the self-employed.

There is however no secondary legislation for established persons with the full breadth of Regulation 1612/68. To the extent that this Regulation deals with employment matters this is no problem. However, it also grants educational rights to families of workers, and social advantages to the workers themselves. The development of these rights for established people relies on Art 43 itself.

However, the analogue of the employment-related parts of Regulation 1612/68 can be seen as the various directives governing recognition of diplomas and higher education qualifications, and the directives governing the recognition of professional qualifications, notably the lawyers' directive.[33] These are the pieces of legislation which govern the working activities of established people.

Each of these documents is moderately complex, and there are also others. Some aspects of them are considered in Chapter 10. However it is not always necessary to dwell on their details, because each is subject to general principles governing recognition of qualifications which have been developed by the Court in its Art 43 caselaw.

4.2.1.2 The use of Art 43

Four issues will be considered: social advantages for established people, the families of established people, qualifications, and regulatory requirements.

4.2.1.3 Social advantages for established people

One must be careful in using the phrase 'social advantages' in the context of establishment, since it is perhaps a term of art that belongs to workers and Regulation 1612/68. However, one can also say that it is a phrase that has entered Community law as

---

33   Directives 89/48, 89/49, 92/51 and 77/249.

describing all the official benefits one gets from residence in a particular member state. In that case, one can ask, do established people get these too?

In various cases the Court has decided that in matters relating to housing, the ownership of property, renting property, and even access to leisure facilities, established people have a right to equal treatment because not to do so would be an obstacle to their ability to move, and so contrary to Art 43. This is evident from a case on registering yachts in pleasure harbours in which the Court said:

> As regards vessels not used for the pursuit of an economic activity ... under Community law, every national of a member state is assured of freedom both to enter another member state in order to pursue an employed or self-employed activity and to reside there after having pursued such an activity. Access to leisure activities available in that state is a corollary to that freedom of movement.[34]

The logic of this is quite clearly that in order to establish as an economic actor, the migrant must also live as a person. Thus discrimination even outside the work area restricts freedom of movement. Since discrimination in the registration of a yacht must be considered to be a fairly marginal example, not something fundamentally impeding one's ability to live, it may be assumed that the Court is taking the same broad approach to the social rights of established people as it took to the social advantages of workers. Indeed, in the case above it is notable that the matter was considered under both Arts 39 and 43, and the Court did not bother to reason differently for each. The scope of social advantages are clearly the same.

4.2.1.4 The families of established people

The fact that Directive 73/148 does not mention educational rights for children of workers might be thought to put them at a disadvantage. However, the similarity of the structure of Arts 43 and 39 mean this should not be so. If Art 39 can be legitimately interpreted to contain the idea that family members have these rights – and this must be the case, since Regulation 1612/68 was enacted on the authority of Art 39 – then so can Art 43. Thus we can deduce that the position of family members of established people should be no different from that of workers. As the Court said in *Reed*,[35] the presence of family members helps a worker integrate into his host state, and therefore facilitates freedom of movement. This logic underlies all family rights, and seems as applicable to established people as to workers.

This view is supported by *Meeusen*.[36] The case concerned the rights of children of economic migrants to receive grants while studying. The Court seemed to assume that the scope of family rights was unaffected by whether the migrant was employed or self-employed.

---

34   *Commission v Ireland* Case C-151/96.
35   See note 18 above.
36   *Meeusen* Case C-337/97.

4.2.1.5 Qualifications

The principles underlying all the directives on recognition of qualifications, as well as situations which fall outside the directives, are fairly straightforward and common sense.

First, where a qualification from another member state purports to cover the same ground as a national one it must be accepted as equivalent, unless it is possible to show it is not. This is the idea of mutual trust again. If the two degrees have the same syllabus, and the same length, then it is not acceptable to say 'but their degrees aren't as good'. Such snobbery, or realism, according to perspective, has no place.

Secondly, where there are differences in the structure of education and work experience, the host state must be prepared to look at the foreign qualifications and experience fairly to assess whether they are equivalent. Thus if the host member state trains its masseurs with a three-year course of which one year is working experience, but the state of origin trains them with a two-year course, but the person has been working for three years, the host state must be prepared to look at the overall picture and accept that the migrant may be just as well qualified as its own nationals.

Thirdly, if there is a genuine shortfall of knowledge or experience found, but not one that is vast, the migrant must generally be offered the chance to make this up. Usually this means the migrant has the choice of two options: that he be allowed to work for an 'adaption period' during which he may be supervised or monitored, and if that is satisfactory he will then be considered equivalently qualified, or that he be allowed to take an examination to display knowledge of the areas not covered by his home qualification. In some situations he does not have the choice – one or other option may be inappropriate.

If, however, the shortfall is really large – for example, in France osteopaths are all qualified medical doctors, whereas in the UK they are not – then it may not be possible to go through this process. Qualifications are simply not comparable for these professions in these countries. In this situation, the only option for the migrant is to challenge the basis of the host state's requirements – for example, saying they are unjustified and disproportionate. This will generally fail, because it is in principle for states to determine the nature of professions in their territory. The principles applicable to such a challenge would be those developed in the caselaw on regulatory requirements, discussed below.

Most of these principles above are evident from reading the Directives. However they were developed by the Court on the basis of Art 43 alone, before most of the Directives came into force. They are still relevant because the Directives do not cover every possible situation or qualification. Moreover, the member states have consistently argued for restrictive interpretations of the Directives, and the general principles are useful in meeting these arguments.

The first forceful statement on qualifications came in *Thieffry*.[37] Mr Thieffry was a Belgian, who had a law qualification which the French authorities accepted as equivalent. Nevertheless they would not accept it as sufficient for enrolment in the French bar, on the sole grounds that it was not French. This is a crude example of direct discrimination, but the Court made a more general statement:

---

37   *Thieffry* Case 71/76.

A person subject to Community law cannot be denied the practical benefit of that freedom [freedom of establishment] solely by virtue of the fact that for a particular profession the Directives provided for by Art 57 [now 47] of the Treaty have not yet been adopted.

Article 47 sets out explicitly the requirement for qualification harmonising Directives, and the process to be used for this.

The general approach was made more concrete in *Heylens*,[38] where a Belgian football trainer was prosecuted in France because his Belgian diploma did not, in view of the French authorities, adequately qualify him. There was a process in France for assessing the equivalence of diplomas, but it was very narrow. If a foreign diploma did not have a remarkably similar form to a French one it was unlikely to be accepted. The Court rejected this. It said:

... the assessment of the equivalence of the foreign diploma must be effected exclusively in the light of the level of knowledge and qualifications which its holder can be assumed to possess in the light of that diploma, having regard to the nature and duration of the studies and practical training which the diploma certifies that he has carried out.

In other words, a realistic and substantive approach, and not a formalistic or legalistic one.

The Court then went further in *Vlassopoulou*.[39] This concerned a Greek-qualified lawyer who worked in Germany for some years and then applied for admission to the German bar. She was rejected for lack of the correct qualifications, and the German authorities moreover considered her Greek qualifications not equivalent – since they contained no German law! The Court said:

If ... comparison reveals that the knowledge and qualifications certified by the foreign diploma and those required by the national provisions correspond only partially, the host member state is entitled to require the person concerned to show that he has acquired the knowledge and qualifications which are lacking.

In this regard, the competent national authorities must assess whether the knowledge acquired in the host member state, either during a course of study or by way of practical experience, is sufficient in order to prove possession of the knowledge which is lacking.

The important point here is that even though Germany was entitled to insist on equivalent knowledge, they had to take account of Ms Vlassopoulou's practical experience working in Germany in their assessment. This is fairly radical. In the strictly national context one cannot usually bypass professional qualifications by showing experience. It shows the importance the Court attaches to the practical, rather than merely the theoretical, removal of obstacles to movement. It will be a very great burden for professionals to take exams and requalify every time they move, and if they are already experienced it will probably benefit no one. Thus they can rely on their experience, as above.

---

38 *Heylens* Case 222/86.
35 *Vlassopoulou* Case 340/89.

4.2.1.6 Regulatory requirements

By regulatory requirements is meant all the rules that govern practising as a lawyer, or doctor, or other professional, and also the rules governing setting up or moving companies. There is an overlap, of course, between these and rules on qualifications, but this is a much broader category, often involving rules well outside any area covered by a directive. Perhaps for this reason the caselaw has been particularly adventuresome.

Of course, as in every other situation, overtly discriminatory rules are outlawed. However, many rules apply irrespective of nationality but cause very real obstacles. Looking at the cases is the best way to show what these are. What is notable from the cases is that sometimes it is clear that apparent equality in a rule is covering up a very differential effect – what one might call indirect discrimination – but in other cases it is not clear that this is the case. Rather like *Bosman*, it may just be that there is an obstacle to everyone, nationals included. Nevertheless, the Court seems to act. Thus the law on establishment is often considered to go 'beyond discrimination'. When this occurs the Court must be relying on the first paragraph of Art 43: 'restrictions on the freedom of establishment ... shall be prohibited.'

An interesting example of a case where the effect of a rule on foreigners was particularly harsh is *Klopp*.[40] A rule of the Paris Bar provided that a lawyer practising there must have only one office, and it must be in Paris. This rule applied to both national and foreign lawyers, but probably rather more tightly on the latter, who would have to renounce their office in their home state if they wished to practise in Paris. This would be a powerful disincentive to moving. Thus the existence of an obstacle was clear.

This case could have been dealt with simply by applying the Art 43 provisions on secondary establishment. Restrictions on these are prohibited, and the Paris rule was a direct contravention of this. However, the Court took a broader and more explanatory approach. It said:

> In view of the special nature of the legal profession, however, the second member state must have the right, in the interests of the due administration of justice, to require that lawyers enrolled at a bar in its territory should practise in such a way as to maintain sufficient contact with their clients and the judicial authorities and abide by the rules of the profession. Nevertheless such requirements must not prevent the nationals of other member states from exercising properly the right of establishment guaranteed them by the Treaty.

> In that respect it must be pointed out that modern methods of transport and telecommunications facilitate proper contact with clients and the judicial authorities. Similarly, the existence of a second set of chambers in another member state does not prevent the application of the rules of ethics in the host member state.

It seems to be broadly applying a justification and proportionality approach, analogous to those we have seen under goods and workers. Does this rule pursue a legitimate aim? Is it necessary? Does it really work? The Court concluded that the rule went too far.

---

40   *Klopp* Case 107/83.

In fact Mr Klopp had complained that the rule was discriminatory, and one would expect that in that case it would be disallowed without further ado. However the Court declined to decide if he was right, saying:

> ... according to the division of jurisdiction between the Court and the national court laid down in Art 177 [now 234] of the EEC Treaty it is for the national court to determine whether in practice the rules in question are discriminatory. The question put by the national court must therefore be answered without giving any opinion on the objection based on a discriminatory application of the national law in question.

Thus discrimination does not seem to have been necessary to the judgment, and so *Klopp* suggests freedom of establishment extends to truly non-discriminatory restrictions. On the other hand, the actual facts do look discriminatory, making it a weak authority.

The situation in *Kraus*[41] was analytically rather similar. A German rule prohibited the use of foreign academic titles. An LLM was in question. The rule applied to Germans and to foreigners, and in fact there may be as many Germans who have studied abroad and gone home to work as there are foreigners who wish to work there. Thus it is not clear who is hurt most by the rule, despite the strong smell of discrimination around it.

In fact, since LLM courses are generally run as money-making activities by UK universities, they may be services within the Treaty meaning. Then this was really a discriminatory restriction on the freedom to provide services. See Chapter 5 for a fuller discussion of this. However, the case was not argued or decided that way. It was again dealt with as an establishment question, on what seemed to be a justification and proportionality basis, and a formula was used which has since been taken up and repeated in a number of cases, notably *Gebhard*.[42]

Gebhard concerned a situation similar to *Vlassopoulou*; Mr Gebhard wished to enroll in the Milan bar, and had worked many years as a lawyer in Italy (he had done this as part of a law firm, and so was not required to be individually enrolled) but had no Italian qualification. They refused to consider his experience. What the Court said was:

> It follows, however, from the Court's caselaw that national measures liable to hinder or make less attractive the exercise of fundamental freedoms guaranteed by the Treaty must fulfil four conditions:
>
> they must be applied in a non-discriminatory manner;
>
> they must be justified by imperative requirements in the general interest;
>
> they must be suitable for securing the attainment of the objective which they pursue, and;
>
> they must not go beyond what is necessary in order to attain it.

This is a very important quotation which seems to set out a framework for all free movement law. It will be returned to in Chapter 8, to see if it really does work as such. However, at the very least it applies to regulatory restrictions on establishment.

What it says is that if the restrictions are applied unequally, they are illegal; this we know. It is obvious from Art 43. Then it says that if they are applied equally, as in *Gebhard*, *Kraus* and *Klopp*, but hinder movement, or make it 'less attractive', they may still be illegal

---

41 *Kraus* Case C-19/92.
42 *Gebhard* Case C-55/94.

if they are not justified and proportionate. This is the essence of the last three conditions. Thus, on the face of it, there is no limit to the type of measure that may be caught by the Treaty, if it makes movement less attractive. Those that apply equally, even those that have no differential effect, may fall, if they cannot be justified.

As with workers, a line will have to be drawn if every national measure is not to be a potential victim of Art 43, but precisely where that line comes, in the area of establishment, is something the Court has not yet said. See again Chapter 8.

4.3 STUDENTS

Students are special, although not as special as they sometimes think. Free movement law was built around things and people which contributed to the economy, and broader rights than this are generally still in their infancy. Yet a right for students to go abroad to study has been around for some time.

This is partly because the exchange of students is a very effective way of strengthening the process of integration. People at a stage of their lives when they are open to new ideas and to learning are exposed to each other, and will form transnational bonds. Also, and not unrelatedly, they will often go on to play an important part in their society. Those who have studied are disproportionately represented in all positions of power and status. Thus moulding them while they are young also moulds the Europe of the future.

As well as this there is an economic argument. The closer the educational links between states, the more likely it is that there will be a convergence of education systems, and of the educational level of citizens. This will enhance labour mobility, and so the effectiveness of the free market. This is why the free movement of students began with vocational training.

Now it has broadened, and Arts 149 and 150 EC provide for a broad range of measures to be taken by the Community to foster co-operation and movement in the sphere of education. This includes things like language teaching programmes, and the well known Erasmus and Socrates programme whereby students spend a year studying abroad. Harmonisation of national systems is specifically excluded; this is a very sensitive area for states that treasure their educational histories and systems, and often regard them as the foundation of their national ethos. Thus it is hoped that by encouragement and gradualism states will grow together, rather than being forced into a mould.

4.3.1 Directive 93/96

This is the major secondary legislation in the area, and provides for a right of residence for students of one member state who wish to study on a vocational training course in another one. The meaning of 'vocational training' is discussed below. The residence right lasts as long as their course. Their spouse and dependent children may come with them, irrespective of their nationality, and may work. A right to maintenance grants is specifically excluded, in Art 3.

Moreover, according to Art 1 the student must have sufficient resources to avoid being a burden on the social security system, and must have sickness insurance. The first of these demands has been considerably softened by caselaw. First, the Court has found that a declaration by the student that she has sufficient funds must be accepted as adequate proof of this – authorities may not demand bank records or other documents. Secondly, if a student makes the declaration in good faith but later in the course falls on hard times and runs out of money, she seems to be entitled to social assistance on the same terms as national students. This emerges from *Grzelczyk*,[43] and had much to do with the student's status as a citizen. The case is discussed further in Chapter 8.

4.3.2 Students and non-discrimination

The Court has gone far beyond the directive above, using the Treaty articles on education, as well as Art 12, the general prohibition on discrimination, to find that there is a general right of non-discriminatory access to education. Thus foreign EU students may not be charged more than, or admitted on different terms from, national ones. It should be noted that the caselaw is largely confined to issues of access. Initial access to grants, which are seen as concerning support during education, rather than access to it, has not been found to be a Treaty right.

The important issue has always been the type of education to which the above principles applied. Initially it was post-school vocational training only, and this was clear from the Treaty. However, the Court interpreted this more and more liberally as time passed. Thus in *Gravier*[44] it was said that any course that prepared for employment was vocational training. Here a course in drawing cartoons was included – and why not? – and in *Blaizot*[45] any university education that was not mere general knowledge was said to be 'vocational', as long as it prepared for a profession or employment. In *Lair*[46] it was said that this included language degrees, since they prepared for teaching.

This is all very reasonable but takes the force out of the word 'vocational'. In the light of these two cases, and in the probable absence of degrees in general knowledge anywhere in the Community, it seems that all university education, and more or less all other post-school education, is included. This is particularly so since the Treaty has been amended over the years and now has much broader wording than before.

It should not be forgotten that EU students are also citizens, and may have rights arising out of this status – see the section below and Chapter 8.

4.4 CITIZENS

4.4.1 Who are EU citizens?

Citizenship of the European Union is created in Art 17 EC. It says:

---

43 *Grzelczyk* Case C-184/99.
44 *Gravier* Case 293/83.
45 *Blaizot* Case 24/86.
46 See note 28 above.

1   Citizenship of the Union is hereby established. Every person holding the nationality of a member state shall be a citizen of the Union. Citizenship of the Union shall complement and not replace national citizenship.

2   Citizens of the Union shall enjoy the rights conferred by the Treaty and shall be subject to the duties imposed thereby.

We see that EU citizenship is dependent upon national citizenship, and it has been accepted that who is a national citizen is something for the member states to decide.[47] Thus in the end, the member states decide who is an EU citizen. European Union citizenship is not autonomous. Moreover, it complements and does not replace national citizenship. This means that there will be no EU passports (just national ones in standard EU form).

Nevertheless, as non-discrimination becomes effective, nationality will become irrelevant within the EU, and the important distinction will become 'EU citizen or not?'. In this sense it clearly will replace national citizenship. Even outside the EU one can see this trend. It is not uncommon any more that a country's immigration rules will treat all EU countries similarly, and the important distinction for these nations will gradually become 'EU or not' as well. Particularly in the light of the standard passport, one can imagine many officials coming to lump Europeans together. Of course these are not formal occurrences. Legally nationality remains, and is the thing that must be filled in on forms, but it plays a decreasing real role.

The important paragraph is the second one. This gives citizens rights and duties. This was intended to give a human dimension to the EU and make the citizens of the member states feel part of the European integration process. They would feel they got something out of it, and had a stake in it. On a psychological level this may be fair enough but it was criticised on the grounds that it was an attempt to distract from the genuine democratic deficit of the institutions. People may have felt part of the thing, but they had little say in it. Moreover, in the beginning at least, the rights that came with citizenship were less than exciting. They will be discussed in the next section.

The duties were in some ways more interesting. It has traditionally been considered a principle of international law that it cannot subject individuals to duties (subject now to war crimes legislation). International law is something existing between states, and any obligations it wishes to impose on individuals must be mediated by those states. Thus if they wish to bind their citizens to follow international norms they must do this via domestic laws. In the UK, for example, Parliament might pass a law that would enforce an international fishing convention. In some other countries, such as the Netherlands, the constitution provides that some international law can be directly effective.

The mention of duties on citizens, although not new – since competition law, among other sections, had been imposing duties on private parties for years – emphasised that the EU is not an international law body, nor just an inter-state one, but a new kind of thing. It may not be a nation, but it does have a bond with its people that entitles the give and take of rights and duties. Again, this was supposed to give a concrete reality to the EU in ordinary people's lives. Indeed, in recent years the fundamental freedoms have been extended to cover more situations where the obstacle is placed by a private

---

47   *Kaur* Case C-192/99.

individual (see Chapter 12). Community law is integrating ever more into national legal systems.

However, in the end, the future or the meaningfulness of citizenship depends not on possibilities, nor on abstractions, but on the content of these rights and duties. These are now considered.

4.4.2 What rights do citizens have?

The less spectacular rights can be dealt with quickly. A citizen may:

Vote in local elections in a member state where he lives but is not a national, and also vote and stand in European elections [Art 19].

Use the consulates of embassies of other EU states when he is in a non-EU country where his home state is not represented [Art 20].

Petition the European Parliament, or apply to the ombudsman, or write to any other institution, in any official language, and get an answer in the same language (!) [Art 21].

Every three years the Commission will write a report on how the development of citizenship is going, and the Council can take measures that it thinks appropriate to help this along (Art 22).

This development is likely to be particularly centred around the major citizenship right, which is contained in Art 18:

1   Every citizen of the Union shall have the right to move and reside freely within the territory of the member states, subject to the limitations and conditions laid down in this Treaty and by the measures adopted to give it effect.

2   The Council may adopt provisions with a view to facilitating the exercise of the rights referred to in paragraph 1 ...

The story of citizenship so far can be understood as the history of the tension between the parts of this article, between the big idea and the conditions and limitations.

The first part of the first paragraph is quite as broad and vague as the articles on workers or established people, and so potentially could be made into an all-encompassing right. There is no mention of discrimination, but the Art 12 general prohibition on discrimination could be used, particularly in the light of Art 17(2). Then there might be a citizen's right to free movement and non-discrimination. See Chapter 8 for a full discussion of this.

Since all workers and established people are also citizens, one can imagine that the specialised Treaty articles conferring their rights could then be done away with, and the same logic that allowed them to bring their families and gain social advantages could be applied to Art 18. Then every EU citizen could go anywhere, and live anywhere, within the EU as if she was a national of that state. This is the Nirvana point, to which we are slowly headed. Not only will it have social benefits, but it will have legal ones; all of the Treaty rules on free movement of workers, established people, and service providers and recipients, may be abolished, and replaced by this nice, tidy, general, constitutional-looking combination of Arts 12 and 18. In the words of the Court in *Grzelczyk*:

Union citizenship is destined to be the fundamental status of nationals of the member states, enabling those who find themselves in the same situation to enjoy the same treatment in law irrespective of their nationality.

However, reality intrudes. The second part of the first sentence tells us that the first part is subject to all the other conditions and limitations in the Treaty. Thus citizens may move and reside freely except where a limitation on movement or residence is implied by another article. In fact it goes further than this; the first part is subject to the Treaty but also to the 'measures adopted to give it effect'. Thus the first part is subject to regulations and directives and any conditions or limitations they might contain as well.

This is an extremely rare, perhaps unique, example of primary law being subject to secondary law. In fact one could go further; there is often talk today of a 'constitution of Europe' and the first part of Art 18 is one of the parts of the EC Treaty that has a constitutional feel to it. It is, in part, a nice broad right for everyone. Therefore we may perhaps say that we have a constitutional provision that is subject to all other law including administrative regulations made by unelected bodies.

In fact it was simply not desired by the member states to introduce a general free movement right at once. Thus the first part should be understood partly as a policy aim, not just a simple black-letter law. It is an agreement to work towards this ultimate goal, but in a piecemeal, and step-by-step manner. In some areas progress might be fast, and in others slow – but each issue would be dealt with individually. Therefore the general right was subject to all the specific measures.

This conditionality is made even more clear by the second paragraph. That measures are to be passed to enable the first paragraph indicates that it is not the general right that it might seem. It might even be taken as a hint that it is not directly effective, but needs to be implemented. This is discussed below, after a consideration of the relevant secondary legislation.

4.4.3 Secondary legislation

A variety of secondary legislation exists covering movement and residence rights for people who do not fall within one of the major categories. This legislation has been passed under various articles, and so is not strictly 'citizenship' legislation. Article 18 is not its legal base. However, in another sense it is citizenship legislation; it is extending free movement beyond a narrow economic idea to a more inclusive one, and it is because this has been done, and almost everyone already has a right to move and reside, that the step to making Art 18 directly effective, and interpreting it broadly, is politically possible. It is no longer such a great leap.

The best known pieces of legislation are the directives covering students and ex-workers and ex-self-employed people.[48] However now there is also Directive 90/364, the general right of residence, which fills in all the gaps between everything else. It provides that any citizen, and her spouse and dependent children, may live in any member state provided they and their family have enough resources not to require public assistance and that they have medical insurance effective in that state. By contrast to the approach in

---

48 Directives 93/96 (students) and 90/365 (ex-workers and self-employed).

Levin, the level of resources required is defined in Art 1 as being above that at which the member state gives social assistance to its nationals, or above the minimum pension. Thus the level required will vary from state to state. The nationality of the family members is irrelevant, and they may work.

The Directive does not mention movement, only residence. For EU citizens this is not an issue, since borders are so open, particularly since the Schengen Agreement, and now its incorporation into Community law. For non-EU family members it might be slightly more of a practical problem. See Third Country Nationals in Chapter 14 for a consideration of this.

The final situation is therefore that only the poor and sick – those who are not economically active and do not have sufficient resources, or who cannot obtain medical insurance – do not have an explicit secondary legislation right of residence. They would have to rely on the direct effect of Art 18. Can they? It depends on the direct effect of Art 18, and the meaning of 'subject to ...'.

4.4.3.1 A new citizenship directive?

It is likely that during 2003 a new directive will be agreed, that will probably come into force in 2004.[49] It will set out rights for citizens and their families to move and reside throughout the European Union. It will replace the directives discussed above, those governing residence formalities for workers and residence rights for established people and service providers, and the family rights of Regulation 1612/68. However, it will not fundamentally change the legal position. It is more a simplification and amalgamation of the secondary legislation.

Nevertheless, there appear to be some important changes. First, citizens residing for longer than six months without engaging in economic activity will still have to have sufficient funds not to be a burden on the state. However, for up to six months they and their families appear, on the wording of the proposal, to have an unconditional right of residence without formalities. This is potentially significant, and the Directive is not clear on what happens if they become a burden on the state during those six months. This new six month easy-residence period is 'intended to cater for the modern, high-mobility lifestyles we are witnessing in the member states' (from the introduction to the proposal), to facilitate the lives of those who, for whatever reason, move often from state to state. Also, after four years of legal residence, a citizen will acquire permanent residence rights.

Overall, while it may still be amended before becoming law, the Directive is likely to be an important but incremental development, in line with the incremental progress found in the caselaw discussed below.

4.4.4 Direct effect of Art 18

This is now settled. In *Wijsenbeek*[50] a Dutchman objected to showing his passport at Rotterdam airport, and part of his argument was based on Art 18. The Advocate General argued that it must be directly effective, and the existence of the 'subject to' bit should not

---

49   COM (2001) 257.
50   *Wijsenbeek* Case C-378/97.

negate this. Member states intervened forcefully to oppose him. They realised that the impact of direct effect might be to extend movement and residence rights to the economically undesirable, and they fear, in many cases, so called benefit tourism: a flood of people moving to the richer or more generous northern European countries because these are better places to be unemployed, or to seek medical treatment. There must be great doubt as to whether this would happen, or how much effect it would have, but there is no doubt that it is a politically and socially sensitive issue. If hospital waiting lists and benefit levels are affected by the presence of many foreign claimants it will not take long for this to translate into public disaffection.

Perhaps because of this sensitivity the Court chose to carefully avoid giving a clear answer to the question of direct effect. It repeated all the parties who had taken sides, and then said:

> ... even if, under Art 7a [now 14] or Art 8a [now 18] of the Treaty, nationals of the member states did have an unconditional right to move freely within the territory of the member states, the member states retained the right to carry out identity checks at the internal frontiers of the Community.

It seems to say that it is not necessary to state whether this right was directly conferred by the article, since passport checks would not be contrary to it. This refusal to answer a hypothetical question is no doubt theoretically admirable, but also frustrating. In other parts of the judgment the Court uses phrases like 'at the present stage of Community law', emphasising that these articles are not to be seen as static. The Court is edging forward, showing the way, but reluctant to rush ahead.

Nevertheless, although the Court does not say 'Article 18 has direct effect', it does say at one point that:

> Article 8a(1) [now 18] of the Treaty confers the right to move and reside freely in the territory of the member states on citizens of the Union, subject to ...

This kind of language can only be compatible with direct effect. A non-directly effective article does not confer rights on individuals. Thus on balance, although one might have expected a clearer statement, *Wijsenbeek* is an authority that Art 18 has direct effect.

This has now been confirmed in *Baumbast*.[51] The case concerned the family rights of a migrant, but of course the scope of their rights depended on the scope of his. He had been a worker, but was no longer. One of the questions asked was whether he could then rely on a directly effective right of residence using Art 18(1). The Court's answer was quite unambiguous. It explained that while, once, it had been necessary to participate in an economic activity to have free movement rights, now that citizenship existed this was no longer the case. Considering Mr Baumbast's position, it said:

> As regards, in particular, the right to reside within the territory of the Member States under Article 18(1) EC, that right is conferred directly on every citizen of the Union by a clear and precise provision of the EC Treaty. Purely as a national of a Member State, and consequently a citizen of the Union, Mr Baumbast therefore has the right to rely on Article 18(1) EC.

---

51 *Baumbast* Case C-413/99.

4.4.5   Subject to ...

However, in the next paragraph in *Baumbast*, the Court said:

> Admittedly, that right for citizens of the Union to reside within the territory of another Member State is conferred subject to the limitations and conditions laid down by the EC Treaty and by the measures adopted to give it effect.

The important question then becomes the precise meaning of 'subject to...' in the second paragraph of Art 18.

To understand what this meaning is, a distinction has to be made between imposing a restriction, and simply not granting a right. For example, in Mr Baumbast's case he had initially been a worker, covered by Art 39. When he ceased to be a worker, the Court found that he could then rely on his citizenship. Art 18 could be used to take over where Art 39 stopped. This is not undermining the restrictions of Art 39, because Art 39 doesn't say that non-workers may not reside, it just does not talk about them. They are outside its scope. Thus Art 18 can be used in this way to fill the gap, and make sure even those outside the economic articles have a movement and residence right.

However, the situation is different if we consider the various specific restrictions on free movement; for example, the exceptions for public policy and so on in Art 39, and the requirement for sufficient resources and sickness insurance in the general residence directive, Directive 90/364. These are positive limitations on rights, and to use Art 18 to undermine these would be incompatible with its second paragraph.

Thus in *Baumbast*, the Court found that while Mr Baumbast could rely on his citizenship for a residence right, as a non-economic migrant he fell within Directive 90/364, and so was subject to its restrictions. His host state could demand that he had sufficient resources and sickness insurance.

However, the Court also said that if the host state did impose such conditions, it must do so in a proportionate way. The UK, the host state in the case, claimed that in fact Mr Baumbast's sickness insurance was not fully comprehensive, and might not cover emergency treatment. They considered this enough to deprive him of his residence right. The Court clearly indicated that in the context of someone who had been resident for quite some time in the country, never been a burden on public resources, and generally complied with all the conditions for residence, to rely on a minor defect such as that would be a disproportionate restriction on free movement.

This is another step towards expanding citizenship rights. Now that direct effect has been overcome, it may be that the Court will begin the slow process of interpreting away the resources and insurance restrictions, to bring true nationality equality even closer.

The only advantage now of being an economic migrant, rather than just a citizen, lies in the specific extra benefits granted. It is not necessary to prove resources, for example, and there is the extensive secondary legislation conferring family and social rights. However, as the cases discussed in this chapter suggest, most of these rights seem to be just specific interpretations of the rights of free movement and non-discrimination, the application of those principles to the actual situation of a migrant. Since these rights are also available to a citizen, it seems that the difference in status between economic and non-economic migrants is now extremely difficult to draw. Of course, in practice it is convenient to have the explicit secondary legislation to rely on. However, in principle, a citizen should be able to claim all the same benefits, just relying on Art 18, Art 12, and the logic of the law. Chapter 8 discusses this in some more detail.

CHAPTER 5

THE FREE MOVEMENT OF SERVICES

The free movement of services is primarily governed by Art 49 EC. This provides that:

> ... restrictions on freedom to provide services within the Community shall be prohibited in respect of nationals of member states who are established in a state of the Community other than that of the person for whom the services are intended.

The first question to ask is 'what are services?'. After this it becomes necessary to look more carefully at the situations to which the article applies; they turn out to be more diverse than one might expect. Finally, some of the peculiarities of this area of law, arising out of the abstract but often personal nature of services, are examined.

5.1 WHAT ARE SERVICES?

A service in ordinary language is something that a person or body does for another person or body. It is a sort of act. Mostly, we know them when we see them. However, in Community law the word is used in a specific sense, and while that sense is mainly the same as the ordinary language one, there are certain specific rules at the boundaries. In other words, there are a few things to know about distinguishing services from other things.

5.1.1 Distinguishing them from other economic factors

The fundamental freedoms are mutually exclusive. While a case may involve a number of them, the articles themselves do not overlap. Thus a case on television broadcasting might involve questions of free movement of goods (the effect of a ban on advertising), of services (the advertising itself) and of establishment (the advertising agency), but what was considered to be the goods under Art 28 would be different from the service under Art 49, and so on.

Sometimes it is not easy to choose between categories. Are e-books goods or services? If I spend six months providing massage in Spain am I established there, or a service provider? Formally, one must ask if the thing is a good, or if the person is established first, and only if the answer is negative consider services. This follows from Art 50, which says that a service is a service if it is not covered by one of the other articles. Services are residual.

In practice the order of consideration makes no difference. The point is to know how to distinguish the categories. Distinguishing services from goods is probably the easiest; services are abstract, goods have physical presence. An e-book would be a service. This is just ordinary language, but it accords with the cases.

Distinguishing services from establishment is more difficult. When a citizen visits a member state, not their own, to provide services they are a service provider. When they base themselves there and stay there for a long period, then even though they are still providing services they are established, and covered by Art 43 (and so not Art 49). Somewhere in-between is a line which can be hard to draw.

The main factor is whether the presence in the host state is temporary or permanent; services that are covered by Art 49 are provided on a temporary basis. However, other factors, such as the presence of an office or staff can also be relevant, although not usually decisive. The Court has said that a service provider may have an infrastructure in a state where he regularly provides services. It is a question of fact in every case. This quotation from *Gebhard*[1] gives an idea of how the Court looks at the matter:

> The concept of establishment within the meaning of the Treaty is therefore a very broad one, allowing a Community national to participate, on a stable and continuous basis, in the economic life of a member state other than his state of origin and to profit therefrom, so contributing to economic and social interpenetration within the Community in the sphere of activities as self-employed persons.

> In contrast, where the provider of services moves to another member state, the provisions of the chapter on services, in particular the third paragraph of Art 60, envisage that he is to pursue his activity there on a temporary basis.

> ... the temporary nature of the activities in question has to be determined in the light, not only of the duration of the provision of the service, but also of its regularity, periodicity or continuity. The fact that the provision of services is temporary does not mean that the provider of services within the meaning of the Treaty may not equip himself with some form of infrastructure in the host member state (including an office, chambers or consulting rooms) in so far as such infrastructure is necessary for the purposes of performing the services in question.

Fortunately, it turns out that the distinction very rarely matters. The basic principles governing services and establishment are the same. This follows both from the wording of the articles, and the caselaw (see Establishment (4.2), in Chapter 4, for more on this). Thus the outcome of a case will not usually turn on which article applies, and the Court very commonly considers them both in parallel, without necessarily deciding between them.

The distinction might be important in two situations. One is where establishment itself is necessary – for example where the rules of a professional association require establishment on the national territory. However the Court is not terribly sympathetic to this sort of rule, so it would have to be well justified, and in any case the rules on establishment expressly provide for secondary establishment. Thus it is possible to be established in two places at once. This is probably rather easier for companies than for people, since if people have too many offices they may come to seem rather temporary in some of them.

The other situation is where a member state tries to impose as many requirements on foreign service providers as on those established on its territory. This is usually disproportionate, and is discussed in the last part of this chapter.

---

1   *Gebhard* Case C-55/94.

5.1.2 Distinguishing them from non-economic things

Article 50 says that services must be provided for remuneration in order to come within the Treaty. They must be economic services. This might seem to exclude many activities not primarily done for money – perhaps charitable or public services, for example. However, it is possible to imagine many grey areas; what about the (legal) street musician who takes a collection, or the travelling preacher who does the same? They want money in the hat, but they can't insist on it. In the second case, the money may be necessary for life, but is not the motivation for the preaching. Does this mean that in these cases the service is not 'for remuneration'?

We can assume, using the principles developed in the context of workers, that the motivation is not important.[2] Moreover, the Court is likely to take a broad approach to the method of payment. It is consistent in concentrating on the underlying question: is this an economic activity? The street musician must be. Probably the preacher is too. There must also be grey areas in the growth field of non-governmental organisations. If an environmental organisation is paid by the state to write a report on an incident or subject, is that an economic service? Perhaps it takes no more than covers its costs, and is not motivated by the money, and is even registered as a charity. If Greenpeace advised the government, we might find it strange to think that it was providing economic services. Yet why are we to say it is not? The state clearly thinks its advice is worth money. The world is becoming too complex for a simple division into economic and non-economic.

Nowhere is this more evident than in the area of public services: those provided by the state. Traditionally these are excluded from the Treaty provisions on services. The provision of health care, education, and other public goods is often not done for money. Even if some contribution is demanded, as the Court said in *Humbel*, the state is '*not seeking to engage in gainful activity but is fulfilling its duties towards its own population in the social, cultural and educational fields*'.[3]

That case concerned university education. It was claimed that because students were required to pay a fee it was an economic activity, and so came within the services provisions. The Court said that it did not. The fee only covered part of the costs, most of which were met by subsidy, and so it was not really remuneration, but more a '*contribution to the operating expenses of the system*'. Therefore the Court was able to categorise the education system as a public duty, as above, and exclude Art 49.

The reasoning is clumsy, but the idea is simple; the state is not in business. However, since Art 49 was written much has changed in Europe and the line between commercial, or economic, activities, and public ones is very much harder to draw. The emphasis on budget control and accounting and even profit within state institutions makes them look much more commercial.

University education is a good example of this. Many postgraduate courses are run to make money for their institutions. The student fees are the primary source of funding, and everything about the course is geared towards getting those fees in. Universities advertise, budget, and generally behave just as if they were commercial actors.

---

2   See *Levin* Case 53/81, and Chapter 4.
3   *Humbel* Case 263/86.

In *Wirth*,[4] the Court repeated its observations from *Humbel*, but added:

> However, as the United Kingdom has observed, whilst most establishments of higher education are financed in this way, some are nevertheless financed essentially out of private funds, in particular by students or their parents, and which seek to make an economic profit. When courses are given in such establishments, they become services within the meaning of Art 60 of the Treaty. Their aim is to offer a service for remuneration.

This clearly includes private colleges and universities, but it could also include many state ones, if they behave in a commercial way. The line is becoming blurred.

It is also fuzzy in health care. In *Kohll*[5] the Court found that dental work done by an orthodontist outside any hospital system, for payment, was a service. This seems obvious enough. However, in many member states public and private provision are hopelessly intertwined, and hospitals which are technically private, or doctors who are legally self-employed, may receive most of their income from the state and be the basis of the public health system.

It is quite normal in Europe that people will receive medical treatment from an institution with mixed private and public characteristics, which will be billed to either a state insurance scheme or a private insurance scheme that is so heavily regulated as to look almost public. It will be very difficult to decide in which of these situations services are being received and in which not. The tendency of the Court is to find that an economic service is provided. In *Geraets-Smits*[6] they said that hospital treatment was an economic service because it was provided for remuneration, even though that remuneration did not come directly from the patient but rather from a third party, in this case the patient's insurance company. The judgment seems to suggest that if the remuneration had been from the state the decision would have been the same. The Court reiterated that the 'special nature' of services such as medical care would not take them outside Art 49.

This matters. As is discussed further in Chapter 14, the services provisions, as all of free movement law, are powerfully deregulatory. If they apply to health and education they will change them, and make them more liberal, less monopolistic, but perhaps also more commercial.

The question has also arisen of whether 'immoral' activities can be services. Most notably, in *Grogan*[7] the Irish government argued that even though abortion was carried out for money in some member states, to categorise it as an 'economic service' was almost obscene. The case concerned the advertising by students in Ireland of abortion in the UK. Abortion is constitutionally prohibited in the Irish republic. The Irish authorities wished to prohibit the advertisement. The students said this would be a restriction on the freedom to go and receive services.

This could have resulted in a full-blown conflict between the Irish constitution and Community law, but the Court managed to avoid this. It found that because the students were not acting on behalf of UK abortion clinics they were not economic actors, and so

---

4   *Wirth* Case C-109/92.
5   *Kohll* Case C-158/96.
6   *Geraets-Smits* Case C-157/99.
7   *Grogan* Case C-159/90.

could not rely on Art 49. Even if they had been, and there had been a restriction on services, the Court would almost certainly have allowed Ireland to escape via the public policy Treaty exception.

However, the controversy lay in the categorisation of abortion as a service – the mere fact of considering what was perceived in Ireland as a purely moral issue in economic terms. This inspired a spate of outraged articles in learned journals, amongst other things, and one can quite see the point. If a member state considers something to be the illegal taking of life, akin to murder, should it really have to see its rules on this measured against the economic yardstick of Art 49? Should the Court not have said that this matter fell entirely outside the article, just as did state education, because it was fundamentally not economic?

The problem was that in the UK it *was* economic; it was a service provided legally for remuneration and done for profit in private clinics. In that context it was unequivocally within Art 49. Therefore if the Court accepted the Irish point of view it would be denying a sector of the economy its Treaty rights. In the end it found this an unacceptable thing to do, and said that:

> It is not for the Court to substitute its assessment for that of the legislature in those member states where the activities in question are practised legally.

That is, the Court refuses to get involved in moral questions. If the activity is a service in one state, the Court will treat that as a service, and another member state will have to rely on Treaty exceptions to justify its restrictions. It cannot simply claim the Treaty does not apply.

5.2 THE THREE SERVICE SITUATIONS

Article 49 covers three situations: the movement of a service provider to another state, where she provides services; the movement of a service recipient to another state, where she receives services; and the movement of services from state to state, while both provider and recipient remain in separate member states. A fourth situation is also possible: where both provider and recipient meet in a third state.[8] Then both cases on moving providers and recipients would be relevant.

5.2.1 The moving provider

If a member state imposes explicitly discriminatory restrictions on service provision – they subject non-nationals to different requirements – they will be caught by the second part of Art 50, which says that:

> A person providing a service may, in order to do so, temporarily pursue his activity in the state where the service is provided under the same conditions as are imposed by the state on its own nationals.

The more interesting situation is where the restriction is not based on nationality, but on some other requirement, quite often the place of residence or establishment.

---

8   *Commission v Greece* Case C-198/89.

An early and important case in this category is *van Binsbergen*,[9] which was also the case where the Court said that Art 49 had direct effect. It concerned a Dutch lawyer, who moved his offices to Belgium. Because he was no longer established in the Netherlands he was not allowed to act in court there; in short, he could not provide legal services. Dutch law only allowed lawyers based in the Netherlands to do court work.

The Court said that the precise point of Art 49 was to remove restrictions on services being provided by people not established in the state in question. Therefore any restriction on service provision that applied only, or differently, to those established in another member state, was potentially caught by Art 49. Only if it could be shown that it was objectively justified and proportionate would it not be contrary to that article.

The Dutch government said its measures were necessary to ensure the proper supervision of lawyers, and so protect the integrity of the legal system. The Court said that if establishment was necessary for this, the measures would be acceptable. If less restrictive means could be used, the establishment requirement would not be allowed.

We see here very familiar terminology. A measure that restricts the provision of services by those established elsewhere must be justified and proportionate to escape.

As with the free movement of goods, the principle of mutual recognition plays a role in determining proportionality. In *Webb*,[10] the Dutch authorities wished to prosecute a UK service provider for providing manpower services in the Netherlands without having undergone the background checks and licensing procedure that Dutch law required. However, the Court said that if he had undergone similar checks in his home state, the Dutch authorities had to take this into account, and it would be disproportionate to impose equivalent requirements again.

The Court is also unsympathetic to national administrative or bureaucratic requirements which may hinder service providers. In *Corsten*[11] the German authorities wished to prosecute a foreign architect for providing services designing parts of buildings in Germany without being entered on the local register of tradesmen. This was a national legal requirement for all skilled tradespersons providing services in Germany, whether German or foreign. However, the Court found it disproportionate to apply this rule to foreign providers, unless the procedure involved no delay, no cost, and no complication for the provider. In a real life bureaucratic system, this seems impossible – so the compulsory registration was as good as illegal.

The German government had claimed that the register served as a control of tradespersons, so that quality could be ensured and the public protected. However, while this might be a laudable aim, their argument was quite wrong; it suggested that they had the option of refusing permission to trade to persons they did not approve of. However, since freedom to provide services was a Treaty right, this was not the case. Many cases turn on similar confusions by member states, who tend to persist in thinking that foreign service providers do so in their land by their permission, when in reality they do so as a result of Community law.

---

9   *van Binsbergen* Case 33/74.
10 *Webb* Case 279/80.
11 *Corsten* Case C-58/98.

Social advantages

Since a service provider may visit her host country regularly, the question of social advantages and benefits can arise. For example, does such a person have a right to housing, or the use of sports or cultural facilities, on the same basis as a national or a resident?

It is important to distinguish here between two situations: discrimination on grounds of residence, and on grounds of nationality. The first may often arise in the context of benefits – for example, an authority may provide housing to those that live within its area – and if this is justified, which it usually will be, since this is a normal way to organise society, then it will not be contrary to the Treaty. Non-nationals do not have a right to a kind of fictional residence; that would put them in a better position than nationals.

However, if nationals are entitled to housing benefits even if they spend only part of their time within that area, while non-nationals are not, then there is discrimination. This was the case in *Commission v Italy*,[12] and the Court found that such discrimination was contrary to Art 49 where it restricted the ability to provide services.

Thus the line taken is a little more restrictive than that for workers. Only discrimination that has some relevance to the services is prohibited by Art 49. Matters concerning housing, and anything else of importance, will be caught by this, since they can make it easier or harder to operate in a country, but truly minor matters – sports facilities again – might not.

However, the position is probably not as restrictive as this suggests, since in the context of the moving recipients, discussed below, the Court has found a very wide right to non-discrimination, and it is suggested that there is no reason why this cannot be transposed to moving providers.

5.2.2 The moving recipient

It was made clear that this situation is caught by Art 49 in the case of *Luisi and Carbone*.[13] These two Italians were prosecuted by the Italian authorities for taking large amounts of Italian currency to France and Germany. They said it was to pay for tourism and medical services, and so restrictions on such movement were contrary to Art 49.

The more obvious provisions for this case are those on free movement of capital, but at the time of the case this was not fully liberalised, and the Court used the service provisions as a way round this. It found that the freedom to go to receive services, and indeed to take money to pay for them, was a 'necessary corollary' of the right to move to provide services. This was because the services articles had as their objective:

... liberalizing all gainful activity not covered by the free movement of goods, persons or capital.

It has since become clear that one does not need to take huge amounts of money to come into this category; all tourists are service recipients, because inevitably they receive some

---

12   *Commission v Italy* Case 63/86.
13   *Luisi and Carbone* Case 286/82.

service (see the cases below). Probably it is fair to say that every member state national in another member state is a service recipient.

The most interesting aspect of the caselaw in this area has been the extent to which the Court has used non-discrimination. One might think that it would require only that people be entitled to receive services on the same terms as nationals. However, in the context of service recipients the Court has gone much further than this, and said that any discrimination against a service recipient is contrary to the Treaty.

In *Cowan*,[14] Mr Cowan was mugged while visiting France, and claimed compensation from the French State under a crime-victim compensation scheme. A French national would have been entitled to this wherever he lived, but foreigners could only receive it if they lived in France. The Court said that this was discrimination contrary to the Treaty:

> By prohibiting 'any discrimination on grounds of nationality' Art 7 [now Art 12] of the Treaty requires that persons in a situation governed by Community law be placed on a completely equal footing with nationals of the member state.

And this principle applied to service recipients applying for criminal compensation, because:

> When Community law guarantees a natural person the freedom to go to another member state the protection of that person from harm in the member state in question, on the same basis as that of nationals and persons residing there, is a corollary of that freedom of movement.

The Court is saying that freedom to move must be understood to include freedom from discrimination in all areas; without that non-discrimination movement is inhibited, and so the freedom to move is limited. What is striking is that the Court is using this general idea – that freedom of movement entails non-discrimination – to trespass on an area, criminal law, not normally within its jurisdiction.

It did this again in the more recent case of *Bickel and Franz*.[15] Here a German and an Austrian were arrested and tried in Italy for minor offences. One was a tourist, one was a lorry driver. It just so happened that the area of Italy where they were on trial has a large German minority, and they have a right in Italian law to have trials in German. Messrs Bickel and Franz also wanted this, but were told the right only applied to Italians of German ethnicity, not to foreigners. They claimed discrimination.

The Court said they were right:

> Although, generally speaking, criminal legislation and the rules of criminal procedure – such as the national rules in issue, which govern the language of the proceedings – are matters for which the member states are responsible, the Court has consistently held that Community law sets certain limits to their power in that respect. Such legislative provisions may not discriminate against persons to whom Community law gives the right to equal treatment or restrict the fundamental freedoms guaranteed by Community law.

Is there a limit to this, or is it truly the case that all discrimination against such people is outlawed? In principle, the Court is consistent that there is no *de minimis* in the area of

---

14   *Cowan* Case 186/87.
15   *Bickel and Franz* Case C-274/96.

discrimination (see Chapter 3 on goods, and *van de Haar*[16]). However, one odd case suggests that in practice there may be a point at which things become too trivial for consideration.

In *Grado and Bashir*,[17] an Italian national complained that the German prosecutor, in his trial for a driving offence, refused to call him 'Herr' although he would do so were he German. This different treatment was discrimination contrary to the Treaty, he said. The German court asked the Court of Justice if this was correct. The Court replied that it could not see how this question was necessary for the German court to make a decision in the substantive case – which was about Mr Grado's driving. Therefore it would not answer it.

This may be technically correct, but it is a strange judgment. Presumably the Italian court felt it was capable of giving Mr Bickel and Mr Franz fair trials in Italian, with the help of translators, so that question could also have been said to be hypothetical. Anyway, the deeper logic, that discrimination inhibits movement, is not consistent with such a technical approach. It is suggested the Court simply did not wish to get involved in such a marginal question.

An important point about all these cases is that the Court uses both the services articles and Art 12. It says that because there is a restriction on free movement, the situation is within the scope of Community law, and Art 12 applies. This is not good reasoning. If a matter is a restriction on services then it may be disposed of using those articles, and Art 12 should not be necessary. The use of Art 12 here is not really correct, but can be seen as part of a unifying and simplifying trend in free movement law; why use so many different articles, when the general non-discrimination one can do just as much work? This is discussed fully in Chapter 8.

5.2.3   The moving service

Sometimes both service provider and recipient stay at home – it is the service itself that moves. This is the case with television broadcasting across frontiers, and selling internationally by telephone. Legally, there is perhaps no need for this category. If a person provides a service to someone it may be that he should be subject to the same law whether he 'sends' it, or provides it in person. This would be a consumer protection perspective.

Indeed, it is not suggested that the legal principles applicable here are any different from those in the categories above. However, the particular situations are conceptually different, and so for that reason it may be helpful to consider these cases together. Typically they involve conflict of regulation situations: in one country it is allowed to advertise alcohol, or cold-call, in another country it is not. The service provider in the first country broadcasts his advertisements, or makes his phone calls, to the second country, where he is then breaking the law. He claims the law is a restriction on services.

The Court's approach to this should be, by now, unsurprising. It asks whether:

... those provisions are necessary for meeting overriding requirements of general public importance or one of the aims mentioned in Art 56 [now 46] of the EC Treaty, whether they

---

16   *van de Haar* Joined Cases 177 and 178/82.
17   *Grado and Bashir* Case C-291/96.

are proportionate for that purpose and whether those aims or overriding requirements could be met by measures less restrictive of intra-Community trade.[18]

Article 46 sets out the exceptions to the services and establishment provisions, and is dealt with in Chapter 7.

In short, can the member state rely on a Treaty exception? If not, are its measures objectively justified and proportionate?

An unusual situation arose in *Alpine Investments*.[19] A financial services company based in the Netherlands wished to cold-call people in Germany to offer them its services (cold-calling is telephoning without being asked, in an attempt to sell something). However, Dutch law does not allow cold-calling. Alpine claimed it was suffering a restriction on its freedom to provide services, contrary to Art 49. The Court found that there was a restriction on services, although it was acceptable because it was justified by the desire of the Dutch government to preserve the reputation of its finance industry, and was proportionate. However, the significance is in the finding that there *was* a restriction. This rule affected Dutch and foreign consumers equally; neither could be cold-called by any Dutch finance company. It also affected all companies operating in the Netherlands equally, wherever their legal place of establishment. It is therefore hard to see that there is any element of discrimination in the rule. It is simply a non-discriminatory restriction on a certain kind of commercial behaviour. Therefore, *Alpine* suggests that Art 49 can be interpreted to go 'beyond discrimination'. This aspect is discussed in Chapter 8, but to fully understand the reason for the judgment it is also necessary to consider the particular problems of services.

5.3 THE PARTICULAR PROBLEMS OF SERVICES

Services are particular in two ways: they are personal, and they are abstract. Both of these raise problems in regulating them, and in deciding what should be encompassed by Art 49. These problems are discussed below.

Services are personal in that they tend to involve a person doing something to or for another person, often within a relationship of trust, or inequality of power or information. The relationships of client with doctor, teacher, or financial adviser are examples of this. Regulation of services involves controlling these relationships, telling people what they may or may not do. This is something that people, and member states, have very strong feelings about. Either they feel that individual liberty is infringed, or that consumers, morality or social values are inadequately protected. The balancing of concerns such as these is implicit, and sometimes explicit, in judgments in many services cases, such as those about education and health care,[20] financial and insurance activities,[21] abortion,[22]

---

18 *de Agostini* Joined Cases C-34–36/95.
19 *Alpine Investments* Case C-384/93.
20 Eg, *Humbel*, *Wirth*, and *Kohll*, notes 3–5 above.
21 Eg, *Alpine Investments*, note 19 above, and *Säger*, note 26 below.
22 *Grogan*, note 7 above.

gambling,[23] advertising of alcohol,[24] and advertising aimed at children.[25] It can be very quickly seen how politically important all these issues can be.

Yet the abstract nature of services can make their regulation particularly difficult. A service is much harder to locate in a particular place than a thing or a person. When neither provider nor recipient moves, but the service is transmitted, which is the proper state to regulate that service? A consumer protection perspective, and perhaps a democratic one, might suggest the destination state. Thus Germany would decide what services German consumers could receive, wherever those services came from. If an English firm transmitted contrary to those rules, it would be liable in German law.

However, a practical perspective would suggest the state of origin might be a better choice. If the firm is located in the UK the UK government is better placed to monitor and control it, and can much more easily enforce regulation. Moreover, the firm then knows that wherever in the Community it transmits its services it only has to worry about one regulatory regime – that of the UK. This makes business much easier and promotes cross-border trade.

One answer is harmonisation, removing the national discrepancies, but this is often very difficult. Member states have strongly held convictions about how services should be regulated. But in the absence of harmonisation the Court still wants, and Art 49 demands, trade in services to continue, and so it has to deal with these issues.

Alpine was really a case about this regulatory question. Financial services are very important, and our whole lives may be affected by decisions we make about our finances, yet they are horribly complex. Thus every member state would agree that a banking or financial institution operating in the Community must be subject to a proper regulatory regime. But, in *Alpine*, should it have been the Dutch or the German?

Initially the Court said:

> Although the protection of consumers in the other member states is not, as such, a matter for the Netherlands authorities, the nature and extent of that protection does none the less have a direct effect on the good reputation of Netherlands financial services.

Then later it said:

> The member state from which the telephone call is made is best placed to regulate cold-calling. Even if the receiving state wishes to prohibit cold-calling or to make it subject to certain conditions, it is not in a position to prevent or control telephone calls from another member state without the co-operation of the competent authorities of that state.

It is acknowledging the practicalities, and choosing a middle path. Dutch regulation is accepted, because it has legitimate interests in regulation, and it is well placed to do so. However, the option is left open that Germany could also regulate. The protection of its consumers is its proper concern.

Therefore service providers may well find themselves subject to more than one regime if they attempt to operate abroad, something which is a powerful deterrent to such trade, and may partly account for the very limited internationalisation of consumer

---

23 *Schindler* Case C-275/92.
24 *Gourmet International,* Case C-405/98.
25 *de Agostini,* note 18 above.

banking, insurance, and finance generally. Moreover, unlike goods law, where the principle of mutual recognition has often been used to overcome regulatory obstacles, the Court showed itself cautious in *Alpine*, accepting the Dutch government's arguments that it had to regulate to protect its own reputation.

Such caution is understandable; there are huge differences in the style and content of different member state regulatory systems, and they are all highly complex. From a legal point of view, banking or insurance or health or education vary much more from state to state than cheese, wine or washing machines, and the barriers created by these differences are much harder to overcome. To say Germany must accept cassis with a low alcohol content may not rock German society. To say that it must accept services from banks or insurance companies operating on English rules may be much more controversial.

Nevertheless, the Court has indicated that there are limits on how far member states can regulate even complex and sensitive services that are provided from abroad. In *Säger*,[26] a UK company wished to perform patent checks on behalf of a client in Germany. They monitored these patents to see if they needed renewal. This service could not be provided in Germany, according to German law, except by companies subject to very strict regulatory requirements. They had to show expertise, and qualification, and trustworthiness, and obtain authorisation. In practice this meant one had to be established in Germany as a German patent agent in order to legally provide these services.

The Court made two points. First, although the desire to protect consumers was legitimate, the German restriction of these services to patent agents was disproportionate. Secondly, if a service provider was subject to all the restrictions of an established person, this deprived the service provisions of meaning and effectiveness.

This has proved to be a very important point, used in many cases since. Many national laws, perhaps being old, seem to assume that companies or persons providing services in their country will be established there. Thus, where the services are regulated, often these regulations will be very detailed and restrictive. This may be quite understandable if the service provider is indeed in the jurisdiction, and so that state is its primary regulator. However, if the service provider is based abroad this becomes an enormous obstacle to movement. Moreover, since such laws take no account of the fact that companies will be regulated in their home states, they are almost invariably disproportionate. Thus there have been many cases following the principles of *Säger*, such as *Corsten*, discussed earlier, in which the Court found that while it might be acceptable to have a compulsory register of all skilled tradespeople established in the area, to require registration for temporary service providers would be a disproportionate burden. If they only intended to provide intermittent services, the cost and hassle of registration might be enough to put them off doing business in that country at all.

The point here is that the service provisions aim to create a competitive market in services, in which the different kinds and forms of provider in each country may compete on each other's ground. If they may only do so when they take the same form as the national provider, the competitiveness of the market is reduced, and in practice foreign providers are excluded. In such cases the principle of mutual recognition is applied. In

---

26 *Säger* Case C-76/90.

general, unless there is a good justification, where services are provided across frontiers, a member state cannot impose all its own requirements on foreign providers, but must accept them if they are legal somewhere else.

CHAPTER 6

THE FREE MOVEMENT OF CAPITAL

Capital is an abstract idea. Following Karl Marx it is wealth that can be used to build up other wealth. However, for Treaty purposes it can be taken to mean the same as 'money'. Therefore restrictions on the cross-border movement of cash, or international bank transfers, are clearly restrictions on the movement of capital. However, the concept goes beyond this. Just as rules about product packaging may inhibit the movement of goods, so rules about investment, or insurance or buying houses, might all inhibit flows of money from country to country. Therefore the scope of the free movement of capital is potentially broad. How broad it actually is now will be discussed below.

6.1 THE DEVELOPMENT OF CAPITAL MOVEMENT

Free movement of capital is governed by Arts 56–60 EC, of which Art 56 is the key. It provides that:

1   Within the framework of the provisions set out in this chapter, all restrictions on the free movement of capital between member states and between member states and third countries shall be prohibited.

2   Within the framework of the provision set out in this chapter, all restrictions on payments between member states and between member states and third countries shall be prohibited.

The other articles of the chapter are not without importance. They set out various restrictions on the broad statement in Art 56. For example, that article will not prejudice restrictions on movement between member states and third countries which existed at the beginning of 1993.[1] In other words it does not override existing arrangements. It just stops states creating new restrictions.

It is also specified in Art 58 that the free movement of capital will not prejudice any restrictions on freedom of establishment which are compatible with the Treaty. Therefore if a legitimate restriction to freedom of establishment exists, Art 56 may not be used to undermine it.

However, Art 56 remains the central article, although until recently it was not directly effective. In fact the free movement of capital has always lagged behind the other freedoms, with restrictions being allowed to a greater extent than for goods, services or persons. This was largely a result of the desire of member states to retain control over capital movements, and the importance they gave to this. They were much more willing to let goods move freely than allow uncontrolled movement of money.

The first sign of judicial frustration with this was perhaps *Luisi and Carbone*.[2] The case concerned a restriction on the movement of money, but the secondary legislation passed

---

1   Article 57 EC.
2   *Luisi and Carbone* Case 286/82, and see Chapter 5.

under the free movement of capital articles had not gone far enough to prevent this. The Court classified the matter instead as a payment for services, and using the more advanced services provisions was able to override the restriction.

In some cases since it has acted similarly, tending to treat capital as a residual freedom, and to use the others first. However, in others, involving both capital and services, they have been treated side by side, as equals. In *Safir*,[3] it was argued that Sweden taxed life insurance taken out through foreign insurers more than that coming through domestic ones. This was an issue that can be argued to involve both the free movement of capital and of services. However the Court decided the case entirely on the services point, noting that it was then not necessary to consider the capital issues. On the other hand, in *Svensson*,[4] which considered different treatment of mortgages from foreign and domestic lenders, the Court considered both capital and services in full, concluding that there was a restriction contrary to both articles.

Whether or not the Court can be said to treat the free movement of capital quite as the equal of the other freedoms, it has certainly come a long way. In *Sanz de Lera*,[5] in what remains the most important judgment in the area, it at last found that Art 56 was directly effective, and used it to override a Spanish restriction on the movement of currency.

In this case Spanish law forbade the export of more than 5,000,000 pesetas without authorisation. In a decision with very strong echoes of *German Beer* and other goods cases,[6] the Court found that to ask for authorisation was disproportionate. The same aim, of preventing money-laundering and major crime, could be achieved by a mere declaration that the money was to be moved. The theme here is information rather than control.

However, the free movement of capital remains at the stage of considering fairly crude restrictions on movement. The caselaw falls broadly into two categories. On the one hand, there are those where a member state imposes an explicit restriction on cross-border movement of money. Generally the Court deals with this as it did in *Sanz de Lera*. On the other hand, there are cases where foreign currency or finance or investment is treated differently from domestic currency or finance or investment. This latter situation has occurred in two cases on land purchase, *Trummer*[7] and *Konle*,[8] and in several on 'golden shares'.

The first land case concerned an Austrian rule that only mortgages denominated in Austrian schillings could be registered in the Austrian land register (this was pre-euro). This meant that if you borrowed in another currency to buy Austrian land, you would have to convert this to AS and enter that sum. The problem was that if currencies fluctuated, the value of the registered mortgage might end up being significantly different from the amount you owed. This could cause problems for both borrower and lender, and so would be a deterrent to borrowing abroad. It was therefore, in the view of the Court, a restriction contrary to Art 56.

---

3   *Safir* Case C-118/96.
4   *Svensson* Case C-484/93.
5   *Sanz de Lera* Joined Cases C-163/94, C-165/94 and C-250/94.
6   *German Beer* Case 178/84, and see Chapter 3.
7   *Trummer* Case C-222/97.
8   *Konle* Case C-302/97.

In *Konle*, an Austrian rule provided that foreigners who wished to buy land in border areas of Austria had to show that it was not going to be a secondary residence, and obtain a permit. The Austrians wished to prevent whole areas of their countryside becoming no more than holiday dormitories, full of foreigners at some points in the year, and empty at others. This is an issue of importance to many states. In Portugal whole rural areas have already been bought by northern Europeans, and Denmark is also sensitive to this occurring along its border with Germany. As a result, both Denmark and Austria obtained derogations from the Treaty, which allowed them to maintain restrictions on the ownership of land by foreigners for some years after they joined the Community. However, those derogations have now expired, and had expired when *Konle* came before the Court.

The Court of course found this restriction illegal, since it is so clearly discriminatory. However, what is useful is that it spelt out that a restriction on buying property is a restriction on the movement of capital. It follows that all restrictions on investment are restrictions on capital. The concept of capital goes beyond mere money. This is not controversial, but it is important. It shows how Art 56 has the potential to become one of the most significant Treaty articles.

The Court also indicated the basic approach to capital restrictions, and once again it will not be surprising:

> ... to the extent that a member state can justify its requirement of prior authorisation by relying on a town and country planning objective such as maintaining, in the general interest, a permanent population and an economic activity independent of the tourist sector in certain regions, the restrictive measure inherent in such a requirement can be accepted only if it is not applied in a discriminatory manner and if the same result cannot be achieved by other less restrictive procedures.

Summarising this, a measure that may restrict capital will be acceptable only if it is non-discriminatory, justified and proportionate.

An interesting twist in *Konle* involved Art 295 EC. This provides that 'this Treaty shall in no way prejudice the rules in member states governing the system of property ownership'. Member states have often argued that where the rules on free movement interfere with matters such as land purchase, or intellectual property, which are aspects of 'property ownership', the free movement rules must take second place. Article 295 indicates that the national property system is to triumph. The Austrian government made this argument in *Konle*.

The Court's response in *Konle* was consistent with its caselaw in other areas. It said:

> ... although the system of property ownership continues to be a matter for each member state under Art 222 [now 295] of the Treaty, that provision does not have the effect of exempting such a system from the fundamental rules of the Treaty.

In other words, member states may have whatever property rules they want, so long as they comply with free movement.

This is not a linguistically justifiable interpretation of Art 295, but it is an effective and purposive one. Rules on property ownership, whether houses, shares, or other types of property, can be so complex and restrictive that if an integrated market is to be achieved they have to take second place to free movement.

It is the shareholding cases that have been the most dramatic. In the simplest, against Portugal, national laws allowed only a limited proportion of the shares of certain recently privatised companies to be held by foreign shareholders.[9] Portugal, like many member states, had in recent years privatised certain industries that had traditionally been state owned, but wished to maintain a degree of control over them. They said this was necessary for economic policy, which really meant preventing important national industries being taken over by owners that they thought undesirable, or operated in a way not in the national interest. However, these aims might be understandable but the discriminatory way of going about them was not. Moreover, economic reasons could not be used to limit a fundamental freedom.

Two other cases concerned so called 'golden shares' in privatised oil and gas companies, held by the French and Belgian governments.[10] Although these governments did not have shareholdings in the companies that would normally give them control, when they privatised them they had retained special rights for themselves, which they said were necessary to protect national energy supply and so national security. The difference between the two cases is revealing. In the Belgian case, the government had essentially reserved the right to intervene when the privatised company proposed to take actions which the government thought might be harmful to energy policy. In the French case, any shareholdings above a certain amount had to be first approved by national authorities.

In both cases the Court found that there was clearly a restriction on free movement of capital, because investment in the companies was likely to be deterred, and could be limited, by the actions of the authorities. However, in both cases energy policy provided a legitimate reason for some restriction. But, while the Belgian rule went no further than necessary, and so was permissible, the French rule was far too vague, and essentially reserved a discretionary power to the authorities to choose who became a large shareholder. This was contrary to legal certainty, and would deter foreign investors, and went far beyond what was necessary to protect the energy supply. It was contrary to the Treaty.

These cases have great implications. Market deregulation as well as the current economic mood puts great pressure on member states to privatise, and so not have to bear the cost of operating huge industries themselves. However, the great fear is that this will make consumers, and the national interest, take second place to the profits of the company and the interests of shareholders. What these cases make clear is that it is perfectly acceptable to take measures to protect important national interests, but one must do so in a clear and proportionate way that protects the position of investors, and cannot be abused and used to cover discrimination against foreigners.

6.2 THE FUTURE OF CAPITAL MOVEMENT

Two very important questions remain largely unanswered in the area of capital. One is the extent to which Art 56 applies to private parties. The other is the extent to which non-

---

9   *Commission v Portugal* Case C-367/98.
10 *Commission v France* Case C-483/99, *Commission v Belgium* Case C-503/99.

discriminatory restrictions will be removed. They are important for related reasons. The rules governing investments and finance are intricate, and often restrict the movement of capital not because there is discrimination, but simply because the system is restrictive. The same rules apply to everyone, but they are rules that make it difficult to do things with money.

Of course, these rules tend to perform a function. They regulate and control markets and business, and so are important. However, there are wide divergences of opinion on how far such rules need to go, and what form they need to take, as is shown by the different rules in different states. If Art 56 can be used to subject such rules to a proportionality assessment, then the Court has a very powerful deregulatory tool, and one which it could potentially use to force the pace of harmonisation – faced with the destruction of their financial rules by the Court, member states have a motivation to agree common rules.

However, many of the rules and practices that close financial systems arise out of the behaviour of private parties as well as regulation. To try and send a payment abroad, or receive a salary into a foreign bank account, or deposit a foreign cheque, to use everyday examples, is to experience the highly national outlook of high street banks. As for buying your insurance from abroad ... better not to think about it. Most things to do with consumer finance are notably national. Is it a coincidence that levels of consumer satisfaction are also notably low in this area, and that banks are constantly accused of anti-competitive practice?

Of course, some of this market division is the result of the different currencies that have been historically present in Europe. However, this has not prevented other sorts of trade, and cannot be a complete explanation. There are also serious obstacles to transacting financial matters abroad, arising from both private and public measures. The possibility that Art 56 could be used to overcome these is an enticing one.

The possibility of applying free movement law to private parties is considered in Chapter 12. On the question of applying Art 56 to non-discriminatory measures *Sanz de Lera* is again of relevance. Rather like in *Groenveld*,[11] in goods, we are faced with an export restriction, this time of money, which is difficult to classify in terms of discrimination.

When a state restricts imports, it is almost invariably doing it to protect its national market in some way, and it is the foreign suppliers who will complain. Discrimination fits this situation nicely. However, in *Sanz de Lera* the measures taken were as likely to hurt Spaniards who wished to go abroad as foreigners who wished to bring out pesetas they had acquired in Spain. Moreover, while in one sense Spanish industry benefits if Spanish money stays at home, an inability to export pesetas is a disincentive to importing other money, and so restricts investment, which hurts Spanish business.

In fact, rather than trying to favour one group of economic actors over another, the restriction in *Sanz de Lera* aimed to protect the state from the activities of wrongdoers, whoever they might be, Spanish or foreign. Further, this was its effect; it was merely that it achieved it in a disproportionate manner. Therefore, this was not really a discriminatory measure, in any sense. It may be that it can then be seen as authority that Art 56 will be used in non-discriminatory situations.

---

11 *Groenveld* Case 15/79, and see Chapter 3.

On the other hand, although the measure may not have been discriminatory, it was explicitly aimed at restricting cross-border movement. This is one of the keys to the application of free movement law (see Chapter 11). Therefore, it does not follow from *Sanz de Lera* that measures that are restrictive of movement, but no more of cross-border movement than other movement, will fall foul of Art 56. The *Bosman*[12] situation may not be realised with capital.[13]

6.3 NOTE ON ECONOMIC AND MONETARY POLICY

The economic and monetary policy of the European Community are dealt with in Arts 98–115 EC. They are two separate, but very related, things. The economic policy provisions embody an agreement between member states on how they will conduct their own, national, economic policies. They are supposed to do this in a way that helps the Community achieve its objectives.

The monetary policy provisions concern the behaviour of the European Central Bank (ECB), and the European System of Central Banks (ESCB), in their administration of the euro. To a very large extent this consists of setting interest rates. The ESCB is composed of the ECB and the national central banks.

Together, these two sets of provisions aim at what is called economic and monetary union (EMU). This is the harmonious coming together of the economic and monetary policy of the member states. The jewel in the crown of EMU is of course the creation of the euro.

This is not, in a strict legal sense, an internal market matter. There is a separate title of the Treaty covering EMU. This is not an empty point; it is quite wrong to see monetary union – the creation of the euro – as an aspect of free movement of capital, because this implies limits to the free movement of capital which do not exist. Free movement of capital is not limited to any particular currency, or even to currency as such. Moreover, it extends to movements from member states to third countries. Its rules also apply to all member states. The euro, by contrast, is a creation of a sub-group of member states, and its requirements do not extend to all states.

However, it would be equally misleading to think that the internal market and EMU are not connected – the one is vital to the other. Therefore, while this is not the place for detailed consideration of economics, nor of the ECB, an outline of EMU and its role in the internal market is given below.

6.3.1 Economic policy

Articles 98–104 EC, and a Protocol to that Treaty, together embody what is often called the 'growth and stability pact'. This is an agreement between member states, made in Amsterdam in 1997, that they would avoid excessive deficits or debt, in the interest of economic stability in Europe. This was also intended to ensure that the euro would be a

---

12 *Bosman* Case C-415/93.
13 See Chapter 4.

strong and stable currency. Another Protocol provides that the UK is not bound by these provisions.

The central provisions of the pact are that member states must have a national debt that is no more than 60% of their gross domestic product, and have a deficit – a difference between the government's income and its spending – of no more than 3% of the gross domestic product. In other words, governments can no longer spend as much as they want. If they break the rules of the pact they can ultimately be fined heavily by the Community.

A degree of economic debate surrounds this. Many economists think that these criteria are good government practice anyway, and member states should not spend beyond their means. Others feel that the strict adherence to these criteria could result in an unjustified squeeze on government spending, affecting public services. There are times, they say, when it is more important to invest in health or education or other public services than it is to have your accounts in order.

It may be that this debate is moot, since how all these requirements are interpreted has at various times been controversial. Compliance with them was a condition for joining the euro, yet Italy and Belgium were allowed to participate with roughly twice the permitted debt. Although Art 103 does allow that temporary excess may be overlooked if the trend is in the right direction, many observers felt that the situation in these countries could not honestly be interpreted as compatible with the pact, and the fact that they were able to join the euro was a triumph of politics over law and economics.

Similarly, since the euro entered circulation several member states have breached the 3% deficit requirement, yet it is too early to say whether any of them will ever be fined. Some member states have been enthusiastic for enforcement action, but others have argued for flexibility, no doubt with a view to their own budget deficits. Mutual back-scratching may yet triumph over fiscal discipline.

The influence of the pact on the internal market comes through the financial discipline it imposes. It conditions the behaviour of governments to some extent, and encourages the prevailing mood of deregulation and liberalism. Governments committed to limited spending are often happy to privatise industries, and are also liable to prioritise economic growth over other factors, such as public services. Thus the pact contributes to the creation of a certain sort of European economy, and to trade and business, even if it may, arguably, also have negative effects on social provision.

6.3.2 Monetary policy

Monetary policy is essentially about the euro. All member states except the UK, Denmark, and Sweden are participating in this project, and since January 1999 their currencies have been formally merged. Notes and coins of these currencies continued to circulate until the beginning of 2002, but they were no more than different denominations of the same currency. Their exchange rates were absolutely fixed. It is therefore fair to say that in this transitional period 1,936 lira *were* 6.56 francs *were* one euro. Only the pictures on the paper were different.

The major benefits that the euro is thought to bring to doing business in Europe are the removal of the risks of currency fluctuations, the reduction of transaction costs, and transparency of pricing. It is also hoped by many that it will be a strong currency. On the other hand, there are certain negative points resulting from the centralisation of monetary policy in the European Central Bank. These are dealt with in turn.

The risk that currency values may fluctuate against each other inhibits trade between member states, and investment from the outside. The German exporter has to worry whether the price he asked in francs will be worth the same in marks when he finally gets it. If he prices in marks the importer has to worry whether he will have to find more francs when the time comes to pay. In practice, large companies may take out a sort of insurance against this, often through speculation on money markets, but this still imposes an extra cost on the transaction. For the Japanese company, wanting to open a factory in Europe, the worry is that it will invest a huge amount in one land and then discover that this has become a rather expensive land relative to the others, and so it is difficult to export within Europe. Since, for most non-European investors, the whole point of such a factory is to get inside Europe's trade barriers against the outside world, and so conquer the European market, this is bad news. Since Europeans want outside investment, this is bad for them too.

The reduction in transaction costs should arise because there will no longer be any need to change money. Not only will this eliminate exchange costs, but it should make transfer of money abroad easier, and so cheaper.

Transparency of pricing refers to the fact that the common use of the euro makes it much more obvious where there are price differences between member states, for goods, service, salaries or anything else. This will tend to encourage trading to exploit these and ultimately to reduce the differences. The theory is that this increases the efficiency of the economy and so benefits Europe.

It is also hoped and expected by some that the euro will benefit Europe by being stronger than any one European currency could be alone. This is not an unqualified good; a strong currency inhibits exports. However, it also decreases the price of imports, and can have a psychologically positive effect. Germans felt proud and secure with their rock-hard Deutschmark for many years, and when one's currency is strong one feels rich abroad.

One way in which the euro may become strong is if it is held in large quantities by those outside Europe. This creates a shortage of the currency, and just as a shortage of milk pushes the price of milk up, a shortage of currency pushes its price up (relative to other currencies) – in other words, makes it stronger. There are a number of reasons why people outside Europe may buy euros. The most obvious are to do business in Europe, or for currency speculation. However, they might also do it because they want their savings in a currency they consider safe, or because they need the euro to do business because it has become a world trading currency. At the moment most of these people buy dollars. This is the currency of oil and aircraft trading all over the world, and it is also the currency that is stuffed in mattresses from Moscow to Jakarta. It also tends to be the currency of choice of international crime. This may sound melodramatic, but the sums involved are not small, and it is thought by many economists that this use of dollars outside the US has added significantly to its strength.

Whether the euro will be able to rival the dollar in these areas to some extent depends upon the strength and vibrancy of the European economy, and the amount of world trade done by Europeans. However, it also depends upon psychological factors such as whether Europe is perceived to be as big and strong as the US, or the euro is perceived to be a 'hard' currency.

The euro may be assisted in a small way by the existence of the 500 euro note. This is one of the highest value notes anywhere in the world, which makes it particularly attractive for smugglers and hoarders, who wish to conceal large amounts in small places.

On the debit side, the creation of the euro has resulted in the loss of currencies that in some cases had very deep historical roots. It has also resulted in a loss of autonomy for member states. This arises because monetary policy – of which the major part is the fixing of interest rates – is now set by the ECB. Although the governing board of this contains the heads of national central banks, the ECB is guided by the overall economic picture, and cannot adapt to small countries or areas where economic conditions are aberrant. Thus in the early days of the euro Ireland's economy seemed to be growing out of control, far faster than was healthy or sustainable, but interest rates could not be used to limit this because the rest of Europe required lower ones.

Moreover, the ECB is obliged to pursue particular objectives. Article 105 EC says that:

> The primary objective of the ESCB shall be to maintain price stability. Without prejudice to the objective of price stability, the ESCB shall support the general economic policies in the Community with a view to contributing to the achievement of the objectives of the Community ...

Since it is part of the ESCB, these obligations bind the ECB.

This is not uncontroversial. Historically, national finance ministers have often been guided in their monetary policy by the need to create jobs, stimulate the economy, and many other highly political considerations. While the ECB is clearly permitted, by the second sentence of Art 105, to take a broad view of its aims to some extent, price stability (roughly equivalent to the control of inflation) comes first. Thus it is possible to imagine a situation where the economy arguably required lower interest rates, but the prices of goods in the shops were stable or rising, and so the ECB was reluctant to act, because lower interest rates often lead to higher prices.

Not everyone would be happy with this. Not everyone agrees that price stability is really the holy grail. It is a particularly German perspective, reflecting the approach of the Bundesbank, although since copied by governments in other Member States, notably the UK. Europe has adopted this price stability focus partly because the Germans were reluctant to sacrifice it, and partly because almost everyone agreed that Germany had run a notably successful currency. The arguments here are economic ones, which do not belong in this book in detail, but it is useful to have some idea that they exist, and that because they are about the economy of Europe they are of relevance to the functioning of the internal market.

As a final note it must be mentioned that the ECB is stated in Art 108 to be independent. It may not take orders or instructions from any member state or Community institution. It must simply pursue the tasks the Treaty gives it. This is included because it is the consensus of the moment that independent central banks take better economic decisions. The argument against it is based on democracy; that it makes the bank unaccountable.

In one sense this is true. There is no direct mechanism for the people or their representatives to control the bank. However, the member states can always make a new Treaty, or appoint a new ECB head. Thus ultimate control remains democratic. Whether this control is effective depends very much on how open and transparent the ECB is, so that it is clear what it is doing and why. In practice, the openness of the ECB is more of an issue than its independence.

CHAPTER 7

EXCEPTIONS TO FREE MOVEMENT

The EC Treaty provides for exceptions to the rules of free movement. They allow the member states to ignore free movement in cases of real urgency, when important national interests are under threat. The precise form of the exceptions varies from chapter to chapter, but they have a great deal in common, including the principles of their interpretation. That is why they are treated together here.

In the following sections, the articles providing the exceptions for each of the categories of free movement are introduced. Then these Treaty exceptions are distinguished from other kinds of apparent derogation from the Treaty. Then the interpretation of these exceptions in the caselaw is explored. Finally the so called 'public service exception' is discussed.

7.1 THE EXCEPTION ARTICLES

7.1.1 Goods: Art 30

Article 30 provides that:

> The provisions of Arts 28 and 29 shall not preclude prohibitions or restrictions on imports, exports, or goods in transit, justified on grounds of:
>
> public morality, public policy or public security;
>
> the protection of health and life of humans, animals or plants;
>
> the protection of national treasures possessing artistic, historical or archaeological value; or
>
> the protection of industrial and commercial property.
>
> Such prohibitions or restrictions shall not, however, constitute a means of arbitrary discrimination or a disguised restriction on trade between member states.

Most of this is self-explanatory. It allows member states to forbid imports of meat from countries where there is an animal epidemic, for example, or to forbid the export of certain works of art which are important to the nation. The difficult bit comes in finding the limits – can all art export be prohibited? This is discussed under interpretation. 'Public policy' is perhaps less obvious than the others, but means something like the public good, as understood by the government. The best way to understand it is just to know the cases, again discussed below.

The last exception, the protection of property, is relevant to cases involving trade marks and patents. Sometimes the holder of these rights can use them to prevent imports, and although this is apparently a quantitative restriction, Art 30 may allow it. This is more fully explored in Chapter 13.

One other article is worth being aware of: Art 296. This provides that:

1   the provisions of this Treaty shall not preclude the application of the following rules: ...

(b) ... any member state may take such measures as it considers necessary for the protection of the essential interests of its security which are connected with the production of or trade in arms, munitions and war material; such measures shall not adversely affect the conditions of competition in the common market regarding products which are not intended for specifically military purposes.

The arms trade is not a free one; it may be regulated by considerations that are not primarily commercial, but are to do with the security of the nation.

As far as free movement of goods goes, the work done by Art 296 can also be done by the 'public security' exception, so it will not often be necessary. It simply serves as a second line of defence for measures which preserve the national supply of arms, but would otherwise be seen as quantitative restrictions.

7.1.2   Workers: Art 39

The exceptions to the free movement of workers are contained in Art 39 itself. Section 3 provides that it is 'subject to limitations justified on grounds of public policy, public security, or public health'. As well as this, s 4 states that the whole of Art 39 does not apply to jobs in the 'public service'. The meaning of this is discussed in the last section in this chapter.

7.1.3   Establishment and services: Arts 45, 46 and 55

Article 45, in the establishment chapter, provides that the chapter will not apply 'so far as any given member state is concerned, to activities which in that state are connected, even occasionally, with the exercise of official authority'. This is analogous to the public service exception for workers. Article 46 says that derogations from the principles of freedom of establishment shall be allowed in the interests of 'public policy, public security, or public health'. Article 55, in the services chapter, says that Arts 45 to 48 also apply to services. Therefore the above exceptions are also applicable to the services rules.

7.1.4   Directive 64/221

This Directive applies to workers, established persons and service providers, and sets out how the public policy, security, and health exceptions shall be applied to them. It is mainly procedural, setting out the rights that migrants have to appeal, and be notified of decisions, and so on, if member states wish to deport or bar them. Broadly, they must have the same access to legal remedies as a national would have if she was faced with an oppressive administrative act. The Directive also provides an annexed list of which diseases can justify exclusion on public health grounds.

Article 3 provides that measures taken against a migrant shall be based purely on their own personal conduct, and mere criminal convictions shall not justify deportation. These are both important points explained in *Bonsignore*[1] and *Bouchereau*,[2] considered below.

---

1   *Bonsignore* Case 67/74.
2   *Bouchereau* Case 30/77.

7.1.5 Capital: Art 58

Article 58 is complicated, and ensures that the general rule on free movement of capital does not have an unreasonably destructive effect on member state tax laws, nor on the supervision of the finance industry. Its major section is s 1(b), which says that member states remain free to:

> Take all requisite measures to prevent infringements of national law and regulations, in particular in the field of taxation and the prudential supervision of financial institutions, or to lay down procedures for the declaration of capital movements for purposes of administrative or statistical information, or to take measures which are justified on grounds of public policy or public security.

The last part, public policy and security, is now familiar enough, but it is notable that monitoring and information gathering powers are also expressly protected. In particular, declarations of capital movement may be required, although these can certainly be seen as an inconvenience and a restriction on movement. We can compare this approach with the law on goods and people, where bureaucratic restrictions on movement have often been removed by the Court. The movement of money seems to be subject to somewhat closer control. This is partly a result of the particular dangers of large-scale money movement: money laundering by criminals, instability of the financial system, economic and currency effects impacting on the whole population. Partly it is a result of the particular ease of transferring money, by comparison with goods, or services. Vast amounts can be moved electronically in almost literally no time. Similar scale movements of goods or services would be much more obvious, and easier to stop, and so such strong monitoring powers are not necessary.

7.2 DISTINGUISHING TREATY EXCEPTIONS FROM OBJECTIVE JUSTIFICATIONS

A rule that seems to restrict free movement can be saved from illegality in one of two ways: either by a Treaty exception, or by being shown to be justified and proportionate. It is important to appreciate that these are quite separate and different mechanisms.

The first difference is that justification and proportionality can only be used to excuse a non-discriminatory measure. This will be remembered from *Gebhard*.[3] By contrast, Treaty exceptions can be used for any type of measure.

In practice, however, they tend to be important mainly for discriminatory measures. This is because the category of objective justifications is an open one – unlike the Treaty exceptions – and it is also more loosely interpreted than the Treaty exceptions. Therefore, a non-discriminatory measure is easier to save using the idea of objective justification than it is using the Treaty. For this reason the Treaty exceptions often do not come into play in these non-discriminatory cases.

---

3   *Gebhard* Case C-55/94.

A second difference between the two is that the Treaty exceptions are true exceptions, whereas objectively justified rules can arguably be seen as never involving any obstacle in the first place. This was explained in Chapter 3.

7.3 INTERPRETATION OF TREATY EXCEPTIONS

There are two main points to make about the interpretation of the Treaty exceptions. First, it is a matter for the Court of Justice rather than national courts – public policy, and so on, are Community concepts. Secondly, the Court is highly restrictive. It does not like to allow derogation from free movement.

7.3.1   A Community concept

Because the Treaty exceptions are designed to protect the very important interests of states, one might expect that the member states, or their courts, would have the last word on them. These would be the areas where they would say 'sorry, this is too sensitive for us to bow to the Community. We do not accept interference here'.

However, this is not the case. The exceptions stand in the Treaty, and so the last word on them is reserved for the Court of Justice, as the body charged with Treaty interpretation. It is to decide whether the concept of public policy includes a particular situation, for example, and can tell a member state that its plea for an exception is not acceptable. It will be seen in the section below that it often does this. It will also be seen though that sometimes it does show a degree of deference. This is an acknowledgment both that member states are more knowledgeable than the Court about what their vital interests are, and that where a member state sincerely feels they are at stake it can be politically unwise to challenge this.

A quotation from *Van Duyn*[4] summarises the approach in the context of public policy and workers, although it can be applied more generally:

> It should be emphasised that the concept of public policy in the context of the Community and where, in particular, it is used as a justification for derogating from the fundamental principle of freedom of movement for workers, must be interpreted strictly, so that its scope cannot be determined unilaterally by each member state without being subject to control by the institutions of the Community. Nevertheless, the particular circumstances justifying recourse to the concept of public policy may vary from one country to another and from one period to another, and it is therefore necessary in this matter to allow the competent national authorities an area of discretion within the limits imposed by the Treaty.

The first principle is therefore strictness of interpretation, by the Court rather than the member states. The second is that some discretion for the member states must be allowed.

---

4   *Van Duyn* Case 41/74.

7.3.2 A restrictive interpretation

As the quotation above makes clear, the Treaty exceptions are holes in the internal market, and for this reason the Court tries to keep them as small as possible. This means that it examines critically whether the member state is really acting in response to a threat to a vital interest, whether that threat is serious enough to justify invoking an exception, and whether the measures taken are acceptable. These points are addressed below.

7.3.3 Is the member state acting honestly?

A member state invoking a Treaty exception must be honestly trying to protect a vital interest, and must not simply be using an excuse to hinder trade. This corresponds to the requirement in Art 30 that reliance on an exception not be a 'disguised restriction on trade'. However, the need for genuineness applies to all of the categories.

It is not often that the Court will openly accuse a member state of dishonesty. However, sometimes it can be read clearly between the lines. In the *Newcastle Disease* case[5] the UK banned the import of poultry meat and products from most member states, claiming this was to control this highly infectious poultry disease. They relied on the animal health exception in Art 30. However, the factual circumstances were disturbing. The ban was introduced just before Christmas, when most turkeys are sold in the UK. It followed a year in which turkey imports had increased dramatically, and the press had been calling for protection for British turkey farmers. The Commission, and France (the largest exporter to the UK) were not informed in advance, so they had no opportunity to respond or challenge the measures. Finally, the measures were against the UK government's own scientific advice. In short, it looked very much like disguised protectionism.

The Court first noted:

> ... the second sentence of Art 36 [now 30] is designed to prevent restrictions on trade mentioned in the first sentence of that article from being diverted from their proper purpose and used in such a way as either to create discrimination in respect of goods originating in other member states or indirectly to protect certain national products.

It then considered the facts, and concluded:

> ... the real aim of the 1981 measures was to block, for commercial and economic reasons, imports of poultry products from other member states, in particular from France ...

> ... the 1981 measures constitute a disguised restriction on imports of poultry products from other member states, in particular from France ...

In other words, the Court simply did not believe that this was really an animal health measure. It was simply a restriction on trade.

Another case which can be seen as about honesty is *Commission v France*,[6] the *French Farmers* case. When angry French farmers took to the streets to block imports of agricultural produce the French government said that clearing the roads for imports and

---

5   *Commission v UK* Case 40/82.
6   *Commission v France* Case C-265/95.

protecting their journey would be too dangerous. It would inflame the public mood and might lead to serious public disorder. Thus the police deferred to the farmers, and allowed trade to be stopped.

This was not argued as an Art 30 public policy point, but it looks very like one, and the things that the Court said are relevant to that article. What it said was that if there really was a risk of uncontrollable rioting or breakdown of public order, then perhaps this would justify non-compliance with Art 28. However, the French state had not shown that this risk existed, and so it was in breach.

This seems to suggest that a *'force majeure'* exception might exist. If a member state is unable to comply with Community law because of public behaviour beyond its control, perhaps they would not be considered in breach of the Treaty. This suggests they might be able to invoke public policy to justify their inaction or action.[7] However, in this case the Court did not believe that was the situation. Reading between the lines, it seems that the French government was putting internal politics above its Treaty obligations, and its claims that it was too dangerous to act were a sham.

7.3.4   Is the threat serious enough?

The Court is consistent in finding that the threat the member state faces must be a serious one, and not marginal. The case of *Bouchereau*[8] is an example of this. It is a case about persons, and some parts of the ruling are only applicable in that context. However, the Court also interpreted 'public policy', and the way that it did so gives a good idea of its general approach to how serious a threat must be before Treaty exceptions may be used.

A Frenchman had been convicted twice of possession of illegal drugs, and the UK judge asked the Court whether this could justify deportation on the grounds that he was a threat to public policy.

The answer was that:

> In so far as it may justify certain restrictions on the free movement of persons subject to Community law, recourse by a national authority to the concept of public policy presupposes, in any event, the existence, in addition to the perturbation of the social order which any infringement of the law involves, of a genuine and sufficiently serious threat to the requirements of public policy affecting one of the fundamental interests of society.

In other words, mere crime was not sufficient. There had to be, beyond that, a serious threat to one of the fundamental interests of society. This must mean that not all criminal behaviour justifies deportation; only the most serious.

Moreover, it was also asked whether past convictions could be enough. The wording of Directive 64/221 suggested they could not. The Court explained here that the point was to see whether the person was a *continuing* threat. Were they likely to act in an anti-social way in the future? Past convictions might be evidence that this was the case, particularly if there were a string of them, but were not conclusive on their own. It was, as UK judges say, something to be decided on the facts of each case.

---

7   See *Centre Leclerc* Case C-231/83.
8   *Bouchereau*, see note 2 above.

If that continuing threat was not present, past convictions would be irrelevant:

> The existence of a previous criminal conviction can, therefore, only be taken into account in so far as the circumstances which gave rise to that conviction are evidence of personal conduct constituting a present threat to the requirements of public policy.

One can conclude overall that there must be an actual, continuing, serious threat to a fundamental public interest, before public policy can be relied upon to restrict free movement. Although this test is vague, it is clearly restrictive.

7.3.5 Judging the threat

Deciding whether the standard set in *Bouchereau* is met, and some action contrary to free movement is justified, is mostly common sense and experience. However, there are a number of particular factors which the caselaw shows to be relevant.

7.3.5.1 The presence of Community measures

If an area is regulated by Community measures it is much harder for a member state to justify extra measures of its own which obstruct trade. The assumption is that the Community regulates properly and so no further national measures are necessary. In theory it would still be open to a member state to prove that in fact its actions were justified, but *Compassion in World Farming*[9] shows how hard this will be.

In this case the UK government considered trying to stop the export of veal calves. They were being sent to other member states where they were going to be kept in cruel conditions, illegal in the UK. The UK was to rely on public policy, public morality, and animal welfare to justify its ban.

While there is no doubt that all these issues were properly involved – the treatment of veal calves is a moral issue of animal welfare – the Court did not allow a ban. The reason was that there was a directive in force regulating the treatment of veal calves, and all member states were obliged to comply with that. Therefore there was no reason for further restrictions. The UK was free to have stricter rules internally, but it could not restrict movement of calves to states that complied with the Directive. The Directive allowed calves to be kept in the confined and harsh conditions that were considered unacceptable in the UK.

What gives this case a twist is that, as well as the Directive, the Commission had also issued a recommendation that in fact member states should enforce higher national standards – as did the UK. However, this was not obligatory. It was argued that the UK should be able to restrict exports to member states that did not meet the recommendation standards. This argument failed. As long as member states complied with the obligatory directive standards, their trade in calves could not be interfered with.

---

9 *Compassion in World Farming* Case C-1/96.

7.3.5.2 Real scientific doubt

This case can be contrasted with *Sandoz*.[10] In this case the Dutch government tried to block the import of foods from Germany that had added vitamins. In Germany it was widely believed that adding vitamins to food was healthy; vitamins are good for you. In the Netherlands it was widely believed that it was not safe; some vitamins can be dangerous in artificially large doses. Public health was therefore relied upon.

Two important points come through from the judgment: that there was no Community harmonisation on vitamins in food, and that there was genuine scientific uncertainty over possible health risks. Bearing these things in mind the Court allowed the ban, subject to the limits of proportionality. In their words:

> ... in so far as there are uncertainties at the present state of scientific research it is for the member states, in the absence of harmonization, to decide what degree of protection of the health and life of humans they intend to assure, having regard however for the requirements of the free movement of goods within the Community.

However, they continued, the principle of proportionality required that they did not go beyond what was necessary to protect health. There must be the possibility of authorisation for marketing of goods where the importer could show that the added vitamins were safe, and served a useful purpose, particularly a 'technical or nutritional' one.

They also said that because the member states had the technical expertise in this area, they must be left a very wide discretion to decide whether the importer had met these requirements.

This is therefore a notably deferential judgment, allowing significant restrictions on free movement, because the Court is satisfied that there are genuine issues of health, the Netherlands is behaving honestly, and at the moment this is a matter where the member states are better placed to decide things than the Community is.

7.3.5.3 Domestic action

If a member state tries to repress imports, but does not repress their domestic equivalent, this is very good evidence that the threat is not actually a serious one. Therefore there is no basis for relying on a Treaty exception. A number of cases have dealt with this point and developed it. They show that, broadly, measures taken against imports must be consistent with internal actions. The Court will not accept a plea for an exception where it can be shown that the member state takes a fundamentally different approach to foreign and domestic goods, or people, or services. For example, blocking pornography imports on grounds of public morality will not succeed if the same pornography is legally made and sold domestically.

This is not quite the same as simple non-discrimination; it is not always possible to treat the foreign and domestic in exactly the same way. For example, because domestic drug dealers are not expelled from the country does not mean that foreign ones cannot be prohibited from entering. The punishments would have entirely different impacts on the two groups – it is generally much worse to be expelled from your home state than

---

10   *Sandoz* Case 174/82.

deported from another. However, it would be necessary to show a reasonable degree of action against domestic drug dealers if foreign ones were to be blocked; in other words, some kind of consistency of policy. Without this, the member state would be open to an accusation of 'arbitrary discrimination'.

The leading goods cases on this point are *Henn and Darby*,[11] and *Conegate*.[12] In the first of these, the UK had imposed a ban on the importation of 'indecent and obscene articles'. Two British entrepreneurs were charged with evading this ban by importing pornography, and they pleaded Art 28 in their defence, to which the UK government replied with the public morality exception of Art 30.

First of all the Court noted that:

> In principle, it is for each member state to determine in accordance with its own scale of values and in the form selected by it the requirements of public morality in its territory.

It then went on to consider the UK laws on pornography, and said:

> ... notwithstanding the fact that they contain certain exceptions of limited scope, these laws, taken as a whole, have as their purpose the prohibition, or at least, the restraining, of the manufacture and marketing of publications or articles of an indecent or obscene character. In these circumstances it is permissible to conclude, on a comprehensive view, that there is no lawful trade in such goods in the United Kingdom. A prohibition on imports which may in certain respects be more strict than some of the laws applied within the United Kingdom cannot therefore be regarded as amounting to a measure designed to give indirect protection to some national product or aimed at creating arbitrary discrimination between goods of this type depending on whether they are produced within the national territory or another member state.

The Court says that although there are loopholes in the domestic law, broadly it bans trade in obscene articles. Therefore there is consistency in the treatment of domestic and foreign goods. Therefore this cannot be seen as a case of arbitrary discrimination. Since member states are entitled to choose their own levels of morality, it is in fact a legitimate reliance on the exception.

On the other hand, *Conegate* concerned the importation not of magazines, but of things, in particular, of 'love-love dolls' and 'erotic vacuum flasks'. The Court once again surveyed UK law. It concluded that as a matter of fact there were no domestic producers of comparable items, but had there been they would have been able to sell them legally, provided they did not send them through the post, and only sold from licensed premises. Therefore, the domestic manufacture and sale of such objects was not actually prohibited. In that case, foreign ones could not be banned either:

> It follows that a member state may not rely on grounds of public morality in order to prohibit the importation of goods from other member states when its legislation contains no prohibition on the manufacture or marketing of the same goods on its territory.

Two cases on persons show a similar approach. In *Van Duyn*,[13] a Dutch scientologist was refused a residence permit for the UK on the grounds of public policy. She had come to

---

11 *Henn and Darby* Case 34/79.
12 *Conegate* Case 121/85.
13 See note 4 above.

work for the Church of Scientology. The UK claimed this was a harmful organisation. However, there were no restrictions on membership of the Church for UK nationals.

The Court had to consider whether this invalidated the plea of public policy, but perhaps surprisingly it found that it did not. First, the UK had taken certain 'administrative measures' aimed at restricting the activities of the Church, and secondly, it had made its opposition well known. Moreover, it was a principle of international law that a state could not expel its own nationals. Therefore precisely equal treatment could not be expected.

Here, the fact that the UK could show it had a history of acting against the Church, and treating it as harmful, was sufficient to show that its ban on Ms Van Duyn was a legitimate act of public policy.

This should be compared with *Adoui and Cornuaille*.[14] Two French women were expelled from Belgium because:

They were waitresses in a bar which was suspect from the point of view of morals.

Public policy was relied upon. The Court found that:

... a member state may not, by virtue of the reservation relating to public policy contained in Arts 48 [now 39] and 56 [now 46] of the Treaty, expel a national of another member state from its territory or refuse him access to its territory by reason of conduct which, when attributable to the former state's own nationals, does not give rise to repressive measures or other genuine and effective measures intended to combat such conduct.

Although there were Belgian laws against prostitution, they were apparently not harsh enough, nor enforced strictly enough, to amount to the 'repressive measures' required to show the state regarded it as a serious threat. Ms Adoui and Ms Cornuaille could therefore return to their employment and self-employment.

The contrast between these cases is striking. No repressive measures at all were taken against UK scientologists, and the 'administrative measures' apparently consisted of little more than a few speeches by politicians. Yet Ms Van Duyn was expelled.

This may have been because the (male) judges were unable to take prostitution as seriously as Scientology as a threat to morals. On the continent this is certainly the prevailing attitude, and Scientology is often taken quite seriously. Alternatively, it may simply be that *Adoui*, the later case, overrules *Van Duyn*, or at least develops it. In any case, *Adoui*'s more precise and logical tests are to be preferred to the vagueness of the Scientology case.

7.3.5.4 Half measures

If a member state takes only moderately restrictive measures, this may backfire; it could be argued that it shows that the threat it faces is not serious. This occurred in *Rutili*.[15] Here the French state wished to ban a migrant from certain areas of France, because of various public order offences. He was a left-wing political activist, and they felt that in the

---

14   *Adoui and Cornuaille* Joined Cases 115 and 116/81.
15   *Rutili* Case 36/75.

countryside he could only be of limited trouble, but he should not be allowed to live in Paris.

The Court said this could not be justified using public policy. If he was a real threat, he should be deported. The fact that he was not showed that he was not taken that seriously. Therefore Art 39(3) was not applicable.

By contrast, in *Olazabal*, the French government also wished to confine a foreign worker to one area of the country.[16] However, in this case they stated that the only alternative was deportation. The Court said that if his behaviour was of the sort that would incur repressive action were he French, and if the authorities would be entitled to deport him, then it was also acceptable for them to take the less draconian measure of simply limiting his right of residence to a certain area of the country, if this solved the public order problem.

The difference between this case and *Rutili* seems to be that in *Rutili* it was in serious doubt whether Mr Rutili's actions were grave enough to justify deportation. If not, then it was also not acceptable to confine him to one area. There is no provision for half-exceptions for half-serious threats. However, in cases where the threat is serious enough to justify reliance on a Treaty exception, then the *Olazabal* approach is correct.

Of course, if national law allowed regional restrictions on nationals, then in principle they could be applied also to foreigners on the same basis. This was also stated in *Rutili*. Then, there would no longer be any discrimination, and there might be no need for Treaty exceptions at all. There would just be enforcement of criminal law. At most, one could claim that there was a restriction on free movement, which must be justified and proportionate.

7.3.5.5 Economic factors

The basic principle is as stated in *Kohll*:[17]

It must be recalled that aims of a purely economic nature cannot justify a barrier to the fundamental principle of freedom to provide services.

The protection of national industry, or the economy, or the financial situation of the government, or other economic considerations, are therefore not within the Treaty exceptions.

However, the position is not quite so simple, because sometimes economic interests blur with other ones. In *Kohll*, the question was whether a person could use his national health insurance to buy health care abroad. The national authorities said this would undermine the financial balance of the health care system, and could undermine it. The Court was sceptical, but said:

However, it cannot be excluded that the risk of seriously undermining the financial balance of the social security system may constitute an overriding reason in the general interest capable of justifying a barrier of that kind.

In other words, the threat of a collapse of the national health care system would justify use of a Treaty exception, even if the threat in question was of an economic nature.

---

16   *Olazabal* Case C-100/01.
17   *Kohll* Case C-158/96.

Another example of this kind of blurring is in *Campus Oil*.[18] Any company wishing to import oil to Ireland had to buy 35% of their petroleum product needs from the Irish State Oil Refinery. The rest could come from abroad. The point of this was to keep the refinery, the only one in Ireland, in business. The problem was that its prices were higher than elsewhere.

Importers claimed this was a restriction on imports (since they were restricted to 65% of the total), contrary to Art 28. The Irish government claimed that public policy and security required that they have an oil refinery. Crude oil was much more easily available than refined oil. Without a refinery their national supplies of petroleum products were much more insecure. The only way to keep the refinery open, since its prices were high, was to impose the compulsory purchase obligation.

The Court allowed this claim, but has been criticised for its decision. It is argued that it failed to distinguish between the strategic interest in having an oil refinery – fair enough – and the economic interest in having it make money – illegitimate as a grounds for exception. It is said that the Irish State could also have kept the refinery in business by subsidising it so that its prices were lower and people bought from it willingly. This would have been less of an obstacle to trade, and so more proportionate. The problem with this is that then the Irish government might have been accused of providing illegal state aid.

Whatever the correctness of this, the case shows how closely economic and other considerations can be interlinked. Another case showing this is the *Preussen Elektra*[19] case, considered in the next sub-section.

7.3.5.6 Environmental considerations

Strictly speaking, the protection of the environment is not one of the grounds of exception in any of the Treaty articles. However, the protection of the life and health of humans, animals, and plants, might be thought to come quite close. It is up to the Court whether it interprets this broadly to include general environmental issues, or narrowly, confining it to situations where a specific direct health threat can be shown. The protection of free trade favours a narrow approach. However, the environment is an increasingly important political issue, and there has been fierce criticism of the Treaty for failing to protect it adequately. In the light of this the Court may be more inclined to interpret 'life and health' broadly.

In one early case it managed to avoid the issue, that of *Walloon Waste*.[20] A Belgian law required that waste be disposed of within the local area. This was because Wallonia – a region of Belgium – was becoming dangerously overfull of foreign waste, with environmental effects. The measure meant that this foreign waste could no longer be imported for treatment or disposal in Belgium. The processing of waste is a business, and waste has a certain value, so this was apparently contrary to Art 28.

If the rule was discriminatory, it would not be open to the Belgian government to argue environmental justification, because this is not in the Treaty. It would have to argue

---

18   *Campus Oil* Case 72/83.
19   *Preussen Elektra* Case C-379/98.
20   *Walloon Waste* Case C-2/90.

public health. The measure does look discriminatory. Foreign waste is expressly banned. However, the Court found that the underlying principle was not nationality but locality, which was not to do with nationality. There was a restriction on trade, but it applied to Belgian and foreign waste equally; neither could be moved across the border of a Belgian region. Thus waste from other areas of Belgium could not be sent to Wallonia either. Therefore the ban was open to any objective justification, and the protection of the environment was a good one.

It is hard to imagine the Court finding an import ban open to justification in many circumstances, and this case is often criticised. However, it enabled an apparently sensible environmental measure to be protected, without breaking with the principle of a narrow approach to Art 30. That article never needed to be considered. A similar approach has been used in subsequent waste cases.

Since *Walloon Waste* the environment has moved further up the political agenda, and recent caselaw suggests that the Court may now be prepared to openly interpret 'life and health' to include the environment. The case in question is *Preussen Elektra*,[21] in which a German measure required power suppliers to buy all the electricity produced by local windfarms. The price was above the market price for electricity.

Just like *Campus Oil*, in this case imports were reduced by making purchase of the national product compulsory. Since energy suppliers had to buy local wind power, they would buy less power from abroad. Article 28 was apparently infringed. However, the German authorities argued that the measure was justified by the protection of the 'life and health of humans, animals, and plants' in Art 30. The Court considered the dangers of greenhouse gases to the world, and the role of windpower in reducing them, and the role of the environment in the Community (an important policy), as well as in world affairs (it mentioned the Kyoto Agreement), and then concluded that there was no infringement of Art 28. It was not entirely clear from their judgment whether this was because they saw the rule as a justified indistinctly applicable one, or because it came within the Art 30 exception. In this sense, *Preussen Elektra* is consistent with the other environmental cases, where the issue of discrimination is glossed over, and the basis of the environmental exception left unclear. However, because the measure does look clearly discriminatory, and the Court did use the phrase 'life and health of humans' in its argument, *Preussen Elektra* may indicate that the Court is prepared to include the environment within Treaty exceptions.

In that case, this is an extremely purposive judgment, since the connection with life and health is extremely indirect, and it is also radical in that it is not a restrictive approach to the Treaty exceptions, but a broad approach.

As with *Campus Oil*, the judgment is open to the criticism that the profitability of the windfarms is confused with their existence, and economic issues with environmental ones. Arguably, if the windfarms had been subsidised so that their electricity was attractive on the free market this would be a more open and transparent and less distorting – and so more proportionate – way of achieving the same ends. Instead of the government requiring private power suppliers to effectively subsidise the windfarms, would it not be more honest for it to do so itself? The answer to this is not simple. It is

---

21 *Preussen Elektra*, see note 19 above.

part of a complex, but important, debate about state aids and regulatory assistance which is beyond the scope of this book.

7.3.5.7 Personal conduct

The conduct of other people cannot be relevant to deportation. This seems obvious, but it was not clear to the German judge in *Bonsignore*.[22] In this rather tragic case, an Italian living in Germany accidentally shot and killed his little brother with a hunting rifle. The possession of the firearm was illegal, and he was convicted of both that, and criminal negligence. No punishment was imposed for the latter, because it was judged that he had suffered enough. However, the national court wished to deprive him of his residence permit and deport him, as a threat to public policy. They said that the deportation might be justified:

> By reasons of a 'general preventive nature', ... based on the deterrent effect which the deportation of an alien found in illegal possession of a firearm would have in immigrant circles having regard to the resurgence of violence in the large urban centres.

In other words, although it was accepted that the death had been an accident, and Mr Bonsignore was neither violent nor a threat to society, his deportation would send a useful message to immigrants that they could not get away with using guns. This was particularly important since violence in cities was increasing.

The Advocate General in this case commented that crimes by foreigners often aroused particular hostility, 'verging on xenophobia', and implied that the national court was giving in to this. The Court followed his cue, and denied the public policy claim. It said:

> With this in view, Art 3 of the Directive provides that measures adopted on grounds of public policy and for the maintenance of public security against the nationals of member states of the Community cannot be justified on grounds extraneous to the individual case, as is shown in particular by the requirement set out in paragraph (1) that 'only' the 'personal conduct' of those affected by the measures is to be regarded as determinative.

> As departures from the rules concerning the free movement of persons constitute exceptions which must be strictly construed, the concept of 'personal conduct' expresses the requirement that a deportation order may only be made for breaches of the peace and public security which might be committed by the individual affected.

This is actually a less obvious decision than it seems. The different tariffs that criminal law applies to different crimes reflect the feeling of the population about how serious those crimes are. Moreover, one of the major functions of punishment is to deter others. It is quite common that a judge will give heavier sentences when a particular kind of crime is becoming a particular threat. Thus 'ram-raiders' received heavier sentences when it was perceived that this crime was becoming an epidemic and it was important to stop it.

Therefore, in several ways, the behaviour of others, and the effect on them of the sentence, are all taken into account when sentencing someone. Nor is it possible to ignore them. Without considering the social context it is impossible to decide what is an appropriate punishment. However, *Bonsignore* clearly sets limits on this, and one of those

---

22   *Bonsignore*, see note 1 above.

limits is clearly that the nationality of the criminal cannot make his crime, or punishment, more serious, nor can it play a part in the wider considerations of the judge.

7.3.6 Are the measures taken acceptable?

The fact that a threat exists which justifies invoking a Treaty exception does not give member states a licence to act as they like. The nature of their response to the threat remains subject to the supervision of the Court, which applies a number of general principles of Community law. The most important of these, which have been important in the caselaw, are proportionality, mutual recognition, and human rights.

7.3.6.1 Proportionality

Measures taken under a Treaty exception must be proportional. In particular, they must go no further than necessary to achieve their aim. An example of a disproportionate measure can be found in *Commission v UK*.[23]

The UK had a system of health checks for ensuring the safety of pasteurised milk products. The checks were at all stages of production, from farm to shop. No other state had such a system. As a result, the UK banned all imports of pasteurised milk products. It said none of them could possibly comply with its requirements.

The Court admitted that this might be true, at that time. However, the UK had to remain open to the possibility of compliance. If imports came with certification meeting all the UK's safety concerns then they would have to be admitted. To not even admit this possibility, to have an absolute ban, was disproportionate. It also had a negative effect because it created a disincentive for other states to set up checking mechanisms as stringent as the UK's. Why bother, if imports would not be allowed anyway?

Another case concerned the Church of Scientology.[24] French law prohibited any foreign investment in companies connected with 'public authority', where that investment might be contrary to public policy, health, security, or a range of other reasons. The decision on this would be taken by a government minister. He had a discretion in deciding if there was such a threat, and if he felt so, could order transactions to be undone.

The Court found this was clearly a restriction on the free movement of capital, and moreover, it was an illegal one. Even though the reasons for exclusion in fact corresponded reasonably well to the Treaty exceptions, such a rule was much too vague. How was a foreign investor – such as the Church of Scientology – to know whether or not their transaction would be acceptable? The rule was contrary to legal certainty. This case could be seen as introducing a new requirement into the Treaty exceptions; national measures relying on them must be reasonably clear, certain and predictable.

Alternatively, legal certainty can here be seen as an aspect of proportionality. Member states must spell out clearly which aspects of their national interest need protection and how, and be careful that they do not impose restrictions beyond this. The French minister

---

23 *Commission v UK* Case 261/85.
24 *Scientology International* Case C-54/99.

had been given far more power to impede investment than he, or the national interest, actually required.

7.3.6.2 Mutual recognition

In *Dutch Plant Checks*[25] the Dutch authorities wished to check imported plant protection products, such as weedkillers or insecticides or fertilisers, for the presence of various toxic chemicals. These were allowed in some member states, but not in the Netherlands. The checks were clearly a barrier to trade, but they were justified on human health grounds.

However, some of the products had already been tested in their country of origin, and had certificates to show this. The Netherlands refused to accept these. The Court said that although it was legitimate to conduct additional tests, where it could not be shown that these tests had already been done, if there was evidence that the relevant tests had already been performed in another member state the Netherlands had to accept these test certificates and results. The protection of human health justified establishing the presence of certain chemicals. However, the principle of mutual recognition required that foreign test results be treated as equivalent to national ones.

7.3.6.3 Human rights

The case of *ERT*[26] was highly controversial when it was decided. The Greek government had given a national television broadcasting monopoly to one company, ERT, and another company, who wished to broadcast, was challenging this monopoly. It said it was a restriction on the freedom to provide services, as well as making various other arguments. The Greek government said that this restriction was justified by public policy. ERT was a non-profit organisation which would broadcast in a way beneficial to the development of the Hellenic people. Another complaint made was that the monopoly was contrary to Art 10 of the European Convention on Human Rights, that providing for freedom of expression, and it is the answer on this point that is the most interesting.

The Court said that if a member state sought to rely on a Treaty exception, this was subject to the use of that exception being compatible with human rights. Thus if the monopoly was a restriction on freedom of expression, contrary to the European Convention on Human Rights, then Community law would not allow it either. A claim of public policy would fail.

This surprised some people because it had always been the position that the Court could only apply human rights considerations to matters within the scope of Community law. However, the Treaty exceptions were 'holes' in the Treaty, so surely they were outside Community law, and not subject to its human rights supervision? This is wrong however. If a member state acts in a way that hinders trade, and relies on Art 30, then clearly its action is within the scope of Art 30. Therefore it is within the scope of Community law, and Community human rights laws apply.

---

25 *Dutch Plant Checks* Case 272/80.
26 *ERT* Case 260/89.

7.4 THE PUBLIC SERVICE EXCEPTION

Article 39 does not apply to jobs in the 'public service'. The establishment and services articles do not apply to activities that involve the exercise of 'official authority'. These two phrases are expressions of the same idea. This is that certain key activities of the state are too sensitive to be opened to foreigners. Member states can legitimately preserve them for their nationals. The question is, precisely which activities and jobs are these? The answer is that only those with genuine national security or policy implications are covered. Mere civil servants as such are not.

The member states began by arguing for a very broad interpretation, and the phrases themselves seem to support this. In particular, 'public service' seems able to cover all state employees. Thus in *Commission v Belgium*[27] the Belgian authorities said that any job with local or national government or public undertakings owned by the government was excluded from Art 39. Nurses, railway workers, municipal architects, all were public servants, and foreigners could be excluded from these posts.

The Court rejected this, and set out the now standard approach to public service and official authority. The exclusion covered:

> ... posts which involve direct or indirect participation in the exercise of powers conferred by public law and duties designed to safeguard the general interests of the state or of other public authorities. Such posts in fact presume on the part of those occupying them the existence of a special relationship of allegiance to the state and reciprocity of rights and duties which form the foundation of the bond of nationality.

The key point of this is that the posts must require a special allegiance to the state and be to do with safeguarding the interests of the state. This is not obviously true of jobs such as children's nurse, or gardener in municipal parks. They have little to do with patriotism or the protection of the state, except in the very broadest senses.

The Court did not list particular professions that were in or out in this case, but subsequent caselaw has made clear its general approach. Judges, tax inspectors, police, policy-making civil servants, even government architects might be in. These are all jobs where the state has to know that the person is reliable; the kind of jobs for which one might be vetted. Nurses, teachers, cleaning staff and railway workers are out. The citizen-state allegiance is not such a feature of these jobs. In the words of Advocate General Mancini, the exceptions cover jobs and activities for which the employees or actors 'don full battle dress'[28] in the service of the state.

As regards establishment and services, activities such as the servicing of warplanes by private companies, or the development of sensitive computer programs for government departments by private computer companies, would clearly be included within the exercise of 'official authority'. The state could insist on using national firms, with national employees. On the other hand, contractors for street cleaning or building car-parks would be out. There is no 'battle dress' involved.

Some member states had problems with the principles in *Commission v Belgium*. The French government even claimed it was a constitutional requirement that French civil

---

27　*Commission v Belgium* Case 149/79.

28　Advocate General's Opinion, *Commission v France* Case 307/84.

servants be French. The idea of an employee of a hospital or a local council having another nationality threatened the very identity of the state. If this is so, it seems the French State is doomed.

However, there are many reasons in favour of the restrictive approach taken by the Court. Three of them emerge from the judgment. The first is simply that many jobs in national civil service simply do not need to be filled by nationals. The interests of the state are not threatened by foreign gardeners. The second point is that the civil service is of different sizes in different states. If public service and official authority included anyone in government employment or acting on behalf of the government, the uniformity of Community law would be threatened, and the internal market distorted. A job in one country might be open to foreigners, but not the equivalent in another, merely because an activity was privatised in one, and not the other. The third point was that in some states such a high proportion of employment is by the state that the free movement of workers and self-employed people could be severely limited by a broad approach. Up to 50% of jobs might be reserved for nationals.

This connects with another point, which the Court was too polite to make but Advocate General Mancini made in his opinion in another case.[29] This is that member states are dishonest in this area. They claim constitutional and philosophical objections to employing foreigners, but in fact they are concerned with domestic politics. Governments have traditionally dealt with high unemployment in certain areas or population groups by creating large numbers of, often low-paid, jobs. Thus the Carabinieri in Italy, and the Gendarmes in France, both paramilitary police forces, have played a very important role in ensuring employment for young men from poor areas, just as London Transport and what was British Rail have been major sources of employment for the ethnic minorities in the UK. Governments do not wish to weaken these politically useful employment tools by opening them to foreigners. However, while this is understandable from a domestic point of view, it is also an expression of nationalism, and a return to discrimination, in opposition to the most basic principles of the Community. The Court inevitably refuses to allow it.

A slightly more complex situation occurred in *Commission v Italy*.[30] In an Italian research centre the senior jobs were clearly of strategic importance and within the public service exception. However the lower jobs were clearly not. The problem was that the senior people were appointed from the junior ones. The Italian government therefore wished to include all the jobs within the exception. The Court did not allow this. It said that Italy could protect its interests by failing to promote foreigners from the junior posts. It was not compatible with the Treaty to exclude jobs merely because they might lead to positions of sensitivity. Only the actually sensitive activities themselves were within the exception.

---

29 *Commission v France* Case 307/84.
30 *Commission v Italy* Case 225/85.

CHAPTER 8

COMMON PRINCIPLES: DISCRIMINATION
AND MARKET ACCESS

Underlying the fundamental freedoms there are two common ideas. One is that discrimination on the grounds of nationality should not occur in the internal market. The other is that nations should become more open to each other. In the internal market context the first is usually just called discrimination, although sometimes people talk about the 'principle of equality' or equal treatment. It is important to remember that it is discrimination on the grounds of nationality that is being talked about, and not, for example, on the grounds of sex or race. The second is often described in terms of 'market access', although when people talk about encouraging further 'integration' in Europe they are talking about a very similar thing. The key is the openness of a nation or national market to outsiders, and to new entrants.

In this chapter these two things are considered in turn. For each one it is shown how it is expressed in the Treaty, and then how that has been interpreted by the Court in its caselaw. Finally, it is asked whether the existence of common underlying principles means that the fundamental freedoms share a common structure. Is there actually one set of rules that can be applied to all the freedoms? This would seem logical, and also help to make sense of the law as a whole. It turns out that the Court is unifying the law, and has almost done so.

8.1 DISCRIMINATION

The key expression of the principle of non-discrimination in the EC Treaty occurs in Art 12. This says:

> Within the scope of application of this Treaty, and without prejudice to any special provisions contained therein, any discrimination on grounds of nationality shall be prohibited.

It is now clear that this has direct effect.

However, non-discrimination is also found in a number of other places. Articles 39, on workers, and 43, on establishment, prohibit discrimination in their respective areas. Article 43 does not use the word, but it does say that foreign self-employed people must be able to set up businesses on the same terms as nationals. Article 49, on services, does not mention discrimination either, but then Art 54, which is within the services chapter of the Treaty, says that any restrictions on services which have not yet been abolished must be non-discriminatory. Finally, Art 28, on goods, does not allow quantitative restrictions on imports – which looks very like another way of prohibiting discrimination based on the origin of the goods, that is, their nationality.

Therefore, it seems as if the provisions creating each of the fundamental freedoms are capable of supporting the idea of non-discrimination on their own. What then is the function of Art 12, and how does it relate to the other articles?

8.1.1 Article 12 and the economic articles

Article 12 is a sort of blue-print article. It is the source of the idea, the platonic ideal, of which other expressions of non-discrimination in other articles are mere copies. There would be no difference in outcome between applying the Art 39 prohibition on discrimination on employment, or applying Art 12 to employment.

In that sense it can seem a little pedantic to worry about which article is the proper basis for an argument. However, it can be important, because it helps us to see which situations that article applies to, which can be important for other matters. For example, where they apply, the economic free movement articles seem to go beyond discrimination. Therefore it is important to know what kind of situations they apply to. That makes it useful to know how the legal territory is divided between these articles and Art 12.

The first point is that Art 12 is subordinate. It applies 'without prejudice' to any other Treaty article. Therefore where another Treaty article allows discrimination, Art 12 cannot subvert this. It does not threaten the Treaty exceptions to free movement.

However, suppose a free movement article does not allow discrimination, but simply does not ban it – because it does not extend that far. For example, suppose that the Court found that a particular situation was outside of the scope of the services provisions – it was not a service, or the discriminatory rule had nothing to do with the provision of the service. Could Art 12 be used then? If so, it would be a sort of gap-filler. Discrimination not covered by the economic articles might fall under Art 12.

The answer to this is in two parts. First, Art 12 only applies 'within the scope of this Treaty'. Therefore a situation must be covered by a Treaty article before you can apply Art 12 to it. To avoid a ridiculous circularity, clearly that must be a Treaty article other than Art 12. Therefore, a situation must be covered by some other article before Art 12 applies. Secondly, in the free movement context, within the scope of each of the individual articles all discrimination is outlawed by those articles themselves.

Putting these together, if the situation is covered by one of the free movement articles, then it looks as if both that article and Art 12 could be used to prevent discrimination. Since Art 12 is subordinate, one should turn to the specific article first (always good practice anyway), and so Art 12 would be irrelevant. On the other hand, if the situation is not covered by one of the free movement articles, then unless one can find some other article covering it, then it is not within the scope of the Treaty, and so Art 12 does not apply either.

In short, strictly, Art 12 has no contribution to make to basic free movement law, although as will be seen, it is sometimes used. Usually this is in situations where people have travelled and experienced discrimination, and the Court allows them to wield Art 12 as a sort of personal right. This is something that is invariably tied up with citizenship – after all, most economic actors are also citizens – and so it is necessary to consider the interaction of Art 12 and Arts 17 and 18.

8.1.2 Article 12 and citizenship

Article 17(2) provides that citizens shall enjoy the rights and duties conferred by the Treaty.

Article 18 provides that citizens may move and reside throughout the EU. Since it is directly effective, one would expect that a citizen exercising these rights could say that she came within the scope of the Treaty. In that case she would be able to rely on Art 12. There would then be a general right to non-discrimination, not limited to economic actions, applying to all moving and residing citizens.

This seems quite straightforward, and may well be correct. However, there is a problem with it, which arises out of the idea of the 'scope' of the Treaty.

Conventionally, the idea of 'scope' has been divided into two aspects – material scope, and personal scope. The personal scope of a particular article was all the people it applied to. The material scope was all the situations or things it applied to. Thus the personal scope of Art 39 may be said to be workers who are nationals of a member state (and their families, and work seekers, and so on), and the material scope may be said to be all rules, acts and measures affecting workers' movement.

It is necessary to come within both the material and the personal scope of the article to rely on it. Therefore it would be the case that an Italian worker complaining about discriminatory treatment by the UK tax office would come within the overall scope of the article, but an Italian worker saying that his freedom to move was restricted by the weather or the food in the UK would not. Similarly, an American worker in the UK complaining about the tax office would not be able to rely on the article.

Now, the personal scope of Art 18 is very simple: citizens, when they are in other member states. However, the material scope is more troublesome. It is clearly matters relating to 'moving and residing' in other EU countries. The problem is how far this goes. On a very narrow reading this could just include specific barriers to crossing borders, transport, renting and buying homes – very clearly movement and residence issues.

On the other hand, if we follow the approach of the Court in the economic articles, this material scope would clearly go a lot further. If social advantages, for example, are relevant to the free movement of workers, then they ought to be relevant to the free movement of citizens. A similarly purposive approach to Art 18 would therefore bring almost all aspects of living abroad within its scope. In that case, Art 12 would apply to all of these, and citizens would have a general right to non-discrimination in all aspects of life when they are abroad within the EU.

Many people assume that this is already the case, and so this may seem an unspectacular conclusion. However, the slow development of Art 18 has meant that there is not a significant body of caselaw on the interpretation of Arts 18 and 12 together, and so the position cannot be said to be clear. The best one can do is look at what few cases there are.

8.1.3 Discrimination: the caselaw

The Court has used Arts 12, 17 and 18, and the economic articles, all together in a mixed-up kind of way. A pattern emerges, but clear reasoning does not. One has to focus on the bigger picture, and not worry about the details too much. Some cases showing this are explained below.

8.1.3.1 Articles 12, 17, 18, and the economic Articles

In situations governed by the economic articles, discrimination is forbidden by those articles. This much we know. However, the Court has also used Art 12 in cases concerning those articles. Sometimes it is just referring to Art 12 as the 'mother article'. It will mention the fact that the rule against discrimination in, say, Art 39, is an instance of the general rule. Or it will decide the case under Art 43, but then mention that Art 12 could also have been used. This kind of use is decorative, and harmless.

However, sometimes it seems to use Art 12 to drive out, or complement, the specific article, and this has happened in cases involving services, usually service recipients. The best example is *Bickel and Franz*.[1] This case, discussed in Chapter 5, involved service recipients who had been arrested in Italy, and claimed discrimination during their trials. In this case the Court found that discrimination in criminal trials might affect the ability of service recipients and citizens to move throughout the Union. Therefore such discrimination fell within the scope of the Treaty, and so Art 12 applied. Therefore it was prohibited.

What is unclear from the judgment is whether the same result would have been arrived at if Mr Bickel and Mr Franz had not been service recipients. If they had just been citizens, relying on their Art 18 right to move, would that have enabled them also to rely on Art 12?

It may be that the Court deliberately avoided giving a clear answer to this. If all citizens could move around the Union and rely on non-discrimination, whether or not they were economically active, this would be controversial. The Court may have wished to introduce the idea of linking Arts 12 and 18 in a context where it made no difference, because in fact the economic article, Art 49, could have decided the case alone.

However, another important case, *Martinez Sala*,[2] suggests that citizens do have a non-discrimination right that is independent of economic activity. In this case a Spanish woman resident in Germany was the victim of discrimination in the handling of a benefit application. She was asked for a resident permit, which she was still waiting for from the authorities, while a national would not have been asked for such a permit. The fact that she could show she was entitled to live in Germany should have been enough. The official paper was not necessary. One of the important points of the case is that it made clear that even this kind of procedural discrimination, which occurs very widely, is discrimination in the Treaty sense. However, the important point here is why Ms Sala was able to rely on Art 12 at all. It may have been that she was a worker, but it was not clear, so the Court did not decide the case on that basis. It said:

> As a national of a member state lawfully residing in the territory of another member state, the appellant in the main proceedings comes within the scope *ratione personae* of the provisions of the Treaty on European citizenship.

> Article 8(2) [now 17(2)] of the Treaty attaches to the status of citizen of the Union the rights and duties laid down by the Treaty, including the right, laid down in Art 6 [now 12] of the Treaty, not to suffer discrimination on grounds of nationality within the scope of application *ratione materiae* of the Treaty.

---

1   *Bickel and Franz* Case C-274/96.
2   *Martinez Sala* Case C-85/96.

> It follows that a citizen of the European Union, such as the appellant in the main proceedings, lawfully resident in the territory of the host member state, can rely on Art 6 [now 12] of the Treaty in all situations which fall within the scope *ratione materiae* of Community law, including the situation where that member state delays or refuses to grant to that claimant a benefit that is provided to all persons lawfully resident in the territory of that state on the ground that the claimant is not in possession of a document which nationals of that same state are not required to have and the issue of which may be delayed or refused by the authorities of that state.

In this quotation the Court takes a relaxed approach to the concept of 'scope'. It says that Ms Sala comes within the personal scope of the Treaty because she is lawfully resident in another member state. This is very vague. However, since they expressly refused to decide whether she was a worker or not, it must be because she is a resident citizen. Then the Court says that citizens enjoy the Treaty rights, including the right to non-discrimination, in all matters within the material scope of the Treaty. Then the Court says that this benefit was within that scope. Therefore the overall situation comes within the Treaty and Ms Sala can rely on Art 12.

However, earlier the Court had said that the benefit was within the material scope of the Treaty only because it was a Regulation 1612/68 social advantage – something granted to workers. Thus Ms Sala, a citizen, within the personal scope of Arts 17 and 18, is entitled to equal treatment in claiming benefits that are within the material scope of Art 39. There is a mixing and matching of articles. This is like saying that because students are within the personal scope of the Treaty, and social security is within the material scope, therefore all students are entitled to equality in social security benefits. Legally this is odd, since the Treaty does include social security, but only insofar as it is granted to economic actors. However, it is what occurred in the recent case of *Grzelczyk*,[3] where social security benefits were in fact extended to students. Here a student from one member state studying in another was allowed to claim benefits while there. It was always believed that students had no such rights. However, the Court used Arts 12 and 17 to provide the right, saying simply that citizens had the rights in the Treaty and these included non-discrimination. Since national students could get the benefit, so could foreign ones. The fact that the Treaty only mentioned social security in the context of workers did not seem to play any role.

The detailed legal reasoning in these cases is unclear, but the broad idea is simpler. The Court is using the principle of non-discrimination in a broad and strong way, and it is beginning to look like a real 'citizen's right', applying very widely. As a consequence, the idea that the Treaty confers different rights on different groups of people seems to be slowly disappearing.

This is perfectly sensible. All the rights granted to economic actors by secondary legislation and caselaw are based on their Treaty rights to free movement and non-discrimination. Since citizens now have those same primary rights, equal secondary ones ought to follow. It has taken a while for this to happen, for political reasons, but these recent cases suggest the time has come.

If that is the case then Arts 12, 17 and 18 will become very important. For most citizens they will be the only law they need to know: 'I am an EU citizen and therefore

---

3   *Grzelczyk* Case C-184/99. See also *D'Hoop* Case C-224/98.

may not be discriminated against in any area of life.' This will do much of the work of the economic articles, and although they may formally continue to exist, one can see that the temptation will be to rely on the citizenship rights more and more. As this occurs, it will become increasingly important to have a clear definition of what exactly discrimination is. This is the next topic considered.

8.1.4 Defining discrimination: intention and effects

Sometimes spotting discrimination is easy. When a rule says 'no foreigners please', there is clearly discrimination on grounds of nationality. However, other situations are more difficult. Sometimes a rule does not mention nationality as such, but it does tend to exclude the foreign – for example, a rule that 'only those with UK qualifications should apply', or 'only those who have lived in France for ten years will be considered'. Are these discriminatory? There are two different perspectives. On the one hand, one can look at the intention of the person or body making the decision. On the other, one can look at the effect of the measure.

Therefore, from an intention point of view, one could ask whether the person requiring UK qualifications intended to exclude foreigners, or whether there happens to be some good reason why they need people from this group. Maybe they are doing research into UK qualifications, and of course they need to interview people who have them. They have no problem with foreigners, as long as they have the necessary UK diplomas. Then one might say there is no discrimination. On the other hand, if the intention was to favour UK citizens, then we would say that there was discrimination.

If we look from an effects perspective, we ask a different question. What was the effect of this requirement? If the effect was to exclude foreigners and favour UK citizens, which of course it will have been, then there is discrimination. If not, not.

One can soften this a little by asking what the effect was, and if it seems discriminatory, then asking whether the measure was justified. If so, perhaps we could say it was not discriminatory. One could call this a justified-effects approach. It is in fact, as will be seen, the approach taken by Community law.

In ordinary life we tend to use a bit of all these perspectives. If we are rejected from a job and the successful candidate was of the opposite sex we want to know what was going on in the selector's mind, and also what the successful candidate was like. If we discover that the selector prefers employing one sex, we will cry discrimination. If we discover the successful candidate was underqualified we may do so too. Even if we come to believe that the selector tried to be fair we may accuse him of unconscious bias, or bias in the system. Intention will suffice to show discrimination, but even without that intention we may feel it exists, on the basis of the outcome, or effects, of the system.

The advantage of an intention-based approach is that it seems very honest. If we find someone meaning to exclude a particular group we feel very comfortable about penalising them. The law gains a certain moral stature. By contrast, if we look at effects we may end up penalising people or bodies for things they did not mean to do. The disadvantage of intention is that it is difficult to know. In criminal law, where intention is often vital, it is an eternally controversial topic, and the subject of convoluted and arcane rules that have grown up in an attempt to deal with the problem that other people's minds are closed to us.

In Community law the need to examine intention is less pressing – it is a less moral sort of law. Moreover, one is generally looking at the actions of states or organisations or groups of official persons. Is intention really a sensible concept in this context? One may well think not. Therefore intention plays no explicit part in defining discrimination in free movement law. Sometimes it is mentioned in a judgment, but it is as a background factor – the good or bad intentions of a member state can be so blindingly obvious that it is difficult not to be influenced by them, and the Court may make a mention of them – but in general it is the accepted and uncontroversial position that discrimination in free movement law is effects-based. Therefore the first question when faced with a possibly discriminatory measure should be: 'Will this measure tend to favour one nationality over another?'

8.1.5 Defining discrimination: equal treatment

If it does, one must then ask whether this is justified. The basis of discrimination is the idea that like situations should be treated alike. Only relevant differences may be taken into account. In some legal systems this is formalised in a principle, the principle of equal treatment, or equality. This can be a very broad principle; thus it may be that one group of workers might be able to challenge different government treatment of another group on the basis of the principle of equality – the argument being that there was no relevant difference between the two groups. In the nationality context, the idea is that nationality is no longer a relevant criterion for decisions within the EU. Therefore if two people, or goods, or whatever, are alike apart from their nationality, there is no basis for treating them differently.

Given this philosophical basis, when a measure divides by some criterion that is not nationality, but favours one nationality, one must ask whether the factor used is a relevant one – or an objectively justified one, in the language of the Court. Therefore, using the example of the residence in France requirement, first we note that this will clearly tend to favour the French over other nationalities. It is not necessary to be technical here. Of course some foreigners will have lived in France for ten years, and some French people will not have, but in general this measure will favour the French.

Then we should ask whether the requirement is justified (and proportionate). Is the job one requiring an intimate knowledge of France? Then the rule may be reasonable. Or is it simply teaching law in a French university? Then there is no need to have lived in France at all.

If the requirement is justified, then we can say that those who have not lived in France are not to be considered alike with those who have, and so the distinction between these groups is acceptable. The consequent tendency to favour one nationality is not to be called discrimination, but is simply incidental. The approach being taken here is what was called above a 'justified-effects' approach.

8.1.6 Defining discrimination: direct and indirect

Direct discrimination occurs when the division by nationality is explicit in the rule. 'Only Belgian margarine may be sold in Belgium' would be an example. This kind of measure obviously divides by nationality, and will only be justified either by a Treaty exception, or if nationality can be shown to be a relevant criterion for the decision being made. If some reason could be shown why Belgian margarine was necessary, this rule might not be called discrimination. This is going to be very very rare. One might imagine a government research project into the quality of Belgian fat products. They could justify buying only Belgian margarine. It also seems to occur sometimes in environmental cases – see here Chapter 7. However, outside of such specialised contexts, nationality will not be a justifiable basis for classification.

Indirect discrimination occurs where the rule in question, on the face of it, divides by some other criterion, but in fact this criterion correlates very closely with nationality. This category of discrimination has been best developed in the caselaw on workers. In *O'Flynn*[4] the Court said:

> Accordingly, conditions imposed by national law must be regarded as indirectly discriminatory where, although applicable irrespective of nationality, they affect essentially migrant workers or the great majority of those affected are migrant workers, where they are indistinctly applicable but can more easily be satisfied by national workers than by migrant workers or where there is a risk that they may operate to the particular detriment of migrant workers.

> It is otherwise only if those provisions are justified by objective considerations independent of the nationality of the workers concerned, and if they are proportionate to the legitimate aim pursued by the national law.

> It follows from all the foregoing caselaw that, unless objectively justified and proportionate to its aim, a provision of national law must be regarded as indirectly discriminatory if it is intrinsically liable to affect migrant workers more than national workers and if there is a consequent risk that it will place the former at a particular disadvantage.

Thus the examples given earlier on UK qualifications, and residence in France, are examples of indirect discrimination, unless they are justified and proportionate, when they are to be considered non-discrimination.

A certain amount of difficulty comes in applying the definition in the context of establishment, services and goods. In all those areas the Court has said that the articles embody the principle of non-discrimination. The requirements of free movement of these things include an absence of discrimination on the basis of nationality. However, the wording of the articles can seem to suggest a more narrow interpretation of discrimination than the one above. For example, Art 43 requires that foreigners be able to establish 'under the conditions' applied to nationals. Article 54, on services, requires that remaining restrictions on services be applied 'without distinction'. Both of these seem to embody the idea of the abolition of direct discrimination, but sit less comfortably with indirect discrimination. It is the characteristic of indirect discrimination that it does in fact apply the same terms and conditions to all nationalities, and treats them without distinction. It just so happens that the terms it sets are rather harder for foreigners to meet.

Partly this problem can be met by saying that the concept of removing restrictions to freedom of establishment and services includes the removal of indirect discrimination,

---

4   *O'Flynn* Case C-237/94.

and this seems quite reasonable. The idea of 'covert' discrimination can also be useful. This was also set out in *O'Flynn*, where the Court referred to:

> ... not only overt discrimination by reason of nationality but also all covert forms of discrimination which, by the application of other distinguishing criteria, lead in fact to the same result.

Essentially covert discrimination is the same as indirect, and overt is the same as direct. They are just different labels which the Court uses sometimes. However, they give a particular nuance, and express the idea that a member state should not be allowed to get off on technicalities, to sneak round the prohibition on discrimination. An absence of formal discrimination will not be an excuse if substantive discrimination lurks underneath.

One can say then that although the services and establishment articles only refer to direct discrimination, where the same result as this is achieved by unjustified, indirect methods, this must also be taken to be caught. Nevertheless, the Court does not speak about discrimination as much in establishment and services cases as it does in Art 39 ones. It tends to use more the language of 'restrictions' following the relevant articles. Partly this is just a different way of describing the same thing; therefore many cases, such as those described in Chapters 4 and 5, on persons and services, which are presented in terms of restrictions could also have been described as discrimination.

This is also true in goods law. Article 28 speaks of import restrictions which, using the same reasons as above, can be taken to include indirectly discriminatory measures. However, the Court tends not to talk about discrimination very much in the goods context, referring instead to obstacles to movement, which is language closer to the article.

However, this different speech is not just a function of the different wording in the articles. It also reflects a slight difference between the sort of rules that are often found in the persons, particularly workers, context, and the more technical regulations that tend to occur in services, often establishment, and goods. These latter regulations, which might include product rules such as in *Cassis*,[5] and regulatory requirements for businesses or professions, can of course be an obstacle to movement, but they seem to have a sort of neutrality that rules about people often do not. That is, where a rule excludes a particular nationality of person, it will tend to be because some characteristic is chosen that has a real link with that nationality. Where it excludes some goods or services or a particular nationality, this may not be so.

Thus, rules about language, or place of residence, or type of qualification, or local experience, might be indirectly discriminatory (if not justified), and one can see that there is a sort of 'intrinsic' link between these things and nationality; of course Germans will tend to live in Germany, have German degrees, speak German, of course foreigners will tend to do all these things less. It seems to follow inevitably from nationality. To imagine a time when this is not so, when there are no more Germans in Germany than other EU citizens, and everyone is equally mixed, is probably to imagine a time when nationality has become meaningless – a really post-national age. In the immediate future, the bond between nationality, and the sort of requirements listed above, seems fixed.

---

5   *Cassis* Case 120/78.

On the other hand, if we consider technical rules on, say, alcohol levels (*Cassis*), or maintaining two law offices, which was forbidden by the Paris Bar, and challenged by a German lawyer in *Klopp*,[6] this is less true. On the one hand, both of these rules did have as their effect that foreigners tended to be excluded, and both were found unjustified. That would seem to make them indirect discrimination. On the other, the link between the requirements and the favoured nationality is less strong than in the people examples above, and this may be why the Court did not describe them as discrimination, but used the neutral language of restrictions and obstacles. It is imaginable that fruit liqueurs might tend to a common alcohol level in Europe, just as it is imaginable that German lawyers might become happy to close their German office and base in Paris, just as lawyers from Bordeaux would do if they wished to practise there. The discriminatory effect of the rules is more contingent, less inevitable, than in the examples above.

This is a rather imprecise distinction, and not clear in the judgments. The closest the Court comes to expressing it is in its use of the idea of a measure that is 'intrinsically liable' to affect one nationality more than another, in the quote from *O'Flynn* above, which is now often repeated. We could say that the requirements in *Cassis* and *Klopp* happened to cause problems for free movement, but they were not 'intrinsically liable' to favour one nationality. The rule in *O'Flynn*, discussed in Chapter 4, was.

The distinction is also difficult to make sometimes. In *Sea Fisheries*[7] the Court found an Irish rule to be discriminatory because it banned large boats from fishing in Irish waters, while small ones could. Irish boats were small, while their main competitors, the Dutch, used large ones. This sits very well with *O'Flynn*, but less well with *Cassis*. Is it intrinsically Irish to sail in little boats? Perhaps the Court was influenced by the transparently obvious protectionist intent of the Irish government.

The position can be summed up by saying that the definitions of direct and indirect discrimination (or overt and covert discrimination) found in *O'Flynn* apply to all the categories. However, the Court uses them more in workers than the others, partly because of the wording of the Art 39, which encourages discussion in discrimination terms, and partly because discrimination occurs more in a personal context; rules about people tend to have the 'intrinsic' link with nationality which seems necessary for discrimination to be found.

Fortunately, it is rarely necessary to worry about the precise line between discriminatory and non-discriminatory, or the precise meaning of 'intrinsic'. As will be seen in the section on 'convergence', at the end of this chapter, the Court now takes a simplified approach that avoids this need. Nevertheless, it still uses discrimination of all types as a decision making tool from time to time, so some knowledge of it is necessary.

Finally, it may be noted that we have moved a long way from a 'pure' effects approach to discrimination. We now look at both justification and the closeness of the link with nationality. They can be seen in terms of effects; a justification indicates that the measure also has positive effects, and a looser link with nationality indicates that the effects of the measure are more contingent, and perhaps less oppressive. Nevertheless, the initial simplicity is lost.

---

6   *Klopp* Case 107/83, and see Chapter 4.
7   *Sea Fisheries* Case 61/77.

8.2 MARKET ACCESS

8.2.1 Open markets in the internal market

Every rule governing economic life excludes players from the market. It may be that it excludes people whom we want to exclude – the dishonest, or the unqualified, or the unsupervised. However, if the rules go further than necessary, or are badly made, they will also exclude those who could make a contribution to that market and increase overall prosperity.

One aspect of excluding more players is that the status quo is preserved to a greater extent. The harder it is for a new company or person to begin business, the smaller is the threat to the existing actors, and the slower is the rate of change in the market. Therefore, if the market is already national in character, then this will tend to be preserved by regulation. This inhibits the integration of Europe and the development of the single market desired.

Sometimes this problem can be dealt with in terms of discrimination. However, in other cases it is hard to do this. For example, in *Bosman*,[8] the obstacle to movement was not discriminatory in any sense. It simply tended to maintain the existing situation, which happened to be that most football players played at home. The same kind of thing occurs in finance, telecoms, and many other areas of life. Rules may no longer discriminate against foreigners, but because they make the whole market less volatile, and make new entry more difficult for everyone, the effect is that the national character of the business area is preserved. For example, starting a consumer bank is a highly regulated matter everywhere. It doesn't happen very much. Most Europeans bank with a nationally owned bank.

Consumer taste also plays a part in this. People will tend to stick with the companies, and things, food and clothes, that they know. Aggressive advertising and promotion is sometimes the only way to persuade them to try something else. Advertising restrictions, which are very common, restrict the possibilities for entry to the market, and so again, preserve the national status quo. They may be as frustrating for the native would-be entrant who wants to compete against his compatriot, as for the foreigner, and so they may not be called discriminatory. Nevertheless, the effect is that national business remains dominant.

Dealing with this kind of rule requires thinking not in terms of discrimination, but of market access. It is a more structural, and more economically-minded approach. The fundamental balance is a familiar one – is the market closing aspect of this rule justified by the other considerations? In other words, does it pursue a justified aim in a proportionate manner?

However, once the aim of opening markets *per se* is accepted for internal market law the reach of the law becomes much broader. Moreover, one begins to significantly interfere with the regulatory autonomy of member states. They must allow the structure of their economic life, which is intertwined with their social organisation, to be assessed for openness and freedom. Even worse, this is not an area where one can be objective. It may be possible to agree on the meaning of discrimination, but deciding structural

---

8   *Bosman* Case C-415/93.

questions of market access is a balance between economic and social values, essentially the stuff of politics. Not only are there different opinions here, but there is no way that one can speak in terms of correct and incorrect. Different visions of society are in play.

All these factors make forays into pure market deregulation daunting for the Court. It is supported by the fact that the Treaty, and the economic articles, are written in broad terms. Their ambitions clearly go beyond mere removal of discrimination, and to the removal of all obstacles to movement between nations. However, it must also be aware of political realities. The member states may not be ready to accept judicial re-ordering of some aspects of their economy, and the practical need for regulation may make this undesirable. A few cases below show how it balances these considerations.

8.2.2 Market access in the caselaw

The starting point is found in a quotation from *Kohll*:[9]

> It must be observed, first of all, that, according to settled caselaw, Community law does not detract from the powers of the member states to organise their social security systems.
>
> ...
>
> ... the member states must nevertheless comply with Community law when exercising those powers.

This approach has been used in many cases. First the Court reaffirms that the member states are free to regulate a particular area however they like. Then it reminds them that this is subject to the limits of Community law.

This is unhappily worded; obviously the member states are not actually free, and Community law detracts from their powers in a perfectly meaningful way. However, the quotation does serve to indicate the balancing between market freedom and national autonomy. It sets the scene for the decision that follows.

The decisions themselves reflect slightly different balances under the different articles. The Court has gone furthest in the market access direction in cases involving workers and services, has been a little more cautious in establishment, and relatively restrictive in cases concerning goods.

The cases at the frontier of Art 39 are *Bosman* and *Graf*.[10] Together they suggest that significant obstacles to market access will be removed even if there is no discriminatory element present. Bosman, the activist of the two cases, demolished the entire football transfer system, and plunged the football world into mild crisis. A completely new (although not dissimilar) system has now had to be created, in negotiation with the Commission. This can be seen as an example of what a purposive market access approach can do.

However, it is important to note that 'private' legislation was in issue here. The Court may well have been more willing to remove the regulations of the international football authorities than it would have been faced with national laws. It may have been even more emboldened by the fact that the subject of the case was 'only' sport. Thus *Bosman* should

---

9   *Kohll* Case C-158/96.
10   *Bosman*, see note 8 above; *Graf* Case C-190/98.

not be taken to indicate that the Court is ready to run rampant through national laws governing more conventionally important things.

In the area of services the Court has gone perhaps further. In *Alpine*[11] it intervened in the Dutch regulation of its financial services industry. On the prohibition on cold-calling it said:

> However, such a prohibition deprives the operators concerned of a rapid and direct technique for marketing and for contacting potential clients in other member states. It can therefore constitute a restriction on the freedom to provide cross-border services.

And continued later:

> Although a prohibition such as the one at issue in the main proceedings is general and non-discriminatory and neither its object nor its effect is to put the national market at an advantage over providers of services from other member states, it can none the less, as has been held above, constitute a restriction on the freedom to provide cross-border services.

This is entirely economic reasoning, and moreover in an area of political sensitivity and practical importance. The Court is no longer thinking in the – very legal – terms of equality, but in terms of marketing and service provision.

In the area of establishment the position is less clear. In a number of cases, among them *Gebhard*,[12] *Kraus*,[13] and *Gullung*,[14] all involving lawyers, the Court has said that even non-discriminatory obstacles must be justified and proportionate, indicating a potentially activist approach. However, the outcomes of these cases are less dramatic than the style of the judgments.

In *Gullung* the matter was, in fact, disposed of by secondary legislation. In *Kraus* the regulation being challenged, which prohibited the use of foreign academic titles, was partly left in place. In *Gebhard* the general principles were set out, but their application to the facts was, in fact, left to the national judge. Of course, in theory this is what the Court always does, but often it sets out the principles in such a way that the national judge is left with no option in his final decision. It tends to leave things more open where the facts are difficult or complex. Moreover, in all these cases there was a greater burden on foreigners than nationals. This may not have been discrimination, but it is something close to it. Therefore the cases do not reflect the pure market-development approach of *Alpine*.

In the area of goods the Court's approach has varied over the years (see Chapter 3), but is now the most restrictive of all the freedoms (or perhaps the least activist). In *Keck*[15] it said that selling arrangements were not restrictions on inter-state trade because they had no greater impact on imports than national goods. This is an explicitly discrimination-based approach. Advocates General have urged the Court to go beyond this, usually in the context of advertising.[16] Advertising restrictions can be a major barrier to market entry, and their exclusion from Art 28 as selling arrangements is a source of

---

11 *Alpine* Case C-384/93.
12 *Gebhard* Case C-55/94.
13 *Kraus* Case C-19/92.
14 *Gullung* Case 292/86.
15 *Keck* Joined Cases C-267/91 and C-268/91.
16 Eg, *Leclerc-Siplec* Case C-412/93.

frustration to would-be importers. Nevertheless, the Court has consistently refused to abandon its *Keck*-based approach. Recently it has allowed challenge to advertising rules under Art 28, but by relying on the *Keck* proviso – that the factual effect of the rules was unequal (see Chapter 2).[17] Thus discrimination-based thinking remains central.

To find the reason for this we probably have to go back to the cases that came before *Keck*, and culminated in it – the Sunday Trading cases and others.[18] The Court described these as about 'socio-economic' life. Unlike the restrictions in issue in *Alpine, Bosman* or *Gebhard*, these are not directly acting on the free movement in question. They are indirect restrictions. The rules in question do not in fact talk about goods at all, but about advertising, opening-hours, working times and so on. Not unrelated to this, they tend also to have important social consequences or rationales – the 'socio' aspect. This makes it inappropriate to deal with such rules under a purely economic article. What happens on Sundays, and whether advertising aimed at children should be allowed, are questions requiring a broader approach, and probably belonging to the legislature.

Together these factors may explain the more legalistic and narrower approach to goods. It is also true that, while excluding selling arrangements from Art 28 is a significant theoretical limit, it is perhaps not of equivalent practical importance. Most types of selling arrangements genuinely do not prevent imports. Advertising is the notable exception, but most countries do allow advertising of most goods. The truly effective barriers to trade are the *Cassis*-type product rules, against which the Court has been highly effective.

It must also be remembered that even if selling arrangements were included, because they are usually non-discriminatory they would be open to justification. Their 'socio' nature means that this would be likely to occur very often, as was indeed the case before *Keck*, in the Sunday Trading and other cases (see Chapter 2). Therefore *Keck* may be an efficient case – reducing judicial workload and litigation, without significantly increasing obstacles to trade.

8.3 CONVERGENCE: FREEDOMS UNITED?

If common underlying principles exist, it would make sense if a common explicit approach to the different freedoms could also be shown. This would be a single set of rules, or maxims, which could be applied to facts falling under any article, and achieve a correct result. It would be helpful to lawyer and students, but also give a sense of coherence and wholeness to the law, and in that sense also help the internal market itself.

Such an approach could not exist in the early days of the Treaty, because the law existed in a context of pre-existing national legislation. Bringing this into line with the Treaty was gradual, and of course the different freedoms moved at different speeds. However, the internal market is now in a much more advanced state of maturity. There is still a great deal of legislative and harmonisation activity underway, and to be begun, but the caselaw principles may be largely in place. As was said in the context of goods, after *Keck* (when it was probably not true), perhaps 'the Court has completed its caselaw'.

---

17 *Gourmet International* Case C-405/98.
18 See Chapter 3.

This is supported by a formula that has been used several times in recent years, originating in *Kraus*, and then restated a little more elegantly in *Gebhard*:

It follows, however, from the Court's caselaw that national measures liable to hinder or make less attractive the exercise of fundamental freedoms guaranteed by the Treaty must fulfil four conditions:

they must be applied in a non-discriminatory manner;

they must be justified by imperative requirements in the general interest;

they must be suitable for securing the attainment of the objective which they pursue; and

they must not go beyond what is necessary in order to attain it.

This seems to give internal market law in a nutshell. It could serve as a convenient guide for a student faced with a set of facts in a practical problem, or as a conceptual framework for the caselaw. Below it is briefly explained how it can be used, and what its limitations are.

Following this quotation, but also using other principles in the caselaw, it seems that there are a series of questions to ask when faced with a set of facts.

1   Is there a measure which hinders free movement or makes it less attractive?

This is a very broad question indeed – the inclusion of 'less attractive' making it particularly so. Clearly there is not a high level of hindrance required. A slight deterrent would be enough. If the answer to this question is yes, we continue. If not, there is no obstacle to movement, and no legal issue.

2   Is it applied in a discriminatory manner?

This question catches direct discrimination, but on the face of it not indirect discrimination. The essence of indirect discrimination, what makes it indirect, is that it is applied equally, but the effects are unequal. Therefore it is not caught here. The question is thus 'is the measure directly discriminatory?'

If the answer to this is yes, the only way to defend the measure is via the Treaty exceptions. If the answer is no, continue.

3   Does the measure pursue a justified aim?

This is not the same as 'is the measure justified?'. It is not 'is it good?', but 'does it try to be good?'.

Of course, measures can usually claim some justified aim – if the member state cannot show that it is at least trying to act legitimately, it is rather foolish to fight the case. Therefore this question is not usually a killer.

However, there are two classes of justified aim. One is the general 'objective justifications', which may be used to excuse any non-discriminatory measure. The other is the Treaty exceptions. These may allow a different range of justifications. Thus the aim of protecting a strategic national industry is too discriminatory and anti-internal market to be allowed as a general justification, but in the context of a public policy claim under the Treaty it might be allowed.

Therefore, if the measure pursues an aim acceptable as a general 'objective justification', continue. If it does not, turn to the Treaty exceptions.

4   Does the measure pursue its aim in a proportionate manner?

That is, is it effective? Does it go no further than necessary? Are its effects generally proportionate to its aims? If the answer is yes, the measure may remain. If the answer is no, it is illegal. Strictly, this means that if the answer to any of the three sub-questions is no, it falls. In practice the Court takes a global view.

A number of notes may be made on the above.

First, a measure presented as a single whole may sometimes be better described as a number of measures bundled together. Things can sometimes be made much clearer by unbundling them – one aspect of the measure may pursue a justified aim, for example, while another may not. It is perfectly possible for a measure to be unacceptable in part, but acceptable in other parts – assuming that this separation is in fact feasible.

Secondly, one must not use this general formula as a way of avoiding secondary legislation. Where harmonisation has occurred, or a directive or regulation exists, this should be relied on first, and the general approach used only to cover areas that the secondary legislation does not, or where it leads to a different result; then there is an incompatibility between the secondary legislation and the Treaty, and the Treaty takes precedence. However, this amounts to declaring a law 'unconstitutional' and is always controversial. Therefore one should not rush to such a conclusion.

Thirdly, we see that indirect discrimination seems to have disappeared from the law. In fact, if an equally applicable rule is unjustified or disproportionate the Court may, as was discussed with reference to *O'Flynn*, declare that it is indirect discrimination. However, this usually amounts to an *obiter dictum*; it makes no difference to the approach to the measure. Whether a measure is justified and proportionate remains the central question. Indeed, one does not even know if the measure actually is indirect discrimination, until the justification and proportionality tests have been done. The only significance of characterising a measure as indirect discrimination will be if a Treaty exception is to be relied on. Then whether or not it is a non-discriminatory but movement-restricting measure, or a discriminatory one, may affect the attitude of the Court (see Chapter 7).

Fourthly, and perhaps most importantly, there is an element of ambiguity in the first question which has to be borne in mind. This concerns the meaning of 'hinders or less attractive'. It seems like a normal language phrase, and in general that is how it should be understood. However, one cannot ignore the fact that there is also caselaw on what constitutes a hindrance (or obstacle, or restriction), which must be respected. In particular, *Keck* and *Graf* have effectively defined two situations where a measure is not to be considered a hindrance. In *Keck* it was where it is a selling arrangement, and in *Graf* it was where its effect was uncertain and indirect. *Keck* is clearly restricted to goods. The principle in *Graf* looks more widely applicable (indeed, *Keck* looks rather like a specialised instance of *Graf*). Further, the discussion in the section above on market access is relevant here. How expansionist the Court will be in classing things as 'hindrances' seems to vary across the categories.

If the above is borne in mind then it should be clear that the formula is indeed compatible with all the freedoms, as it is expressed to be. It is just a convenient way of expressing what should now be a familiar distinction between the treatment of discriminatory and non-discriminatory restrictions, a distinction used in every category of free movement. The presentation may vary a little, with judgments in goods cases in particular tending to have a distinct style and method, often using the language of 'mandatory requirements' rather than justification and emphasising discrimination less than is typical in the other categories, but the substance of the freedoms does fit within this common approach. The aspects of the internal market are converging towards common rules.

8.4 CONCLUSION

There are common principles behind all the economic articles, which result in a common legal approach. This is summed up in the *Gebhard* formula, which can be applied to situations falling under any of the economic articles. Potentially it even seems applicable to the non-economic Art 18.

However this does not mean that all similar fact sets will lead to the same results. There are broader considerations to do with the need for regulation and political sensitivities, which may mean that some discrepancies between categories remain.

CHAPTER 9

COMPETITION AND THE INTERNAL MARKET

Competition law is now taught and practised as a subject on its own, separately from the law of free movement, the subject of this book. However, the two things are conceptually, and sometimes practically, inseparable. The implementation of competition law is important to the actual realisation of free movement by individuals, companies, goods and services. The ideas behind it are important to the process of harmonisation, and to the vision of a single European market. It is therefore necessary to have some idea of what competition is about.

This chapter aims to give a very brief explanation of what topics are conventionally considered to fall under 'competition', and what their connection is to the internal market, without going into the details of competition caselaw. It also tries to outline the theory behind competition law, and how it leads to harmonisation and the removal of obstacles to movement. This is a preparation for the next chapter, which deals with the practical aspects of harmonisation. The relationship of free movement and competition Treaty articles is looked at first, and then the influence of broader competition ideas.

9.1 COMPETITION LAW AND FREE MOVEMENT LAW

The Treaty provisions on competition law are found in Title VI. This contains articles regulating four matters: competition between undertakings, state aids, indirect taxation, and approximation of laws. Usually only the first, or first and second, of these are really given the name 'competition'. However, there is a reason for grouping all four things together, and below it is very briefly explained what they are, what they have in common, and how they relate to the internal market.

9.1.1   What is in Title VI?

Competition between undertakings refers to the fight between different market players for success. These are usually commercial companies, but they may also be state undertakings that engage in some commercial activity. What is key is that they compete for customers and profit. The Treaty articles aim to ensure that this competition is maintained, and not removed. This removal could happen either through undertakings agreeing together not to compete (cartels), or through one or more undertakings becoming so strong that they no longer need to, and either crushing their rivals, or otherwise preventing challenge to their position (abuse of dominance). Therefore Arts 81 and 82 tightly regulate these situations. Anti-competitive agreements, and abuse of dominance, are prohibited.

State aids are subsidies provided by the state to undertakings. These of course influence the market, by affecting the strength and position of market players. Therefore they are also regulated, and largely prohibited, except in cases of particular need or justification.

Article 86 deals with the situation where an undertaking is granted a monopoly, or some special or exclusive rights, by a state. The former state monopolies in telecoms and water are examples of this kind of situation, and companies operating ports or airports might be another. These companies obviously gain a competitive advantage from their rights, perhaps to the extent of completely excluding competition, but Art 86 makes clear that they remain subject to the Treaty – they cannot abuse any dominant position they may acquire. However, if undertakings operate a service of 'general economic interest', such as the examples above, then Art 86 also provides that they are only subject to the Treaty insofar as it does not prevent them fulfilling their task. Thus they may sometimes be exempted from the other competition articles. The Court will supervise this, however, to make sure that the possible exemption is not abused.

Indirect taxation is dealt with by Art 90, which has already been discussed under goods. It is a competition matter, because an extra taxation burden on imported goods makes them less able to compete against domestic ones on price.

Approximation of laws is another phrase for harmonisation, which is discussed in Chapter 10. It relates to competition because different national laws impose different costs or burdens on companies operating there, and so create competitive advantages or disadvantages for companies according to where they are located. Such 'distortions' of competition, as they are often called, can be removed by replacing the different national laws with a single harmonised one. This is fully explained in 9.2 below.

9.1.2 Competition and free movement: the relationship

All of the things in Title VI threaten to re-erect obstacles to the internal market, which will undermine the removal of the legal obstacles by the free movement provisions. Thus although national laws may allow free movement across borders, agreements between undertakings, or the market-distorting effect of unequal taxation or state aid, may inhibit this.

Also, all the articles in this Title deal with things which would affect the operation of the internal market by causing market position and success to be determined not just by the commercial merit of the undertaking, but by other factors. These could be factors resulting from state behaviour, such as subsidy or tax benefit or favourable laws. They could also be factors resulting from the activities of the undertakings themselves, such as anti-competitive agreements.

Thus although competition law, and the other matters in Title VI, are subjects of their own, they should also be seen as part of the internal market. Distortions of competition hinder free movement. Therefore Art 3(1)(g) says that the Community shall include:

A system ensuring that competition in the internal market is not distorted.

On the other hand, free movement is also necessary for fair competition between undertakings. If foreign products are excluded from a market, or disadvantaged on that market, this protects the national producers, and the financial strength resulting from this protected base can also give them a competitive advantage if they wish to export or expand abroad. Thus the maintenance of an internal market is also part of competition policy. Hence the harmonisation articles in the competition title refer to measures necessary for the common market. Free movement and competition are therefore intertwined aspects of the same task: of creating a single, free market-based economy. Neither the single, nor the free market-based, can be achieved on its own.

9.1.3   Competition and internal market law: differences

The rules on competition, harmonisation, taxation, and free movement together regulate the internal market. The way this task is divided between them can be expressed in different ways.

First, it is often said that competition law and state aids are to do with the functioning, or maintenance, or operation of the internal market, by contrast with the free movement articles and the rules on taxation, which are to do with its creation or establishment. Here we see the idea of a legal framework creating the market, and then economic actors 'operating' it. Harmonisation straddles both categories; sometimes it is necessary in order to fully 'establish' the market, sometimes it addresses 'operational' problems. This distinction is found in the Treaty, which talks about the creation and the functioning of the internal market in different places, as if they are different things (see, for example, Arts 14 and 94 EC).

Secondly, since most undertakings are private, it has been observed that, broadly, free movement law, plus state aids and taxation, prevent state interference with the market, while competition law prevents private interference. Thus there is a kind of public/private distinction to be made between free movement law and competition law.

Thirdly, a distinction can be made between legal and economic thinking. Free movement law is lawyers' law, based on primarily legal concepts. Competition law is an extension of economics, the law tending to merely reflect economic theory. This can be seen in Arts 81 and 82, the competition articles. They are based on economic theory, and as a result apply only to situations having significant economic effects. Thus anti-competitive agreements are prohibited only when the market share of the undertakings involved is above a few per cent of the total market, and the effect on inter-state trade is measurable. Abuse of dominance only becomes an issue when an undertaking has a very large market share. Thus in general, only fairly big business need worry about competition law. In order to know whether these articles apply in a given situation, there is always a great deal of economic analysis and data-gathering. The market situation is almost always crucial to the outcome of a case. By contrast, where discrimination is found, the free movement articles do not require noticeable economic effect. There is no *de minimis*.[1] Even where non-discriminatory obstacles are under consideration, although the Court does ask if they are 'uncertain and indirect'[2] they are assessed on the basis of their form, and the way they work, not their economic impact. No economists are called to provide evidence.

The free movement law can therefore be seen as legalistic and rights-based, assessing measures in strictly legal terms. A lawyer ignorant of economics could apply it. In competition law, on the other hand, the market survey is everything, and non-legal considerations play a much greater role.

---

1   *Van de Haar* Joined Cases 177/82 and 178/82.
2   *Graf* Case C-190/98.

9.1.4 Competition and free movement: overlap

Despite these different ways of drawing lines between free movement and competition law, they sometimes overlap. There are various situations where both may apply. One is the private situation, of which *Bosman*[3] is the most striking example. The transfer rules which restricted movement were also an expression of the dominant position of the football associations, and also an agreement between the clubs, the market players, which restricted their competition. The Court did not decide the competition law issues, because the case was disposed of on the free movement point, but there was no doubt that the articles potentially applied, and in the creation of new transfer rules the competition lawyers have been as involved as the free movement ones.

Another kind of situation is the public undertaking which engages in commercial activity. This could be an economically active branch of the government, or a company in which the state has a majority share or *de facto* control. If it is large enough, and behaves in an anti-competitive way which restricts movement, and most anti-competitive behaviour restricts movement, then it will fall under both branches of law. *ERT*[4] is an example of this. The public monopoly on television broadcasting both kept out foreign service providers and, by suppressing competition, led to an abuse of a dominant position.

We see here how free movement and free competition are intimately linked. Just as free competition can be seen as part of an internal market, so free movement can be seen as one aspect of maintaining competition. It just depends which way you want to look at it.

9.2 THE INFLUENCE OF COMPETITION IDEAS

Competition law, like internal market law, represents ideas about how the economy and society should be ordered. These ideas and their history are diverse and complex, and mostly far beyond the scope of this book. However, one of the most basic ideas is of great relevance here.

9.2.1 Competition: a basic idea

In a very simplified form, this idea is that competition leads to improved efficiency. Many mechanisms and theories contribute to this. From a Darwinian perspective, we might say that in a competitive market the best businesses will survive and prosper, while the worst will fail, leading to evolution of the economy towards higher quality, and greater prosperity. This is rather like one of the classic arguments for freedom of speech: that arguments compete, and the worst are rebutted and the best survive, and so wisdom increases.

A psychological approach might say that competition causes us to want to win, to do our best, and so overall efforts are increased, also improving overall prosperity.

---

3   *Bosman* Case C-415/93.
4   *ERT* Case C-260/89.

Another perspective might be that competition is a sort of trial-and-error approach to things. Instead of central planning of the economy, which assumes that someone knows best, different companies or individuals propose different products, and the consumer picks and chooses and gradually decides which ones meet his needs, and the companies adapt to this. Thus competition can be seen as an empirical, inductive way of running an economy, rather than a theoretical, deductive one.

In any case, the premise is that competition will make things better, and that if it is reduced by anti-competitive behaviour, this will be at the expense of competitor businesses, who will suffer unfair conditions, and more important, of the consumer, who will suffer reduced quality or increased price products.

9.2.2 The idea in the Treaty: harmonisation

The Treaty therefore aims to remove distortions and restrictions of competition. The harmonisation provisions provide that where distortions of competition exist, as a result of disparities between national laws, action can be taken to remove them. As close as possible to a level playing field must be created for competing economic undertakings.

A typical 'distortion' situation might be where one country has tax, environmental or labour rules that impose costs on companies, while another country does not. This would clearly create a competitive advantage for the company based in the lower cost country. It can produce its products more cheaply. Since, as a result of free movement law, it can also export them to the higher cost country, it can probably do well there, being able to undercut the domestic industry, which has to comply with the expensive production laws. Also, in its home market, it is likely to be able to fight off imports, because these will come from countries with higher production costs, and so be more expensive.

This state of affairs can be seen as undesirable for several reasons. First, there are economic arguments about whether it is efficient. It may be that companies then succeed or fail not according to their merits, but according to the country they are based in, and the overall effect will not be to produce a Europe of the fittest and best economic actors. Balancing this argument there is the idea of regulatory competition, which says that having different legal systems creates a fight between them, which results in better regulation, and ultimately benefits the economy.

Secondly, there may be political reasons not to like such distortions. Do we want a Europe where companies migrate to escape high standards, perhaps leaving unemployment behind, and creating constant uncertainty? One of the fears here is that there might be a 'race to the bottom'; in order to avoid domestic industry being harmed by competitors from cheaper countries, member states will lower their own standards, and so the costs on their own companies – until everything except profit has been undermined, and labour, environmental, and social standards are washed away.

Thirdly, one can see such distortions as 'unfair'. Why should a perfectly good company go out of business because its competitors in other member states, which may be no better at their job, have to pay less tax or fewer social costs? Consumers may feel companies can look out for themselves, but this fairness argument appeals to industry, and also to unions, who see foreign competition as threatening their livelihood and jobs.

In general, the Treaty chooses to provide for the removal of such distortions. The position, put very simply, is that there is competence to harmonise when distortions resulting from different national laws are 'appreciable'.[5] Thus, not every difference between member state laws justifies harmonising, but if the effect on competitive position is 'appreciable' then it does. This is obviously a very broad ranging – and very vague – position, which has been the basis of huge amounts of secondary legislation. One of the most important and common sorts of harmonisation is of environmental rules, and so environmental costs, but there is also legislation on social and labour matters, and purely economic trading rules, which are justified, or partly justified, by arguments about distortions of competition.

As well as this, internal market harmonisation may also be justified by obstacles to movement. Situations such as in *Cassis*,[6] where disparities between national product rules obstruct movement, can be remedied by replacing the national laws with Community ones. Hence there are now very many Community product standards.

How much harmonisation actually occurs within these boundaries depends largely on two factors. The first is the procedure that must be adopted. As will be seen in the next chapter, some harmonisation measures require unanimity, and some just a majority of the Council. This may depend on the type of measure, or the area it applies to. Obviously harmonisation is easier to pass where only a majority is needed.

This links to the second factor – politics. Even if harmonisation is seen as essentially economic, of course it can be a very sensitive matter, sweeping away national rules and giving an impression of centralisation in Brussels. Moreover, while high cost countries may often be enthusiastic about a measure, because it removes the 'unfair' advantage of companies in low cost member states, those low cost member states may be opposed for the same reason. Tax harmonisation, of tax on company profits, and taxes on savings, is a good example. These taxes have a very great impact on the location of businesses and capital. High tax countries feel very strongly that there should be harmonisation to prevent this 'unfair' and 'harmful' tax competition. Low tax countries feel that this 'healthy' competition between tax regimes is essential to European economic wellbeing. Companies and savers have a view, as do those who want more tax available for public services. It becomes apparent that the passing of harmonisation measures is just like any other political legislative process, involving horse-trading, with many lobbies and interests playing a role.

9.2.3 Has the Treaty got it wrong?

It remains controversial how much harmonisation there should be. At one extreme, one could argue for a single European set of laws. At the other extreme, why harmonise at all? The arguments sketched above deserve a slightly closer look. In particular, the removal of distortions of competition may not be a wise thing to do, economically at least.

One argument why it may be wrong is that dealing with different laws is all part of the competitive process. The company that can adapt, move, find the best national

---

5   *Germany v Parliament and Council* Case C-376/98.
6   *Cassis* Case 120/78.

environment and fit into it, is the best one. Competition should not be like wrestling, a controlled fight in a controlled environment, but like street fighting, simply the selection of winners, however they may win. This argument says that 'fair' competition is a contradiction in terms. It is just a reduction of the ways in which companies can compete, which will result in flabbier companies.

Another argument against it is that even if competition in purely business matters is made 'fairer', competition in other, perhaps more important, areas is eliminated. For example, competition between legal and tax systems no longer takes place after they are harmonised. This is a powerful argument. The basic idea of competition, that it increases efficiency, can be applied beyond economics. Thus, it can be argued that the existence of different national laws in a single open market leads to legal competition. This will result in the survival of the best legal systems, and the adaption of the others to their mould, and an increase in overall legal quality. This can be an important part of social change. As companies choose whether to go to a high tax country with a structured civil law system and benefits for their workers, or a low tax, low benefit country with a loose but flexible common law system, they are acting as consumers in a market for social and legal systems, choosing what they need, and contributing to the evolution of society.

If competition is indeed believed to be an effective way of delivering what the consumer wants, and if democracy is important, then it must be questionable whether it is correct to deny competition in these very important things, by harmonising them, in the name of competition in mere business. Which matters to us more?

Competition between legal and social systems is also defended on purely economic grounds, where it is usually termed 'regulatory competition'. Economists indicate that there is a trade off between the benefits of harmonisation – which include reduced cross-border transaction costs, and also economies of scale which result from companies being able to merge and expand cross-border more easily – and harmonisation costs. One cost of harmonisation is the reduction in competition between laws. When these do compete that creates pressure for them to adapt to the needs of companies, which generate wealth. Without that competition the laws may become less company-friendly, and less efficient, and so the legal framework may not be such a good one for wealth creation.

Also, if law-making is centralised in Brussels, this may make law-making in some ways less accessible – less transparent and accountable – and so less responsive to society's needs, including its economic needs. Thus centralisation may be equated with isolation, with the possible consequence that the law does not really reflect events or needs efficiently, and so once again hinders wealth creation. On the other hand, it can be argued that centralisation is necessary to produce laws taking account of the needs of Europe as a whole, and not just bits of it.

9.2.4 Or is it right? The 'race to the bottom'

Two other arguments can be made in response to these. One is that harmonisation does not reduce competition at all – it just moves it to the political arena. Politicians decide how and when harmonisation should occur. However, companies can still participate in this process, by lobbying, or by persuading the public – the voters – of their case. This kind of adaptability and ingenuity is what marks the clever company.

A more important argument is that without harmonisation there will be a 'race to the bottom'. The country with the lowest standards and taxes will become the cheapest place to operate, and so business will rush there, and other countries will have to lower their standards to survive. In the US this has been called the Delaware Effect. That small state has very business-friendly laws, and as a result a disproportionate number of American companies are officially headquartered in Delaware. Many politicians call this 'harmful' competition, because they think it results in the lowering of social and environmental standards, since businesses only think economically. However, other people think that high social and environmental standards can actually be defended economically, so that companies will not run away from them anyway. It may be in their business interests to operate in a clean and protective environment; perhaps it enables them to attract better employees, for example. It is a matter of great controversy among economists how much the race to the bottom actually occurs, or would occur.

In any case, it could be said that if social competition results in lowering standards, surely that is because that is what people want. After all, companies will not want to alienate their customers, so if the people really want high standards, and are prepared to pay for them, they will get them. However, this argument gives disproportionate power to the rich, who are the most influential as consumers and customers.

Of course, the fact that the people want low standards, presumably in return for low costs, even if it is true, may not be good enough. Environmental damage in particular does not confine itself to one time or place. Poisoned air or water may linger for future generations, and also travel into other areas. Therefore it can be argued that no one group of people has the right to do such poisoning, even if they democratically wish to.

9.2.5 A middle way

As can be seen, this is an endless and complex debate, which extends far beyond the scope of an internal market book. The proper role and nature of competition is one of the most developed and complicated areas of economic and legal theory, and more than a subject of its own. However, an internal market lawyer cannot ignore it entirely, because it is part of the philosophical foundation of that market.

Nevertheless, she can steer a middle way. Although there are people who oppose any harmonisation, and those who think it must be almost total, most people probably agree that the real exercise is a balancing one. Although each situation will be unique, and the environment and some social protection measures may be considered to be too important for free consumer choice, generally, compulsory harmonisation should be resisted where possible, partly in the name of competition, but also because it is undemocratic, and because it is contrary to the principle of subsidiarity. Moreover, where harmonisation is necessary, market pressures will often lead to it occurring voluntarily.

However, sometimes this will not work. Governments may find other countries' laws intolerable, and not be prepared to keep their borders open to them. Then compulsory harmonisation will be necessary for there to be an internal market at all. At this point economics breaks down, and political reality takes over.

Currently the vogue is to emphasise minimum harmonisation, and framework harmonisation. The former sets minimum standards in important areas, but leaves countries free to set higher ones if they want. The hope is that this prevents a destructive race to the bottom, or at least limits it, while also allowing some reflection of local preferences, and some regulatory competition.

Similar ideas underlie the use of directives giving a framework for national implementing laws, but not spelling them out in detail. These indicate the aims that the national laws must attain, but not how they should do it. The idea here is that enough standardisation will result to enable free movement of goods – since any goods manufactured according to national rules implementing the directive must be accepted in other member states – and create a reasonable amount of equality of economic conditions between member states, but there will still be room for national implementation to reflect national legal styles and preferences, and so still room for some competition to produce the most efficient and satisfactory way of achieving the directive's ends.

CHAPTER 10

THE PROCESS OF HARMONISATION

The theory behind harmonisation was introduced in Chapter 9. Now the practicalities are considered. Although these fall largely within the procedural law of the EU, an overview of how harmonisation works, and the role it plays in the Community, is very helpful in understanding the internal market as a whole.

This chapter first looks at what harmonisation is, and the different types of harmonisation. Then it looks at the approach taken by the Commission, and how this has changed; there have been important developments here. It then becomes more legal, and briefly explains how the legal base for a harmonisation measure is chosen, and the legislative process. After this the role of the Court in harmonisation is discussed. Finally two examples are given of areas where harmonisation has played an important role. These are the recognition of qualifications, and e-commerce. The aim is to show what the rather abstract language of harmonisation means in real and contemporary situations.

10.1 WHAT IS HARMONISATION?

Harmonisation is the creation of harmony. Harmonisation of laws is therefore the elimination of problematic disparities between national laws. This does not necessarily mean just making all laws the same, although this is one method. It can mean making them similar enough that they can smoothly fit together, or fitting them within a common framework.

In the internal market there are a number of types of harmonisation at work. First, there is what might be called 'informal' harmonisation, through voluntary mutual recognition. If a member state decides to accept degrees from other member states, then, although the education systems remain different, there ceases to be an obstacle to movement. A degree of harmonisation has been achieved. This kind of behaviour can also be seen as implementation of Art 10 EC, which provides that:

> Member states shall take all appropriate measures, whether general or particular, to ensure fulfillment of the obligations arising out of this Treaty or resulting from action taken by the institutions of the Community. They shall facilitate the achievement of the Community's tasks.

> They shall abstain from any measure which could jeopardise the attainment of the objectives of this Treaty.

Secondly, there is judicial harmonisation. Where the Court strikes down national regulations that create obstacles to movement, as in *Cassis*,[1] it is also harmonising. Once again the movement from legal system to legal system is made smooth. This kind of harmonisation is also called 'negative harmonisation', because it is the removal of

---

1   *Cassis* Case 120/78.

legislation, but not its replacement by anything else. Where national legislation is replaced by Europe-wide rules, this is called 'positive harmonisation'.

Thirdly there is legislative harmonisation. This is perhaps the most important type, and certainly the type that is most commonly thought of as harmonisation. It consists in the issuing of directives or regulations by the Community which eliminate harmful legal disparities.

Legislative harmonisation can be divided into various sub-types. These are not so much watertight categories, but different ways of talking about harmonisation. 'Total harmonisation' refers to the situation where all rules governing an area come from the Community. National legislation is entirely replaced, and member states lose competence to make new legislation in the area covered. This is by contrast with 'minimum harmonisation'. This occurs when Community rules set minimum standards across the Community, but member states retain freedom to set stricter ones. This kind of harmonisation is useful for environmental, technical, or safety rules, where some states wish to be very strict.

Optional harmonisation occurs when Community rules set standards which may be relied upon, but do not have to be. If optional technical standards exist for making washing machines, then if a manufacturer makes his machine to these standards he can rely on being able to sell them throughout the Community. All member states must accept them. However, member states can still set their own standards internally, and if a manufacturer wishes he can manufacture to these standards instead.

This may seem an odd arrangement, but in some countries national standards may be high, and this may be a good marketing point. A manufacturer may actually wish to be able to boast 'manufactured to German standard XYZ'. On the other hand, if he is manufacturing for many markets it will be easier to use the Community standard, which will still be acceptable. Alternatively, national standards might be lower. If the manufacturer has no export ambitions, it may save him costs to manufacture to the national rules.

If harmonisation is minimum or optional, then it is not called total. Total harmonisation is a phrase kept for the situation when no national rules exist any more.

The last type is 'partial harmonisation'. This is not really a legal category. It just means that some aspects of an area of activity are harmonised. For example, some rules concerning the manufacture of pharmaceuticals are harmonised. Pharmaceutical production may be said to be partially harmonised. One should be careful with this phrase because it can easily lead to confusion. For example, it is tempting to think that if pharmaceuticals are partially harmonised, then some aspects of pharmaceuticals must be totally harmonised, but this is not so; the harmonising rules may be minimum or optional ones.

These harmonisation rules are often said to perform one of two functions in the internal market: they are either concerned with establishing the internal market, or with its functioning. This distinction comes from the Treaty, where Art 2 talks of establishing a common market, and Art 3 refers to the approximation of laws necessary for its functioning. Then the most general harmonisation article, Art 94, concerns itself with national laws that 'directly affect the establishment or functioning of the common market'.

146

Although it is far from obvious from the words themselves, it seems to have become accepted that the establishment of the common (or internal) market refers to the removal of barriers to free movement. This is the stuff of the caselaw. Discrimination, product rules, and so on, are things which may affect the establishment of the market.

The *functioning* of the internal market is a slightly broader concept, and includes national laws which do not directly inhibit free movement, but may 'distort' competition. Things like working conditions, tax rates and employment practices may not have a direct enough effect on movement to be caught by any of the economic articles. However, they might make it advantageous to operate in one country rather than another, and so would affect flows of money, people and goods, and so are seen as 'affecting' the 'functioning' of the market.

These ideas rely on a number of assumptions about how a market should and does operate, which have been discussed more in Chapter 9.

10.2 THE OLD AND NEW APPROACHES TO HARMONISATION

Harmonising legislation coming out of the Community has changed its character over time. It has become simpler, and less authoritarian, but also less precise. This change, which has occurred for both practical and ideological reasons, and has advantages and disadvantages, is the subject of the next two sections.

Early harmonisation measures tended to look like national legislation imitated at a supra-national level. They were complete sets of rules, including all the technical specifications necessary. Harmonising rules concerning a particular product category, for example, would essentially perform the same function as the national rules they replaced, but by being the same over the Community would eliminate the trade barrier.

However, it became apparent that harmonising like this would be a never-ending process, and would not succeed in establishing the internal market. First, national governments proved themselves faster at generating regulations than the Community. This may be contrary to the image in the popular press, but in fact national governments employ vastly more staff of all kinds than the Community does, and so are able to produce more paper. Thus the Commission would complete a directive on safety specifications for washing machines, for example, which would cover, say, wiring and insulation and build strength, on the basis that these were the aspects regulated in the member states. However, as soon as they finished they would discover that member state X had decided that watertightness and button-design also had to be regulated, and had issued a whole lot of technical rules on these. These would, of course, be an obstacle to importation to that country, and so the whole process would begin again.

This was exacerbated by the high speed of technological development that has occurred during the life of the Community, which has not only led to constant change in the nature, and so the specification, of goods and services, but also the coming into being of entirely new categories of goods and services. Moreover, these new areas, such as computers, telecoms and e-commerce, are usually extremely complex and technical ones. Finally, the liberalisation of many aspects of economic life, which is part of the creation of the internal market, has led to enormous growth in certain industries, which in turn has generated regulatory activity. For example, the manpower and money devoted to issues in the regulation of financial services, in governments, universities, and the industry itself, is staggering by comparison with the situation 30 years ago.

As well as these social developments, the nature of the Community meant it found it hard to keep up with the member states. It required, at that stage, unanimity in the Council before measures could be passed, which meant long periods of horse-trading and compromise had to be endured before anything could be achieved. If a member state felt particularly doubtful about a particular area it could simply block harmonisation entirely. Of course, even the most committed Europeans tended to feel this way about areas where their home industry had particularly much to lose from the incursion of foreign competition.

As a result of all these factors, harmonisation failed to deliver what had been hoped. In the old Art 14 EC it had been envisaged that the necessary approximation of laws (another phrase for harmonisation) would be complete by 1969. It was not. Nor was it nearly so.

A period of Community stagnation was entered, in which national rules seemed to have vanquished harmonisation, and a genuine internal market seemed distant. Regulations may have been generated, but a harmonised market was not. This coincided with a period of social and economic woe and Europe began to seem bogged down and directionless. In the 1970s the term 'eurosclerosis' was coined: too rich a diet of state control and regulation, resulting in hardening of the arteries of trade, and loss of vitality. Then came a turn-around. In 1979 Mrs Thatcher was elected prime minister of the UK and *Cassis de Dijon* was decided by the Court of Justice. No doubt they were unconnected, but they were both part of a changing mood. Liberalisation and deregulation began to wax, while the economically dominant and controlling state began to wane.

In 1985, in a now legendary White Paper (a policy document),[2] the Commission announced a 'new approach' to harmonisation. Instead of setting out detailed rules covering a whole area, directives and regulations would simply specify the essential ends to be achieved, particularly concentrating on safety, and only covering what was really necessary. Member states would then be left to implement these requirements in their own way. Free trade would be assured by the principle of mutual recognition, pronounced in *Cassis* to be part of Community law. Even though specifications might continue to vary from state to state, they would all be in compliance with the really important points – which would be in the directives – and so member states would have no reason not to accept imported goods. The harmonising directives would serve to guarantee mutual recognition.

Thus, in a new 'harmonisation-lite' directive on, for example, once again, washing machines, instead of having committees of experts drawing up pages of technical specifications, the directive would simply set out the essential requirements; the machine must be waterproof, not catch fire, be able to be dropped from a height of two metres without breaking, and not be poisonous to young children or animals (for example). The member states could then employ their own experts to translate this into national specifications.

---

2   COM(85) 310, 14 June 1985.

Moreover, harmonising legislation would only be issued when it was really necessary. In many cases the principle of mutual recognition alone should be enough to ensure member states admitted imports.

In the White Paper, the Commission acknowledges that this new approach is not just needed for practical reasons, but also meets broader political criticisms. The old approach was 'over-regulatory' and 'could stifle innovation'. They also acknowledged that for free trade to occur it was not necessary to have central standardisation of all relevant rules. Certain key points were enough.

This can be seen as the application of the legal doctrine of proportionality to harmonisation: actions must be effective and not exceed their aims. It is also in line with the principle of subsidiarity: as much specification as possible is decentralised to the member states. It can also be seen as part of an anti-authoritarian political trend. It should now also be seen in the context of the economic arguments in Chapter 9.

10.2.1 Criticisms of the new approach

The reasons for the new approach, and so its good points, have already been set out. They can be summarised by saying that it is more efficient and less centrist. An important aspect of this is that it is cost-effective. Simpler directives are cheaper to produce.

However, there are a number of criticisms which have been voiced. They centre around two main points: the new approach is undemocratic, and it leads to a lowering of standards.

The lack of democracy results, it is claimed, from the involvement of private bodies in national standard setting. In many countries trade and industrial organisations, and companies, have a significant input into translating the European requirements into technical specifications. Member states work with these organisations for two main reasons. First, now that the end-requirements are Community wide, standards cease to be a national political issue. Therefore there is less motivation for governments to take a great interest in their implementation. Secondly, the business organisations have the technical expertise necessary for implementation – because they are the people working in the area. It makes sense to use this expertise and allow much of the work to be done by them – thereby also saving money.

Because these private bodies are involved so deeply in national standard setting, inevitably they also have some influence on the Community requirements too. These are the outcome of discussion and negotiation between the member states, which draw on their national knowledge – which is rooted in the private bodies. The outcome is that industries can do quite a lot to make sure that the standards set for them are convenient, and it is sometimes argued that the interests of the consumer or of society in general are under-represented. Pre-harmonisation, when national governments had complete control of all standards, it is suggested a broader range of views influenced the standard-setting process.

The argument about lowering of standards divides in two. One the one hand, some claim that member states implement Community requirements with different levels of diligence. In practice, one state may take a very relaxed and loose approach to interpretation, another a strict one. This leads to the presence of lower-standard goods on the market, which puts pressure on the high standard states to take a looser interpretation too, so that their national industry is not disadvantaged by higher costs. This argument essentially says that the mutual trust which is the basis of mutual recognition is not always justified. Some nations really don't do as good a job as others.

The second reason why standards may be lowered is that the new approach is liberalising and deregulatory in spirit. It follows the *Cassis* judgment, and the idea that restrictions must go no further than necessary. As we have seen in the cases, this has meant that product specifications have often been replaced by labelling requirements, and the general trend has been to treat consumers as if they are capable of making sensible decisions if information is available. If they know what is in food, it is up to them whether to eat it or not. We have also seen, for example in the *Danish Recycling*[3] case, that freedom of movement has been awarded exceptionally high weight in the balancing process, sometimes to the detriment of other interests – in this case the environment.

The criticism of this is partly just that freedom of movement should not be given such priority. This is a simple political point. More complex, it is also said that consumers are not actually so well protected by minimalist rules, such as labelling requirements. People tend not to read labels, they don't always understand them, and they may assume that anything they can buy is fine. They are used to being looked after by the state, and not to taking responsibility for their own welfare when buying goods. An interesting twist on this argument is that consumers may vary from country to country. Minimal requirements may serve the cautious consumers of one land adequately, but not protect those in another. Yet allowing national variations to persist harms the market. Therefore, it is said, standards should be uniformly high.

10.3 THE LEGAL BASE

All legislative harmonisation must have a legal base. This means there must be one or more articles in the Treaty which provide for that harmonisation. Deciding which these should be can be difficult, and arguments over whether the right one has been chosen, or whether the article actually covers the directive issued, often occur. These have resulted in a rich and complex caselaw, which is part of the administrative or procedural law of the EU.

That is not something to cover here, but it is important to know why the legal base matters. One reason is that some articles provide for harmonisation by 'qualified majority' voting – if a specified majority of the Council are in favour – while others require unanimity. Therefore, whether a member state can block a measure may depend on which article is relied on as the legal base.

Another reason is that different procedures provide for a greater or lesser role for the Parliament in creating and passing the measure. The Parliament guards its privileges fiercely, seeing itself as the voice of the people in the Community, and can be relied upon to challenge a measure if it thinks it should have been adopted using a more Parliament-friendly procedure.

---

3   *Danish Recycling* Case 302/86.

Here, the main articles used for internal market harmonisation are mentioned and their role very briefly explained.

Article 40 provides for directives or regulations to achieve the aims of Art 39. Article 44 provides for harmonising directives in the area of establishment. Article 47 provides more particularly for directives dealing with mutual recognition of qualifications. Article 52 provides for directives liberalising particular services. Article 93 provides for harmonisation of indirect taxation, where necessary for the common market, and to be agreed unanimously by the Council members.

As can be seen, these articles do not cover the whole internal market. The articles confine themselves to establishing the common market – dealing with direct obstacles – and do not even cover all the ground there. For example, not all services restrictions are to be dealt with by 'liberalisation'. Quantitative restrictions on goods, and capital, are not covered at all. However, this does not mean that attainment of the internal market is not covered by the Treaty. Two general articles fill the gaps left by these specific ones. These are Arts 94 and 95.

Article 94 provides for harmonisation (by Directive) by unanimity of any laws directly affecting the establishment or functioning of the common market. It is therefore broad, but difficult to use – it needs complete unanimity. Although upon reading it seems to be the 'default' harmonisation article, in practice it only needs to be used if no other article is available. Therefore it is more of a 'fallback' article.

Article 95, by contrast, says that it is to be used 'in derogation from Art 94'. This might suggest that it is only to be used exceptionally, since derogations are generally narrowly construed and applied. However, it is actually understood to mean that where Art 95 can be used, it should be used in place of Art 94. It is, in fact, much more used than Art 94. The main reason for this is that it requires only majority voting. A secondary reason is that it allows both directives and regulations to be passed, although there is a tendency to use directives where possible. Article 95 is, nevertheless, only to be used where there is no specific harmonisation article that can be relied upon. Therefore it would not be used for qualifications, for example.

The major limitation of Art 95 is that it only covers goods, services and capital (except tax). Persons are specifically excluded by Art 95(2). This is because when the article was written persons were considered a sensitive area, and it was decided to harmonise only by unanimity. In fact now Arts 40, 44, 47 and 52 have all been updated to majority voting, so that the only area of the internal market where unanimity is still required are indirect taxation, and matters which fall under no other article and so have to be done under Art 94.

Article 95 also contains the possibility of derogation from harmonised rules that have already been passed. Article 95(4) and (5) provide that if a member state feels the need to maintain, or introduce new, conflicting national measures, for one of the Art 30 reasons, or for the protection of the environment or working environment, it may notify the Commission of this. The Commission will then approve or reject the member state's proposal within six months. If it approves it, it may then recommend adapting the harmonised rule to take account of the particular problem.

The function of these derogations is partly to protect the important interests of member states, but also to assist the harmonisation process. If member states know they can derogate in times or situations of need they will be more likely to agree in the first place.

Finally, Art 308 should be mentioned. This provides that:

> If action by the Community should prove necessary to attain, in the course of the operation of the common market, one of the objectives of the Community and this Treaty has not provided the necessary powers, the Council shall, acting unanimously on a proposal from the Commission and after consulting the European Parliament, take the appropriate measures.

This is a long back-stop. If for some reason a measure really cannot be brought under Art 94, Art 308 will come into play. This could be because the 'objectives of the Community' go beyond the mere establishment and functioning of the common market, the subject of Art 94. The extent to which this is the case depends on how broad an interpretation the common market is given. In early years Art 308 was used quite often, but recently, as Treaty amendments have resulted in more and more specific bases for harmonisation, and as the idea of removing distortions of the conditions of competition has been increasingly used within Art 94 and Art 95, it has been less necessary. Indeed, there have been many calls for its abolition, saying it represents an insufficiently precise, and so potentially too broad, transfer of competence to the Community. Another use of Art 308 is when a matter otherwise within Art 94 needs to be dealt with by a regulation; Art 94 only provides for directives.

The confusing and illogical distribution of these articles is a result of history. The Treaty has been gradually changed over the years, and articles added and removed and changed, more with a view to pragmatism than form.

A note should be made on direct taxation. This is tax directly on people or companies, notably income tax. It is to be contrasted with indirect taxation, which is taxation on goods or services or on particular transactions, such as VAT. Direct taxation varies greatly across the Community, and is one of the most enormous obstacles to free movement there is. An individual, or a company, may pay twice as much tax in one country as in another, which naturally has a significant influence on decisions about where to live and work. Since all workers pay tax, the effect on the internal market of the existence of differing tax regimes cannot be overstated.

However, since the only article under which harmonisation of direct taxation could occur is Art 94, which requires unanimity, it may be assumed that it will not occur, or at least only in very marginal cases (perhaps the taxation of interest on savings, for example). High tax countries would block low harmonised rates in order to protect their public services. Low tax countries would block high ones. This can either be seen as a victory for subsidiarity and democracy, and even for competition, or as a glaring hole in the internal market. These views are discussed in Chapter 9. However, on either view, it is an important issue.

It should be noted that some harmonising measures can be seen as restrictions on free movement. For example, a directive harmonising advertising rules and prohibiting misleading advertising might have the effect of weakening rules in previously strict states, but strengthening them in previously lax ones. This could lead to a product or advertisement being prohibited in a member state on the basis of the harmonising measure. In this sense, the harmonisation is itself reducing free movement. When this occurs, the measure itself, and the national implementing measures, are subject to the same principles as any other restriction on free movement: they must be justified and proportionate. In addition to this they must, of course, be properly enacted according to a harmonising Treaty article. In other words, they must genuinely advance the internal market, and not just restrict it. Thus although a directive may restrict in some ways, by creating common rules it may on balance progress the cause of free movement, and be a legitimate measure.[4]

10.4 THE EFFECT OF HARMONISATION

Harmonisation measures under Art 94, and in most other situations, are directives. Harmonisation under Art 95 and some other articles may be by directive or regulation.

Regulations become directly effective law in all the member states from the 20th day after their publication, or from the date stated in the Regulation. Directives will contain a deadline by which they must be implemented. After that date the Directive may be directly effective, if it is clear enough. If it is, then even if it is not implemented, it may be relied upon in national courts in actions against the state, but not against private parties. The idea here is that the state should not be able to escape its responsibilities by failing to implement the Directive, but that private parties should not be bound by something not clearly part of the law.

Once a measure is in force, either as a regulation, or by implementation, or through direct effect, the member state loses all competence to legislate in a way contrary to the measure. All the ground that the measure covers now belongs to the Community. How significant this is depends on whether the harmonisation is total or minimum or optional, and how broad the area it covers is.

In principle, once harmonisation has occurred it should be very difficult for a member state to rely on a Treaty exception to derogate from the harmonised rules. The idea would be that the concerns expressed in those exceptions would have been met and adequately satisfied by the measure. The provisions in Art 95 allowing for exceptional derogation are probably intended to cover the unexpected or short term, perhaps emergency, situation, rather than to allow member states to avoid harmonising measures as a matter of general policy.

Finally, if a product is manufactured according to one member state's interpretation of the Community standard, other member states are required to accept it. There is a presumption that each member state's interpretation is adequate. It would be for a resisting state to prove the contrary.

---

4   See *Estée Lauder* Case C-220/98 and *Germany v Parliament and Council (Tobacco Advertising Directive)* Case C-376/98.

10.5 THE RELATIONSHIP BETWEEN JUDICIAL AND LEGISLATIVE HARMONISATION

The relationship between judicial and legislative harmonisation exists on two levels: the strictly legal and the largely political. The latter has been historically important, but the former may be more important today. They are both outlined below.

The political interaction arises out of the impetus to the internal market that can come from the Court. *Cassis* and following cases revitalised the single market and spurred the Commission to its White Paper. If the member states become too slow in passing harmonising measures they run the risk that the Court will step in and do their work for them.

Moreover, the Court harmonises negatively – it removes legislation but does not create new. Many member states dislike this intensely, and fear of it is a motivation to agree consensual positive measures. The fear of uncontrolled – or rather uncontrolled by the member states, controlled by the Court – negative judicial harmonisation is that a 'race to the bottom' will occur.[5] By simply applying the principle of mutual recognition, and saying that foreign goods must be assumed to be acceptable, the Court creates a competitive advantage for low-standard countries. Their goods will be cheaper to make, and can invade the markets of high-standard ones. Chemical Australian beer made under franchise in the UK can be sold in Germany and undermine high quality, high price, German breweries. This puts pressure on Germany to relax the rules applying to its domestic producers, so that they can compete on price. Before we know it, doomsayers claim, standards are abandoned in the rush to be competitive. Natural harmonisation will occur at the lowest standard of any of the member states.

Of course this can only occur if the Court would not find the high national standards justified and proportionate – otherwise they can be maintained. However, critics of the Court do not agree with its notions of justification. They allow much more importance than the Court does to consumer protection and the desire of particular countries to have extra high safety, quality or environmental standards.

The legal interaction occurs when a judgment is given in which a national measure is declared an obstacle to movement. If it is found that the measure may remain, because it is justified and proportionate, then the judgment can be relied upon by the Commission as authority that harmonisation is necessary – an obstacle exists that the Court cannot remove. Therefore the Commission may begin preparing Community-wide rules.

If the Court finds the measure unjustified, and removes it, then that is authority that it was an obstacle to movement, but not necessarily that harmonisation is necessary – since the obstacle is now removed. However, since member states can continue to apply the struck-down rules to their national industries, and similar rules may be found in other member states, where the Court may not yet have considered them, the Commission may still feel that there is a 'distortion' which affects the functioning of the market. The mere existence of different rules for national producers and importers, which is the result of

---

5   See Chapter 9.

this kind of judgment, is evidence for this.[6] Therefore it may still begin the harmonisation process.

Thus the Court's judgments serve as a kick-start, identifying problem areas, and providing authority for harmonisation to go ahead.

10.6 EXAMPLES OF HARMONISATION: RECOGNITION OF QUALIFICATIONS

The history of Europe is full of expatriate academics, from Erasmus in Oxford, to the enormous migration of Jewish intellectuals to the UK before the Second World War, to take two examples. This shows that, at least sometimes, possession of foreign qualifications was not taken as proof of incompetence. However, in more immediately useful areas of life, such as trades and professions, there has often been more restriction. In the middle ages guilds controlled who could perform certain tasks, and skilled persons were not only restricted to working in their own nation, but sometimes within a certain area of it. A doctor or carpenter could not simply set up shop wherever he wanted. In recent decades this latter attitude has been the prevailing one. Without any basis other than prejudice, or sometimes nationalism, member states have tended not to accept foreign qualifications as equal to their own. They have preserved skilled work for graduates of their own colleges and universities.

As was discussed in Chapter 4, the Court developed general principles to deal with this, requiring member states to genuinely assess foreign qualifications for equivalence, and to allow procedures for missing knowledge or experience to be acquired. However, the area is complex, and reliance on such a general approach risks different results in different lands. Some will accept the spirit of the approach, and be generous, while others will attempt to disqualify people for the merest technical difference between their qualification and the national one.

Therefore a number of Directives were adopted by the Community regulating the area of mutual recognition of qualifications. The legal bases were usually Arts 40, 47 and 55. Articles 40 and 47 have been described above. Article 55 extends Art 47 to apply to services. Thus workers, established people, and service providers, could all be covered by the Directives – all the groups of people who might have qualification recognition problems.

The first Directives to be passed dealt with particular professions – doctors, dentists, hairdressers, and architects, for example. Rules were laid down on when a national qualification should be accepted by other member states as equivalent to their own. However, this profession-by-profession approach was clumsy and slow, and each harmonising step had to be fought for against national professional bodies, and so a more general method was adopted in the late 1980s. Two Directives in particular resulted, which were typical of the 'new approach' in their methodology; they were broad, flexible, and put more day-to-day decision making power in the member states' hands. The Directives are 89/48 and 92/51.

---

6   See *Pistre* Joined Cases C-321–24/94 and Chapter 11.

The first covers people who want to practise a profession in another member state where that profession is regulated, that is, there are legal requirements imposed on people who practise it. These may be just that one cannot use a particular title without certain qualification – the titles of lawyers and doctors are usually protected like this – but it may also be that one cannot perform the activity at all unless qualified. Thus in most member states only qualified lawyers may give paid legal advice.

If the person has completed at least three years of post-secondary higher education, resulting in a qualification – referred to as a 'diploma' – and has qualified to practise the profession in one member state, then she can rely on the Directive. Therefore it may be that the diploma was sufficient, or it may be that the person has also gained practical experience or completed other professional training. The important point is that she is recognised as qualified at home.

What the Directive then says is that she may not be refused permission to practise because she is inadequately qualified. This is a very simple application of mutual recognition. However, in Art 4 the Directive then goes on to deal with some exceptions to this.

Where her training is more than a year less than the host state training, the host state may ask for proof of professional experience. If a certain period can be shown, the qualification must be accepted. Article 4(a) lays down how the required period is to be calculated. It is related to the difference in length between the host and home state qualification times, and there is a ceiling of four years.

Where there is a 'substantial' difference between what is covered by host and home state training, or the profession in the host state covers activities that are not included within the profession in the home state (for example, in some countries opticians are eye-doctors, while in others they are eye-testers) the host state can insist that she take a test covering this missing content, or do a period of supervised work (described as an adaption period). It is up to the mover to choose which she prefers, unless the profession is one where a 'precise knowledge' of national law is necessary. Then the host state may insist on a test.

There are then a number of provisions dealing with essentially bureaucratic obstacles. These provide for the recognition of foreign certificates of good character, and health, and for the use of the host state professional title, and for the adaption of any oaths that may be required for admittance to the profession. This last covers the situation where a profession may have some residual tradition according to which practitioners swear loyalty to the monarch or constitution. This may be inappropriate for foreigners, and so the oath will be adapted – perhaps they merely have to promise to be honest and respect the law, for example.

The narrowness of this Directive is that it only covers professions requiring three years of post-school college training. Many jobs are regulated, and skilled, but have a lesser institutional component, even if they may require several years of on-the-job practical training.

These were brought into the Community system by Directive 92/51. This takes the same approach as Directive 89/48, but covers two different groups of people. The first contains those who have a diploma resulting from a post-secondary course of at least one year, and who are able to practise their profession in their home state. The second contains those who do not meet the first requirement, but do have a certificate saying they have completed some form of post-secondary training, and are able to practise their profession. This second group covers those jobs that do not require extensive college training, but may be mostly apprenticeship, with a certificate of completion.

For each of these groups there are provisions similar to those in Directive 89/48. The situation where a job requires a 'diploma' in the host state, but only a 'certificate' in the home state, is also covered, and procedures laid down to ease the transfer. Essentially, a choice of test or adaption period is allowed.

Together, these two Directives seem to cover almost any post-secondary job qualification obtained in a member state. Another, very short, Directive, 89/49, covers member state nationals who have comparable qualifications they obtained in third states. The Directive 'urges' member states to recognise these, but does not require them to.

What is notable about the harmonisation described above is that it does not involve the standardisation of laws or education systems. Member states remain free to organise qualification how they like. This is an example of harmonisation achieved through fitting diverse national systems into a common framework.

More technically, it can be described as optional minimum harmonisation. It is optional, because there is no obligation to structure training in a way that fits into the Directives. If a profession requires a three-year diploma in most member states, another member state remains free to allow qualification after one year of training. People qualifying in this state will then have a problem moving, because they will meet the requirements of the second Directive, but the profession they wish to practise will fall under the first Directive in the host state. Nevertheless, no Community law is infringed. It is up to the education providers – probably the states – to choose whether to 'manufacture their product' in a way that guarantees it mutual recognition.

The harmonisation is minimum, because member states are free to require longer training periods for a particular profession, if they wish to. They may have ten-year training if they feel this desirable! However, if a foreigner complies with the minimum requirements of the Directives, then they will have to admit her – subject to tests and adaption periods.

This means that if there is a very significant discrepancy between length of training in different countries, this creates a reason to go abroad to train – to short-cut the long period. A German would-be lawyer might find it a quicker overall process to study and qualify in the UK, and then take the extra tests at home, for example. The existence of these competitive pressures tends to lead to a natural harmonisation, as countries move towards similar levels of training.

The Directives here are very typical of the new approach; note how general they are, how free they leave the member states, and how harmonisation is achieved with the minimum of compulsion or interference. Note also, however, how it could be argued that the possibility of short-cutting could lead to lowering of standards. Is a three-year course plus an added-on test really equivalent to a fully integrated and planned five-year course? There is more to education than the mere facts that are likely to be found in the aptitude tests.

10.6.1 Recent developments

Several of the provisions of the directives are the result of recent amendments and should have been implemented by member states by January 2003. These address particular problems that were being experienced. In particular, where a member state claims that there is a 'substantial difference' in qualification standards, they are now required to assess whether this is compensated for by existing experience. The Directive also sets out time periods for them to take decisions on these matters.

There is also an improved procedure for the publication of lists of qualifications that are to be automatically accepted. This is something done by the Commission, which can be extremely helpful to the migrant profession.

Finally, where a member state has recognised a qualification gained in a non-Community country, this is now seen as introducing a 'Community element'. Therefore other member states are required to take this recognition into account and assess whether the qualification is acceptable to them. They cannot simply reject it as 'non-Community'.

10.7 EXAMPLES OF HARMONISATION: E-COMMERCE

E-commerce is something of growing economic and social importance, and something to which it is not always easy to adapt existing laws. Directive 2000/31 aims to overcome some of the obstacles to a Community-wide electronic market by making clear how existing laws are to be applied to e-commerce, and providing new law where necessary. After an explanation of the nature of e-commerce, the Directive and its most important provisions are outlined, and it is shown how they work.

10.7.1 What is e-commerce?

E-commerce is the doing of business via electronically transmitted data. Mainly this means over the internet, but data transmission over dedicated telephone lines is also included.

The business can be of any type. Buying goods over the internet, or paying to access or download sound, text or pictures are both e-commerce.

Note that a commercial element is necessary. Uncommercial data communication is not included within e-commerce. Web pages that are free to access but are funded by advertisements is a difficult area. If the advertisements have links, it looks as if the pages are part of electronic business. If they do not, the situation may be more arguable. In any case, for the purposes of the Directive, advertising-funded web-pages are covered.

10.7.2 Directive 2000/31

A number of pieces of Community legislation are relevant to e-commerce in some way or another. Data protection, encryption, and the protection of human rights – with reference to hate speech and freedom of expression especially – all impact to a greater or lesser degree. However, the main instrument of regulation is Directive 2000/31. The legal bases of this are Arts 47, 55, 95 and 251. A somewhat simplified summary of the Directive follows, emphasising the key points.

The purpose of this Directive is set out in Art 1(1):

> This Directive seeks to contribute to the proper functioning of the internal market by ensuring the free movement of information society services between the member states.

Article 2 provides definitions, and then Art 3 makes clear that the Treaty rules on services apply to e-commerce:

> Member states may not, for reasons falling within the coordinated field, restrict the freedom to provide information society services from another member state.

Article 3 also provides for the now-familiar public policy etc exceptions.

Article 4 provides the first new law:

> Member states shall ensure that the taking up and pursuit of the activity of an information society service provider may not be made subject to prior authorisation or any other requirement having equivalent effect.

This imposes a liberal approach on the member states. They are not to think that the internet is something for them to ration, any more than telephone conversations or post are.

Articles 5 and 6 could be seen as consumer protection articles. Article 5 provides that what are called 'information society service providers' (those doing e-business) give certain information to the authorities, such as their names, place of business, and so on. This is analogous to the requirements on a 'physical' business to register themselves and comply with certain formalities. Article 5 also provides that where business is done on the web, prices must be clearly available. Article 6 makes further provisions along these lines.

Article 7 deals with 'spam': unsolicited commercial email. The sender has to be identifiable, and people have to be able to opt-out – to enter themselves on a register, which senders will check regularly. Names on that register will then be removed from email lists.

This article can be criticised as unrealistic. Users of the internet will know that opting out does not work. Many senders of spam are only encouraged by contact indicating that one does not want any more emails. An alternative approach was suggested – an opt-in approach. Under this all unsolicited commercial email would be prohibited, unless people had indicated they did not mind. This was rejected as too illiberal – it might interfere with business. It can also be seen as an infringement of free speech. Can I not send letters to whoever I want?

Article 8 requires that rules governing 'regulated professions' be adapted, where necessary, to allow professionals to conduct their activities over the internet. Those qualified to give advice, for example, must be allowed to do it electronically too.

This is without prejudice to the principles governing those professions. Thus if lawyers are not allowed to advertise, they will not be allowed to advertise on the web. The aim is simply to assimilate the web to the paper world – what can be done on one should be possible on the other.

Articles 9–11 are perhaps the most important in the Directive. They ensure that contracts can be concluded over the internet, and that national contract law will not be a hindrance to this. Certain contracts may be excluded, notably wills and contracts for land, but in general the principle is that e-contracts should be as binding and useable as paper ones.

The general aim is set out in Art 9(1):

> Member states shall ensure that their legal system allows contracts to be concluded by electronic means. Member states shall in particular ensure that the legal requirements applicable to the contractual process neither create obstacles for the use of electronic contracts nor result in such contracts being deprived of legal effectiveness and validity on account of their having been made by electronic means.

The rest of Art 9, and Arts 10 and 11, elaborate the basic requirements that member states must implement to achieve this. In particular, orders must be acknowledged, and contracts must be available in a form that enables them to be stored and printed. Orders and acknowledgments are to be deemed to be received when the party to whom they are addressed is able to access them. This does not eliminate all contractual issues – countries may differ on whether receipt of the order or of the acknowledgment concludes the contract. However, while allowing such legal variations, a common view of the basic facts is imposed.

Note that contracts concluded exclusively by email are not included in these articles. An emailed confirmation to an order placed through a website would not take a contract outside the Directive, however.

One of the essentials for some contracts in many legal systems is a signature. An earlier Directive provided for standards governing electronic signatures.[7] These are essentially numbers or codewords which can be used as a signature. They should be safe provided they are encrypted and of sufficient complexity and so on, and the earlier Directive dealt with these matters. If member states require signatures on contracts, Directive 2000/31 now requires that they accept electronic signatures. This follows from the quotation above. Anything else would not be allowing contracts to be concluded by electronic means.

Articles 12–15 deal with one of the most controversial aspects of e-commerce, the liability of intermediaries. Intermediaries are those who run the network which carries the information. This includes the owners of servers (the large computers that hold information), operators of communication lines, and web-hosting companies.

All these people may store or transmit information provided by others, and if that information infringes laws on libel, obscenity, hate speech or religious rights, for example, they run a risk of liability. This threat has almost closed down some internet providers in some countries. In Italy, France, and Germany, there have, at different times, been threats from national courts or authorities that liability would be imposed for content carried, stored, or delivered to other users. Particularly hot issues are neo-Nazi web pages that infringe many countries' laws on denial of the holocaust, and child pornography.

The intermediaries' problem is that it is very difficult for them to monitor what is on, or passes through, their computers. They point out that telephone companies are not

---

7   Directive 1999/93/EC.

liable for the content of telephone conversations, and insist that if they have to monitor all content, this will effectively stop the internet.

On the other hand, the characteristic of the internet is that information is available world-wide. Thus many of the original suppliers of offensive information are outside the jurisdiction of the offended courts. Their only way of stopping the infringement of their laws is via the control of intermediaries who are physically located in their countries. The ability to hold them liable would be a powerful weapon, and motivate the intermediaries to monitor information themselves.

The Directive has ultimately, and controversially, chosen a liberal approach. Broadly, intermediaries are not liable for illegal data provided it did not originate from them, and they did not know about it, and they did not change it in any way. In short, if it went through their pipes without touching the sides, they aren't to blame.

On the other hand, they may be liable if they have interacted with the data. This might cover the situation where a server hosts a bulletin board, on which people can post comments. That would require a degree of participation from the server, and so it could not claim complete lack of involvement.

Moreover, if they do discover illegal data, they have an obligation to remove it or disable access to it as soon as possible.

Article 15 makes clear that there is no general obligation on the intermediaries to monitor data, and member states may not impose one. This is included because monitoring significantly slows data transmission, and the operation of the internet would be put at risk by such an obligation, and with it the whole development of e-commerce.

Finally, the remaining articles deal with the practicalities of implementation. The deadline for implementation was January 2002.

10.7.3 The approach of the Directive

Once again, this is a minimalist Directive. The quotation from Art 9 is a good example of how the important goals have been set out, but the means of ensuring them left largely up to member states. The actual standardisation of national laws is kept to a very low level. In particular, national contract laws are standardised only to a very minor extent, and national laws on content are not standardised at all, although these two areas are vital to e-commerce.

The approach to dealing with these two issues is similar. The Directive sets out certain basic requirements which functioning e-commerce requires. Regarding contracts, e-contracts must be valid, and there must be certain standard procedural safeguards. The components of the e-contract, the order and reply, must be clear and accessible. Regarding content, intermediaries must have some protection from liability, so that they can function.

Member states must not act in any way that threatens these requirements. However, providing they respect them, they are free to apply, and even develop national law. What is legal on the web, and what kind of contracts may be concluded, and how they are to be interpreted, remains a national matter (subject to other Directives, such as the Unfair Contract Terms Directive), so long as essential free movement is unimpaired.

The criticism of this approach is that problems will remain. Lawsuits arising because websites accessible in one country infringe its laws on expression, or because of conflicts of contract law, may still occur. However, the Directive places a high degree of confidence in the ability of national courts to deal with these using existing law, and insofar as they do not do so in a justified or proportionate way, they remain subject to the Treaty requirements of free movement – as restated in Art 1 of the Directive. The fundamental principle, that e-commerce is valid, legal, and possible, across borders and without unjustified restrictions, is no longer legally open to question.

CHAPTER 11

THE WHOLLY INTERNAL SITUATION

Community law only applies to situations within the scope of the Treaty. In the internal market context that means situations with some connection to free movement between member states. A restriction on movement of goods from France to Germany is within the Treaty. A road-block between two villages in Italy probably is not.

In deciding whether a situation is within the scope of Community law the first thing to do is to look at the facts. Has anything cross-border occurred? If not, Community law will probably not apply. It will be a wholly internal situation. In that case the member state government is free to deal with the matter however it sees fit, and the Court has nothing to say about it.

This can create what is called reverse discrimination. A migrant, or an imported good, may be able to rely on Community law rights, where a national or national product cannot. The nationals may actually be in a worse legal position. In theory the Court is not concerned about this; member states are free to persecute their own nationals, provided they do not hinder the movement of foreigners, or foreign products. However, reverse discrimination is very divisive, and creates tensions and problems which could damage the internal market, and eventually harm the movement of foreign persons and goods. Thus the matter might be within Community law after all. In some situations which look like reverse discrimination the Court has found a reason to intervene. *Pistre*,[1] discussed below, is an example of this.

Another situation arises where domestic law applies a rule equally to national and foreign goods or people. Sometimes the national court sends a preliminary reference question to the Court about this rule, in a case where all the facts are domestic. The Court could refuse to answer this, saying the situation is internal. However, sometimes it does answer, because it knows that the same rule is going to be applied to non-internal situations as well, and so it wants the national court to know its view. *Keck*[2] is an example of this kind of situation.

In practice, once the Court has given an answer, the national court will apply it, even though if the facts are domestic Community law does not oblige this. Thus the Court's view on selling arrangements was applied to *Keck*, even though the national court could have ignored it in that case, as long as it applied it in other cases, where the facts were non-internal.

Thus the real scope of the 'wholly internal situation' is smaller than pure theory might suggest. Many situations that seem at first glance internal are, in fact, governed by Community law.

In this chapter three issues are considered. First, when are the facts of a situation within the scope of Community law? Secondly, how does the Court react to reverse discrimination? Thirdly, some cases where the situation was internal, but the Court nevertheless answered questions put to it, are considered.

---

1   *Pistre* Joined Cases C-321–24/94.
2   *Keck* Joined Cases C-267/91 and C-268/91.

11.1 FACTS WITHIN THE SCOPE OF COMMUNITY LAW

A statement of the basic position can be found in *Saunders*.[3] The UK government had confined a UK citizen to Northern Ireland (a part of the UK) as a result of a criminal conviction. She was not allowed to come to the mainland of the UK, and claimed this was contrary to the free movement of workers. The Court said:

> ... the provisions of the Treaty on freedom of movement for workers cannot ... be applied to situations which are wholly internal to a member state, in other words, where there is no factor connecting them to any of the situations envisaged by Community law.

In this case a national was being troubled by her own government, at home. There was no Community law element. The aim of Art 39, the Court said, was to ensure equal treatment and free movement for migrant workers, not domestic ones.

It took a similar approach in *RI-SAN*,[4] in the context of services. Here an Italian company complained about the process of awarding contracts of an Italian local authority. It said there were no proper tendering procedures; contracts went to friends, rather than the best bidder. This was an obstacle to free movement of services, because it kept out foreign suppliers.

This may or may not have been true, but the Court did not consider it, because the complaining company was also Italian. It said:

> ... the Treaty does not apply in a situation such as that in the main proceedings in which all the facts are confined to within a single member state and which does not therefore have any connecting link with one of the situations envisaged by Community law in the area of the freedom of movement for persons and freedom to provide services.

A third example is *Morson and Jhanjan*.[5] These two people were non-EU citizens, who applied to come and live in the Netherlands, where their children already lived and had Dutch nationality. They relied on Regulation 1612/68, according to which Treaty workers have the right to bring their 'ascending dependants' to live with them. However, they lost, because their children were not EU migrants, but worked in their home state – the Netherlands. The Court said that the free movement articles, and the secondary legislation, could not be applied to situations unconnected with Community law, and:

> ... such is undoubtedly the case with workers who have never exercised the right to freedom of movement within the Community.

Therefore, workers at home are not within the Treaty. This is quite controversial, since it means that a German or British worker within the Netherlands can bring all her family to live with her, regardless of their nationality, while a Dutch one cannot. The political implications are obvious. The Community may be seen as providing a backdoor to unwanted immigration, and nationals may be resentful that they have lesser rights than foreigners.

---

3 *Saunders* Case 175/78.
4 *RI-SAN* Case C-108/98.
5 *Morson and Jhanjan* Joined Cases 35 and 36/82.

As well as this, a motivation is created for people to go abroad expressly in order to acquire rights. If you wish to bring your non-EU family to live with you, and your national government makes this difficult, the answer is to go and work in another member state, and rely on your Community rights. When laws begin to have this sort of distorting effect on people and society, one must begin to question their good sense (or the good sense of the national laws). The extent of the distortions and problems can be seen in the next three cases, which contrast with those already discussed.

In *Surinder Singh*,[6] a British woman went to work in Germany, where she relied on Community law to bring her husband from India. She then returned to the UK, and the British authorities refused him residence and wished to deport him to India. They said Community law had no application, because she was once again back home, and the situation was purely internal.

The Court rejected this. It said that when EU citizens returned to their home state after exercising their Treaty rights to work abroad, they must be in at least as good a position as if they chose to go to another member state instead. Therefore, since the Treaty allowed workers to have their spouses with them in their host member states, they must also be allowed to have their spouses in their home state. The reason for this was that otherwise EU citizens would be deterred from going abroad in the first place.

The logic of this judgment is strange and unclear. First, it only applies to those who have already exercised a Treaty right. It seems that they can bring this right home with them, and that they keep it when they return. The reason for this is that if they could not, it would be a deterrent to work abroad. This is non-obvious, since the returning worker is no worse off than before she left. She is just worse off than she was abroad. The deterrent is not to going abroad, but surely to coming home!

However, thinking less legally and more humanly, after a person has spent a period living with their spouse it is relatively cruel and harsh to ask them to separate when they return home. Human rights considerations should be relevant here.

Furthermore, many non-EU people live in member states in situations of dubious legality. They may have some residence rights, but revocable ones, or even be outside the law. For them, going abroad is a very high-risk activity, since their return will bring them to the attention of the authorities, without any guarantee that they will be admitted to reside.

The reality is then that spouses of people without permanent residence rights will be deterred from going abroad unless they know they can also bring their partners home. The Court's judgment was right, although only lightly explained. However, it is a problematic judgment because it creates two classes of national: those who have been abroad and have Community rights, and those who have not, and do not.

It also leaves a number of questions unanswered. Do all Community rights come home, or just those to do with family members? How long do these rights 'adhere'? Could Mr Singh have stayed for the next 40 years with his wife in the UK, on the basis perhaps of one year in Germany?

---

6   *Surinder Singh* Case C-370/90.

A more recent case, *Carpenter*, has not answered these questions.[7] It concerned a British man, established in the UK, but providing services to do with advertising to companies throughout the Community. His wife was not a Community citizen, and for reasons of domestic immigration law the UK authorities wished to deport her.

The Court of Justice was asked whether this would violate Art 49. The UK government said the situation was wholly internal. Mr Carpenter was established in his own country, and his wife was with him in that country. This was not covered by the directives on family rights, and was outside the scope of Community law.

The Court agreed that the directives could not apply, but said that Mr Carpenter came within the scope of the Treaty because he was providing cross-border services. Since deporting his wife would affect his life, it could also be said to affect the conditions under which he provided those services. It might also be a violation of his human rights. Therefore the deportation was forbidden.

This is a very political judgment, which extends the concept of freedom to provide services abroad to include the conditions of family life of the service provider in his home state. While socially progressive, it is textually much harder to defend, as well as invading member state sovereignty to a great extent. It should probably be seen in the context of a desire to undo the 'injustice' of the internal exception; since Mr Carpenter's wife would have had rights anywhere else in the EU, perhaps she should also have them in the UK. Perhaps, more practically, one could also make the argument that the ability of a service provider to travel abroad to provide his services is very strongly affected if his wife is no longer able to care for his children at home, as Mrs Carpenter did.

Two questions are raised. One is the same one as *Singh*; how long would Mrs Carpenter's right last after her husband's cross-border activity stopped? Given the Court's discussion of human rights, one would think they must last quite a long time. The other question is how many matters can now be claimed to fall within Art 49. If Mr Carpenter felt that national laws to do with, say, renting offices, or operating a company, were impeding his business, could he plead Art 49? These are the sorts of things that if they occurred abroad, might be obstacles to movement. Does *Carpenter* now suggest the same idea can be applied at home, so long as you do some business abroad, and so fall within the Treaty? Logically, it seems it does.

Another set of cases has concerned economic actors returning home and suffering disadvantage because qualifications or experience acquired abroad is not accepted. The defending member state always tries to claim that since the person has come home, the matter is now internal.

An example is *Scholz*,[8] where an Italian national had worked in the civil service in Germany, and then in Italy. Her grade and pay were calculated with reference to the number of years of experience she had, but the Italian government refused to take into account her years of experience in Germany. She claimed, successfully, that this was discrimination, contrary to Art 39. The Court said:

---

7   *Carpenter* Case C-60/00.
8   *Scholz* Case C-419/92.

Any Community national who, irrespective of his place of residence and his nationality, has exercised the right to freedom of movement for workers and who has been employed in another member state, falls within the scope of the aforesaid provisions.

The situation of Mr Knoors[9] was similar. He was Dutch, but had qualified as a plumber in Belgium. When he went back to the Netherlands he was refused permission to work as a plumber because he did not have the Dutch qualification. If he had been Belgian, this would obviously be contrary to freedom of establishment, but the Dutch government said that as he was a Dutch person in his home state the situation was outside Community law. The Court said that if this was right, freedom of establishment would not be 'fully realised'. Therefore it was not right. Mr Knoors could rely on Art 43 just as if he was Belgian.

The Court provided no further reasoning in the judgment, but its decision can be supported. If nationals could not exercise such rights on returning to their home states they would be very strongly deterred from qualifying abroad. Since when people go to study abroad they often work there for a period as well, the overall effect would also be to reduce the number of workers and self-employed people going abroad, which would be contrary to the Treaty. This is particularly true of vocational training such as Mr Knoors', which often contains a significant work element. Therefore Mr Knoors should not be seen as outside the Treaty. Having exercised Treaty rights working in Belgium he was within it, and would stay within it when he came home. Anything less would damage the internal market.

The same arguments can be made about *Kraus*,[10] where the German government wished to ban the use of foreign academic titles. Although the case concerned a German in Germany, because he had studied in the UK, exercising his Community right to study abroad, there was a non-internal element, and he could bring Community law home. Any other approach would be a deterrent to moving abroad in the first place.

In both these cases, the home state governments were worried about 'abuse'. They thought their nationals would go abroad and gain 'inferior' qualifications which they would then use at home, to the detriment of the innocent consumer, and gaining an unfair advantage over their peers. In both cases the governments were confused. If there are genuine and important differences in qualifications both basic principles and secondary legislation allow member states to require this difference to be made good. The member states cannot be taken seriously in their claims of concern for standards. They were simply reflecting the thoughtless nationalism which is very common in the EU regarding qualifications. Suspicion of foreign ones remains very high.

Perhaps encouraged by these cases, there have been a number of recent creative but doomed attempts to attack the internal exception. One of these was *Uecker and Jacquet*.[11] The situation was essentially the same as *Morson*, but the claimants argued that Community law had moved on. With the development of citizenship, even German workers at home in Germany, who had never worked abroad, could be said to be within the scope of Community law. They were EU citizens, following Art 17. Therefore, as

---

9   *Knoors* Case 115/78.

10   *Kraus* Case C-19/92.

11   *Uecker and Jacquet* Joined Cases C-64/96 and C-65/96.

workers, they could rely on Community law to bring their non-EU family members to live with them.

The Court answered that:

> In that regard, it must be noted that citizenship of the Union, established by Art 8 [now 17] of the EC Treaty, is not intended to extend the scope *ratione materiae* of the Treaty also to internal situations which have no link with Community law ... Any discrimination which nationals of a member state may suffer under the law of that state fall within the scope of that law and must therefore be dealt with within the framework of the internal legal system of that state.

The Court here reaffirms that it is not interested in how member states treat their own nationals, if they have not exercised Treaty rights at least. It also says citizenship does not extend the Treaty to cover situations beyond the Treaty, a completely empty statement! What the Court seems to be trying to say is that citizenship does not extend the Treaty to cover new situations. If this is so, it makes a joke of citizenship, but it may be that it is, or was, the view of the Court.[12] In any case, the substantive judgment can be defended, since even if the claimants were within the scope of the Treaty as citizens, they were not Treaty workers, since these must be migrants, and so they still had no basis for relying on Regulation 1612/68.[13]

The Court has taken the same approach in the law on goods. In *Mathot*,[14] a Belgian law required Belgian butter to bear the address of the producer, while foreign butter had no such obligation. This actually put Belgian producers at a disadvantage, because Belgian supermarkets did not like such labelled butter. Therefore the Court said the rule did not infringe Art 28. Only Belgians suffered, and imports were not restricted.

Another unsuccessful case was *Werner*.[15] Mr Werner was German, and worked in Germany, but lived in the Netherlands. He suffered from German tax law, which he said discriminated on the basis of residence. The judgment is complex, but the suggestion is that a Dutchman might have had a stronger case. The Court said:

> The only factor which takes his case out of a purely national context is the fact that he lives in a member state other than that in which he practises his profession.

One might think this is enough, remembering *Knoors* and *Singh*, to put him in as good a position as a foreigner. However, they had both exercised Treaty rights abroad – they had worked. Mr Werner worked at home, and his residence in the Netherlands was not pursuant to any Treaty article. Therefore he did not have as strong a case as Mr Knoors to be able to rely on Community law. This seemed to have been important; the Court seemed to regard the matter as essentially internal.

Finally, the case of *Kremzow*[16] is one of the most unlikely attempts to rely on Community law. Mr Kremzow, an Austrian, was in prison in Austria for murder. He had successfully claimed before the European Court of Human Rights that he had not had a fair trial and his sentence was therefore unlawful. However, the Austrian government

---

12 See Chapter 8.
13 But see *Martinez Sala* Case C-85/96 and Chapter 8.
14 *Mathot* Case 98/86.
15 *Werner* Case C-112/91.
16 *Kremzow* Case C-299/95.

had not released him. He claimed that as an EU citizen, he had a right to move freely within the Community. An unlawful infringement of that right – by imprisoning him – should result in damages under Community law. Since Community law respected human rights, and his detention was unlawful in the eyes of the Human Rights Court, it ought to be unlawful in Community law too. The Court accepted that human rights were part of Community law, and violations were unacceptable. However, Community law could only apply where a situation had some connection with it, and a hypothetical possibility of moving was not enough.

This is very dubious reasoning. If a member state banned its nationals from going abroad to work, the Court would not reject that as an internal situation. It is unlikely it would say their connection was hypothetical since they had not yet worked abroad; that would be circular. Even if the member state only stopped them from going abroad for pleasure, the Court would probably allow Art 18 to be applied to that situation. It is very hard to see this kind of restriction on free movement being allowed. Therefore, as a matter of law, it ought to have conceded Mr Kremzow's point. There was clearly an obstacle to his movement abroad, and thus a situation within Community law. Of course, the obstacle may have been justified; it does not follow that Community law would insist on his release.

The Court also said that it could not look at whether there was a violation of human rights according to Community law, because national criminal legislation fell outside the scope of Community law. This is inconsistent with cases like *Bickel*[17] and *Cowan*,[18] where the Court has intervened in criminal law happily in order to preserve free movement.

What made them reluctant to take a strictly legal approach to this case was probably that Mr Kremzow was in prison for murder. Moreover, it was a one-off case; there was no general anti-movement principle being applied. Therefore, we must assume, the Court decided it was not worth getting involved. This was not a worthy cause.

Moreover, the aim of the Austrian government was not to restrict cross-border movement, nor to discriminate; it was to protect society from a murderer. While this aim should not be relevant to the question of whether there is an obstacle to movement within the Treaty, which is just a matter of effect, it clearly does influence the Court.

11.2 REVERSE DISCRIMINATION AND 'NORMAL' DISCRIMINATION

We have already seen in *Knoors* and *Singh* that where a Treaty right has been exercised the Court will not allow reverse discrimination. However, where there is a genuinely internal situation, as in *Uecker*, the Court does not object to reverse discrimination. In general, reverse discrimination is not against Community law. There are certain situations though where the existence of reverse discrimination can present a legal problem. These are when the extra legal burden placed on the domestic product results in consumers seeing it as somehow different or better. Then, reverse discrimination divides the market along

---

17 *Bickel* Case C-274/96.
18 *Cowan* Case 186/87.

national lines, and can even give an advantage to national products, that is, it can result in 'normal' discrimination.

An example may make this clear. If a law insists that all beer made in Germany be made according to purity rules, while foreign beer can be imported even if it is not, then it looks as if there is an extra cost burden on German producers – an example of reverse discrimination. However, it may be that the effect of this rule is that the public come to know that German beer is quality beer and can be trusted, while foreign beer may be impure. It may be that the extra burden actually results in a marketing advantage for German beer, and has the effect of creating a divided market, in which consumers perceive the national and foreign products quite differently. From a broad internal market point of view, these kinds of divisions are very negative, and hinder European integration. From a more precisely legal point of view, we can say that apparent reverse discrimination actually results in an advantage for German beer, which is then 'normal' discrimination.

This may seem far-fetched, but that it occurs is shown by the fact that many companies manufacture their goods to higher national standards, when lower Community standards would be legally adequate. They like to be able to say 'made to British standard XYZ' because for some goods, to be perceived as quality is worth the extra costs. One can also see how this might happen with people and services, if extra qualifications were required for nationals, or extra regulatory burdens placed on national suppliers. It might increase their costs, but it would also increase the trust people placed in them. Imagine if national doctors had to study ten years before they could practise, while foreign ones were admitted after the normal seven. Would this be an advantage or a disadvantage for the nationals? Who would you go to?

Nevertheless, the caselaw in this area has concerned goods, and the leading case is *Pistre*.[19] In this case, a French rule said that ham could only be sold as 'mountain ham' provided that it came from certain kinds of areas. The pigs had to live on a steep slope and had to be high up, and so on. Apparently this is expensive, but makes the ham taste better. The problem was that the ham had to come from a designated 'mountainous area' and these were picked by the French government and, of course, were only in France. The French authorities said that the point of these rules was to protect consumers. When they bought 'mountain ham', they thought they were getting a particular kind of traditional quality French product, and the rules ensured this was true. However, it meant that foreign ham, even if it came from the steepest, highest bits of Europe, could never legally be called 'mountain ham'.

What made the case unusual was that it was accepted by all sides that the French authorities did not actually apply these rules to foreign products. They probably realised it would be an obstacle to trade. Thus if German or Italian ham was marketed as 'mountain ham', this would be allowed, even though the French authorities could not control the authenticity of the description, and technically it was against French law. The main aim of the rules was clearly to prevent misdescription by domestic producers, who actually kept their pigs in pens at the bottom of the hills. The case was brought as a result of a French producer being prosecuted for misuse of the name. He claimed the rule was

---

19   *Pistre*, see note 1 above.

contrary to Art 28. The French government said that the situation was wholly internal. It did indeed look like it.

However, the Court said that:

> Accordingly, whilst the application of a national measure having no actual link to the importation of goods does not fall within the ambit of Art 30 [now 28] of the Treaty, Art 30 [now 28] cannot be considered inapplicable simply because all the facts of the specific case before the national court are confined to a single member state.

> In such a situation, the application of the national measure may also have effects on the free movement of goods between member states, in particular when the measure in question facilitates the marketing of goods of domestic origin to the detriment of imported goods. In such circumstances, the application of the measure, even if restricted to domestic producers, in itself creates and maintains a difference of treatment between those two categories of goods, hindering, at least potentially, intra-Community trade.

In other words, there could be a link with Community law, even when the facts were internal. The link could be because the rule in question gave a marketing advantage to domestic goods. In this case only French goods could legally use the 'mountain ham' label.

The argument that in practice the rule was not applied to foreign goods did not succeed. It was worded so that it could be, and that was enough to create the violation. Just showing that the rule was not used against foreigners was not good enough. Clearly member states must not just *behave* compatibly with Art 28, but their laws must be compatible too. In any case, if the law had only applied to French products this would not have made any difference; they would still have had the marketing advantage.

Since the rule was discriminatory – only French ham could get the designation – consumer protection was not available as a justification, and none of the Treaty exceptions applied. Therefore the French authorities could not insist that Mr Pistre remove the 'mountain' designation. To do so would be maintaining the division between foreign and domestic goods, thereby giving the domestic an advantage.

It is worth noting that it is difficult to see what kind of rule should replace the one abolished. If 'mountain ham' is to be kept as a controlled designation, which seems reasonable since in France people recognise it as a kind of product, clearly it must be legally available to domestic and imported ham alike. However, the French authorities have no way of controlling the authenticity of imported mountain ham. Thus the clever French consumer may continue to buy only the national product, knowing that only this is really subject to control. To prevent this kind of market division the use of 'mountain' would have to be made totally free, but then the product category would be degraded, and consumers would be misled.

One thing *Pistre* shows is that a rule only applied internally could still be contrary to Art 28. A more clear cut example of this is the *German Quality Products* case.[20] This brand was made available to German products complying with national standards, and when it was complained that this was discriminatory, because foreign products could not receive it, it might have been argued that the matter was wholly internal – a national law applied only to national goods. However, since it gave those goods a marketing advantage by

---

20 *Commission v Germany (Quality Products)* Case C-325/000.

comparison with imports, the effects were clearly not just internal, and the measure was contrary to Art 28.

The case, although a black-and-white discrimination one, in which the internal argument was not in fact made, is interesting because it may represent an attempt by a national marketing body to exploit the divisive effect of the internal situation. Since national goods are subject to national standards, while foreign ones are not, why not turn that from a burden into a bonus for the national product, by giving them a special mark of quality? This is a way of bringing to the consumer's attention that only national goods always conform to the standards they are used to, while foreign ones may be diverse and strange. Thus the internal exception itself threatens to create new, psychological, obstacles to movement, exploitable by clever marketing – unless Art 28 steps in.

11.3 ABSTRACT QUESTIONS

Sometimes the facts of a case are not connected with Community law, not even indirectly like *Pistre*, and yet the Court still answers questions. Why does this occur, since the general rule is that the Court only has jurisdiction over Community law matters, and should not answer hypothetical questions?

The classic example of this is *Keck*.[21] A French man was prosecuted for selling products at a loss. He was prosecuted in France, and the products were not imported from another member state. He claimed that the prohibition on sale at a loss was an obstacle to trade.

However, even if he had been right, the Court's ruling would not have been applicable in his case as a matter of Community law. If he had been right then the French authorities would not have been able to stop importers selling at a loss, but they would still have been able to stop Mr Pistre, since his was a wholly internal situation.

In fact, as we know, the Court found that selling arrangements like this were not obstacles to trade anyway, but why did it answer the question, since the national court would not have been bound to apply its ruling in the particular case?

The answer is pragmatic; it answered the question because it wanted the national court to know the answer. It can be seen as part of the Court's continuing education programme for national courts.

More than this, it also understood that the answer was necessary to the national court, not as a matter of Community law, but as a matter of French law. In practice, there was just one law on selling at a loss in France, which applied equally to domestic and imported products. The French authorities had no desire to create a distinction between these groups, and French law required them to treat them equally. Therefore, if as a matter of Community law the sale-at-a-loss ban could not be applied to imports, then as a matter of French law it could not be applied to domestic products. Therefore, even though this was a wholly internal case, the national court needed to know how this rule stood in Community law.

---

21 *Keck,* see note 2 above.

This reasoning has been confirmed in the case of *Guimont*.[22] A French law only allowed cheese to be sold as 'Emmental' if it had a certain kind of rind. The law applied to domestic and imported cheese. There was no question of discrimination, just a straightforward product rule which might be an obstacle to trade. It is important to understand that this case is not like *Pistre*. In that case, the importers could not legally get a 'mountain ham' designation. However, in this case they could perfectly legally use the name 'Emmental'; they just had to have a rind. They were in no worse a position than domestic producers, and there was no question of any kind of marketing advantage being created for the domestic goods.

Therefore, the Court would not be troubled by the situation where this rule was applied to French producers but not importers. In that case the importers could put a rind on and be in just as good a marketing position as domestic producers, or they could save some money, leave the rind off, and still call their cheese Emmental. The choice was theirs. The discrimination would be entirely against French producers.

In the actual case, the complainant was a French producer, being prosecuted for selling without a rind. Therefore, even if the rule was not a good one, we can be sure that the Court would not have objected to the application of the rule to him, and to his prosecution. That was a wholly internal situation, outside the scope of Community law.

Nevertheless, the Court said:

> ... it is clear from the Court's caselaw that such a rule falls under Art 30 of the Treaty only in so far as it applies to situations that are linked to the importation of goods in intra-Community trade.

> However, that finding does not mean that there is no need to reply to the question referred to the Court for a preliminary ruling in this case. In principle, it is for the national courts alone to determine, having regard to the particular features of each case, both the need for preliminary ruling in order to enable them to give their judgment and the relevance of the questions which they refer to the Court. A reference for a preliminary ruling from a national court may be rejected only if it is quite obvious that the interpretation of Community law sought by that court bears no relation to the actual nature of the case or the subject-matter of the main action.

> In this case, it is not obvious that the interpretation of Community law requested is not necessary for the national court. Such a reply might be useful to it if its national law were to require, in proceedings such as those in this case, that a national producer must be allowed to enjoy the same rights as those which a producer of another member state would derive from Community law in the same situation.

So, since a national producer might be entitled to the same rights as an importer, according to national law, a national court might need to know what rights an importer would have. Therefore the Court would answer the question whether this rule could be applied to an importer. It found that it could not. Nevertheless, it remains the case that Community law does not require that the national court apply the Court's ruling against Mr Guimont.

---

22   *Guimont* Case C-448/98.

CHAPTER 12

PRIVATE ACTORS

An important question in internal market law is whether the free movement articles bind private actors. If a non-governmental body or person acts in a way that creates an obstacle to movement, is this contrary to the Treaty?

There are many practical ways in which private actors can inhibit cross-border movement. A chain of supermarkets might decide to buy only national goods, thereby significantly reducing imports. A bank might make it very difficult or expensive to transfer money abroad, thereby creating an obstacle to the movement of capital and also to goods and services, which have to be paid for. A large employer might decide it has a preference for national employees, or national qualifications, inhibiting movement of workers, and also of students (recipients of educational services, perhaps), who will be put off studying abroad if they think employers at home will not appreciate them.

Two questions can be asked: can action be taken against such private actors directly, as if they were state bodies, based on the free movement articles? And can action be taken indirectly, by demanding that the state bring the private actors into line?

In the case of employment the answer is fairly clear. Article 39 prohibits all discrimination in this area, and Art 7 of Regulation 1612/68 says that any individual or collective contracts of employment that discriminate will be void. This seems worded to apply to contracts with private employers as much as public ones, and has been understood this way. Thus private actors are directly prohibited by the Treaty from nationality discrimination in employment.

However, in the cases of the other articles it is less obvious. Can measures or restrictions by private actors contravene Arts 28 or 43? Even further, does Art 12, the general prohibition on discrimination, bind private bodies?

A general answer does not seem to be available yet. There are an increasing number of situations where the law extends beyond purely public measures, but one cannot simply say that the free movement articles apply to private actors in just the same way as to states.

Here it is first asked whether private actors ought to be bound. Then some different possible situations are explored: bodies that are semi-public/semi-private; bodies that are private but have quasi-legislative powers; truly private bodies and individuals; and then indirect control of private actors, via the state.

12.1 SHOULD PRIVATE ACTORS BE BOUND?

It is important to consider what kind of individual actions might be caught if the free movement articles did apply to private actors. Would I be prohibited from choosing never to buy French cheese, or only banking with British banks? If so, the infringement of personal liberty is so high that it can be argued the Community lacks the legitimacy to impose this kind of rule; it is not democratically accountable enough to have earned the right to make such laws. Supposing I have a corner shop that decides to only stock national goods? We might feel that is also my choice.

On the other hand, if only major supermarket chains or big businesses would be prohibited from such discrimination, then that may be a different situation. Without such a prohibition, big business has the power to make a very big hole in the internal market, and significantly impede its development. Moreover, limiting companies is not as authoritarian as limiting people. We may feel that the liberty/democracy/market development trade-off is more acceptable here.

The existing law does not show us how to draw a clear line between these situations. At the moment the Court says there is no *de minimis* principle applying to discriminatory measures impeding free movement.[1] While this may be fine for governments, it is not good enough for private actors. Thus if free movement law is to apply in the private sphere there has to be development of the law.

A reason not to develop this way may be found in the structure of the Treaty. It is sometimes said that the rules on competition law regulate the action of private actors in the internal market, while the free movement articles regulate the state. One body of rules ensures that the state does not maintain obstructive laws, while the other ensures that within the level playing field created companies behave in a fair and acceptable way. Free movement creates the field, competition controls the players. Some of the examples cited above, such as the supermarket chain refusing to buy foreign goods, might already be caught by competition law (it might be an abuse of dominance, or there might be anti-competitive agreements with national producers). Therefore it might seem that extending internal market law would interfere with the rules on competition.

However, the line between them is not a clear one. First, competition law at the moment only applies to very significant actions – minor anti-competitive behaviour is ignored. Most private actions, even discriminatory ones, are outside its domain. Secondly, it is not true that competition law only applies to private actors; via the rules on state aids and public undertakings it also binds the member states.

Therefore, it does not seem radical to extend internal market law to private actors. The public/private distinction is already confused. This is also true in the broader non-legal context; with economic liberalisation and privatisation the boundary between public and private bodies is ever more blurred, and private actors are ever more dominant in the economy. Moreover, the basic ideas of the internal market, of wealth creation through unobstructed trade, do not contain any division between private or public obstacles.

The approach of the Court seems to be to extend the law to include private actors, but cautiously. Thus there seems to be a limited and step-by-step extension of the law. The following sections show how this has occurred and how far it has gone.

12.2 APPLYING FREE MOVEMENT LAW TO PRIVATE ACTORS

The cases in which attempts have been made to apply free movement law to private actors can be grouped into various categories. These are not watertight divisions, and

---

1   *van de Haar* Joined Cases 177 and 178/82.

some of the cases are relevant to more than one. They are just ways of highlighting the important issues.

12.2.1 Mixed public/private bodies

Sometimes the problem is just deciding whether a body is public or private. It may have some characteristics of each, and may attempt to evade the law by claiming that it is private and that the rules do not apply. In general, if it performs a public law function, or is created or controlled by the state, the Court will find that it is public. It is not impressed by technical legal arguments about the status of a body, but more by its broad nature and role. Does it smell of the state?

Thus the *Buy Irish*[2] case concerned the behaviour of the Irish Goods Council, which was encouraging people to buy Irish goods. This was clearly discriminatory behaviour, and undoubtedly contrary to Art 28 if it was a public body.

In Irish law it was a private company. However, the state gave 'moral and financial' support, and its marketing efforts were part of a broader campaign by the government to support Irish goods. The Court looked at the overall picture, and found that there was clearly a state campaign which infringed Art 28, and that:

> Regardless of the means used to implement it, the campaign is a reflection of the Irish government's considered intention to substitute domestic products for imported products on the Irish market and thereby to check the flow of imports from other member states.

In other words, because there was a government-sponsored campaign, even where 'private' means were used, such as the Goods Council, they were to be attributed to the government. The behaviour of the Council was against the Treaty.

This was a case brought by the Commission against Ireland, so strictly it cannot be concluded that a private action against the Goods Council itself would have succeeded, but the Court did not seem impressed by its 'private' status, so it may well be that it would.

In the *Apples and Pears*[3] case, the question was the extent to which the UK Apple and Pear Development Council was subject to Art 28. It was a growers' organisation, which existed for the benefit of growers and was financed by them. However, it had been set up by the government, which required growers to pay contributions to the Council. Thus it looked a bit private, a bit public. The Court said:

> In fact, a body such as the Development Council, which is set up by the government of a member state and is financed by a charge imposed on growers, cannot under Community law enjoy the same freedom as regards the methods of advertising used as that enjoyed by producers themselves or producers' associations of a voluntary character.

> In particular, such a body is under a duty not to engage in any advertising intended to discourage the purchase of products of other member states or to disparage those products in the eyes of consumers. Nor must it advise consumers to purchase domestic products solely by reason of their national origin.

---

2 *Buy Irish* Case 249/81.
3 *Apples and Pears* Case 222/82.

Therefore, the public law link gave the Council direct Treaty responsibility, and it was bound by Art 28.

In *Royal Pharmaceutical Society*,[4] the situation was more clear cut. This is a professional body governing pharmacy in the UK, not technically part of the state. However, it was created by statute and it has legally enforceable disciplinary powers. An appeal lies from its decisions directly to the Court of Appeal.

Therefore, it clearly performs public law functions, and can be seen as an outsourcing of pharmacy regulation. The Court found that its actions could be 'measures' according to Art 28.

12.2.2 Private rule-making bodies

Some bodies are unequivocally private, and have no connection with public law or the state, but they perform a function which, for certain groups of people, is almost legislative. They make rules which in reality control certain areas of economic life. Unions might come into this category, which may have a sort of limited legislative power within the workplace. Another example might be professional bodies such as Bar Councils, which regulate the activities of barristers. However, the situations which have come before the Court have mostly involved sport, in particular the regulatory bodies of football and of cycling, in *Bosman*[5] and *Walrave and Koch*.[6]

Walrave was brought by two Dutch pacemakers. These are people who ride motorbikes in front of professional racing cyclists, in order to reduce the wind resistance, and to provide them with a steady pace to follow. They normally worked with Spanish cycle riders, but the Union Cycliste Internationale, which sets the rules for international bicycling competitions, changed its rules so that both motorbike and pedal bike had to be ridden by people of the same nationality. Thus Mr Walrave and Mr Koch were out of a job, and complained.

The judgment of the Court is so clear that it is worth quoting extensively:

> The main question in respect of all the articles referred to is whether the rules of an international sporting federation can be regarded as incompatible with the Treaty.

> It has been alleged that the prohibitions in these articles refer only to restrictions which have their origin in acts of an authority and not to those resulting from legal acts of persons or associations who do not come under public law.

> Articles 7 [now 12], 48 [now 39], 59 [now 49] have in common the prohibition, in their respective spheres of application, of any discrimination on grounds of nationality.

> Prohibition of such discrimination does not only apply to the action of public authorities but extends likewise to rules of any other nature aimed at regulating in a collective manner gainful employment and the provision of services.

> The abolition as between member states of obstacles to freedom of movement for persons and to freedom to provide services, which are fundamental objectives of the Community

---

4   *Royal Pharmaceutical Society* Joined Cases 266 and 267/87.
5   *Bosman* Case C-415/93.
6   *Walrave and Koch* Case 36/74.

contained in Art 3(c) of the Treaty, would be compromised if the abolition of barriers of national origin could be neutralized by obstacles resulting from the exercise of their legal autonomy by associations or organizations which do not come under public law.

Since, moreover, working conditions in the various member states are governed sometimes by means of provisions laid down by law or Regulation and sometimes by agreements and other acts concluded or adopted by private persons, to limit the prohibitions in question to acts of a public authority would risk creating inequality in their application.

Although the third paragraph of Art 60 [now 50], and Arts 62 [now 52] and 64 [now 53], specifically relate, as regards the provision of services, to the abolition of measures by the state, this fact does not defeat the general nature of the terms of Art 59 [now 49], which makes no distinction between the source of the restrictions to be abolished.

It is established, moreover, that Art 48 [now 39], relating to the abolition of any discrimination based on nationality as regards gainful employment, extends likewise to agreements and rules which do not emanate from public authorities.

The Court says here that rules that regulate employment or the provision of services are caught by the Treaty whether they come from public or private bodies. It seems to say that not just Art 39 applies to private bodies, which was less controversial, but also Art 49, on services, and even Art 12. This is quite far-reaching. The Court justifies this by saying that if private bodies were excluded freedom of movement would not be realised. Moreover, there would be unevenness across the Community, since some states govern situations by public law where others use private.

This is a very purposive judgment, which upset many in the sporting community. They thought sport should be able to regulate itself, in as discriminatory a manner as it wished. Their distress was brought to a peak years later, by *Bosman*. As was discussed in Chapter 3, Mr Bosman challenged the football transfer rules, which were stopping him leaving his Belgian club to play for a French one. These rules were created by UEFA, the Union of European Football Associations, and enforced in Belgium by the Belgian Football Association. Both are private bodies. The Court repeated its arguments from *Walrave*, but the football associations raised a new objection. UEFA argued that applying the free movement articles to private bodies made the Treaty:

... more restrictive in relation to individuals than in relation to member states, which are alone in being able to rely on limitations justified on grounds of public policy, public security or public health.

This looks like a good point but, perhaps surprisingly, the Court replied that:

That argument is based on a false premise. There is nothing to preclude individuals from relying on justifications on grounds of public policy, public security or public health. Neither the scope nor the content of those grounds of justification is in any way affected by the public or private nature of the rules in question.

It is perhaps difficult to see a private organisation claiming that its actions are necessary in the interests of public security, but it seems that it is open to it to claim that public policy, that is, the general good, supports its behaviour. Perhaps UEFA could have said that the maintenance of the transfer rules, which it said were good for football, was also required by public policy, since football is so important to so many people? However it did not, and the justifications it did offer for them were rejected, and the transfer system dismantled.

Therefore, *Bosman* and *Walrave* establish that a body with power to set rules over an area of economic life will be subject to the free movement articles, and will also be able to benefit from their exceptions.

12.2.3 Ordinary private actors

Most private bodies and individuals are not quasi-legislative. They may be able to impose rules on their employees, or perhaps people they contract with, but they do not fall into the same regulatory category as the cases above. They are not part of the 'collective regulation' of employment or services referred to in *Walrave*. The most orthodox position is that stated in *Vlaamse Reisbureaus*.[7] The Court said, in an *obiter dictum*, that Arts 28 and 30 'concern only public measures, and not the conduct of undertakings'.

This restrictive approach could be peculiar to goods, but there is no obvious reason why that category should be different, and there is, in any case, reason to doubt whether *Vlaamse Reisbureaus* is correct. In *Dansk Supermarked*[8] the Court took an opposite approach.

The facts were quite complex, but essentially there was an agreement between a Danish buyer, the supermarket, and an English producer, not to export certain products to Denmark. A third actor bought the products in the UK and exported them to Denmark. The supermarket went to the Court to block this. Questions of competition law were involved, but the Court also looked at Art 28 and said:

> It must furthermore be remarked that it is impossible in any circumstances for agreements between individuals to derogate from the mandatory provisions of the Treaty on the free movement of goods.

Therefore the supermarket could not rely on its agreement in order to keep the goods out of Denmark, Art 28 prevented this.

The only way this can be correct is if Art 28 applied to the agreement, so that the agreement not to export was a 'measure having equivalent effect'. If the Court is saying the article is that broad, this is a very radical judgment. This kind of anti-competitive practice is normally dealt with by competition law; it seems that internal market law is competing. However, this case has not been followed, nor widely cited, and it can only be concluded that the position in goods is unclear.

The most recent developments have come in the area of people, in the case of *Angonese*.[9] Like *Bickel*,[10] the story takes place in that area of Italy where there are both German and Italian native speakers. It is usual there for young people to take a public examination, after which they get a certificate of bilingualism. Many employers require this before they will employ people.

---

7   *Vlaamse Reisbureaus* Case 311/85.
8   *Dansk Supermarked* Case 58/80.
9   *Angonese* Case 281/98.
10 *Bickel* Case C-274/96.

Mr Angonese was from this area, a native Italian speaker, but he had been to study in Austria, and as a result he had never taken the examination. It was not disputed that he was actually bilingual, but a local private bank refused to consider him for employment because he did not have the certificate. He claimed this was contrary to Art 39.

Before it considered whether the rule was potentially discriminatory, the Court considered whether Art 39 applied to private actors in this kind of situation. On the particular facts of the case, the Regulation 1612/68 prohibition of discriminatory employment agreements was not relevant. It was just a pure question of whether Art 39 in general applied in the private sphere. First:

> It should be noted at the outset that the principle of non-discrimination set out in Art 48 [now 39] is drafted in general terms and is not specifically addressed to the member states.

And even if it was:

> The Court has also ruled that the fact that certain provisions of the Treaty are formally addressed to the member states does not prevent rights from being conferred at the same time on any individual who has an interest in compliance with the obligations thus laid down.

And:

> Such considerations must, *a fortiori*, be applicable to Art 48 [now 39] of the Treaty, which lays down a fundamental freedom and which constitutes a specific application of the general prohibition of discrimination contained in Art 6 of the EC Treaty [now, after amendment, Art 12 EC]. In that respect, like Art 119 [now 141] of the EC Treaty it is designed to ensure that there is no discrimination on the labour market.

> Consequently, the prohibition of discrimination on grounds of nationality laid down in Art 48 [now 39] of the Treaty must be regarded as applying to private persons as well.

In summary, since the article is worded generally, and its aim is to prevent discrimination on the labour market, it applies to private actors. This is particularly so because Art 39 is one of the fundamental freedoms, and part of the general prohibition on discrimination in Art 12.

The question is whether this can be applied to the other articles. If it is possible to say that the aim of Art 28 is to prevent discrimination against imports on the goods market, and that Arts 43 and 49 aim to prevent discrimination in the provision of services, then it seems that the Court's reasoning should translate, and it would be arguable from *Angonese* that all the economic articles apply fully to private actors.

However, employment is special. It seems more wrong for an employer to reject a job candidate for reasons of nationality than it does for a shop to buy national goods, or a company to contract for national cleaning services. The link between buyer and seller, or contractor and service provider, is more distant than that between employer and employee, and in general the actors are less important to each other. Thus the moral obligation not to discriminate seems weaker. This is one of the reasons why Art 39 has always been more readily applied to private actors than the other articles, and why Art 43 has been the next most readily used (for example, *Walrave*). The line between an employee and a contracted service provider is sometimes more legal than real.

The other reason why Art 39 is ahead in this respect is that the free movement of persons, especially of workers, is particularly important from a political, as well as an economic perspective. It binds Europe. As well as this, the dangers of discrimination are much greater in employment than in goods. People are more likely to reject a good foreign job candidate for nationalistic reasons than they are to turn away a well-made good-value foreign product in favour of an inferior national one. The balance of self-interest and nationalism is different.

Therefore, despite the Court's general reasoning, it is probably hasty to conclude too much from *Angonese*. Rather, it remains the position that for goods, services and established people the application of the Treaty to private actors is unclear.

12.2.4 Indirect control of private actors

Whether or not a private body or person can itself be held accountable to the Treaty, in some situations the state can be held responsible for them. If private actors impede free movement, sometimes that state will be in violation of the Treaty article if it does not remove the obstacle to movement that the private actor has created.

The famous example of this is the *French Farmers* case, *Commission v France*.[11] This case was a result of the persistent attacks on imports and importers by angry French farmers over a period of around ten years. They felt that imports of cheaper agricultural products, including strawberries, tomatoes, and lamb, particularly from Spain and the UK, were 'unfair' and were ruining their livelihood. As a result, they blocked ports and roads entering France, attacked foreign lorries and burned their contents, and completely stopped trade in these products between France and other member states.

Whether or not one thinks the farmers had a point, it is difficult to imagine a more direct and deliberate attack on the internal market and a more conscious rejection of its basic principles, or a more vivid realisation of the idea of an 'obstacle to free movement'. There was no doubt that importing to France was, in the words of the Court in *Gebhard*,[12] hindered and made less attractive.

Such public demonstration has been a traditional way of dealing with dispute in France since the revolution. Most strikes or industrial disputes are accompanied by marches and road blockages. The public tend to have sympathy with the demonstrators, and in order not to inflame feelings further and lead to riots or worse the authorities tend to also give them a great deal of leeway. Thus during the agricultural demonstrations it was common to see on the television pictures of groups of heavily armed and protected police watching passively while farmers stopped a foreign truck, invited the driver to leave it, turned it over and set fire to it.

Unsurprisingly, carriers, importers, foreign producers, and other member state governments were incensed. They regarded France as little more than a lawless bandit state, in which the government and the delinquent and criminal farmers were in league against foreigners, free trade, honesty and the rule of law.

---

11 *Commission v France* Case C-265/95.
12 *Gebhard* Case C-55/94.

It was difficult to take action directly against the farmers, because although what they were doing was criminal damage under any legal system, it was hard to get hold of someone worth suing. The individuals turning the lorries over did not have the money, and could not be brought to justice without the assistance of the police, which was not forthcoming. The farmers' leaders and organisations probably also did not have enough money to be worth suing, and anyway could not be held directly responsible.

Thus attention turned to the French State. Finally, after years of pressure, the Commission brought an action against it for violation of Art 28. It claimed that although private actors were creating the obstacles to trade, the state had a positive obligation under that article to take action to remove the obstacles. This has been a common approach in human rights law for years. The European Court of Human Rights regularly finds member states liable for failing to protect individuals from the actions of others. However, it was a first in internal market law.

The French government said that it was very difficult to do anything, because the farmers roamed in small bands that were difficult to find in time, but it was doing everything it could. This was rather undermined by a statement from the French Agriculture minister, reported in the judgment, that:

> ... although he disapproved of and condemned the violence by the farmers, he in no way contemplated any intervention by the police in order to put a stop to it.

The government made a number of other rather weak points, saying that it could not insist that the police arrested people because they had to have discretion, and the real problem was the devaluation of the peseta.

The Court, although polite, was clearly contemptuous of the French approach. In an enjoyable and clear judgment it rejected all the excuses offered, and found the French government had been clearly inadequate and in violation of the Treaty. However, the important legal point was that this was irrespective of the private origin of the obstructions. The Court said:

> The fact that a member state abstains from taking action or, as the case may be, fails to adopt adequate measures to prevent obstacles to the free movement of goods that are created, in particular, by actions by private individuals on its territory aimed at products originating in other member states is just as likely to obstruct intra-Community trade as is a positive act.

> Article 30 [now 28] therefore requires the member states not merely themselves to abstain from adopting measures or engaging in conduct liable to constitute an obstacle to trade but also, when read with Art 5 [now 10] of the Treaty, to take all necessary and appropriate measures to ensure that that fundamental freedom is respected on their territory.

The Court went on to say that it could not tell a member state *how* it must remove the obstacles, or *what* action it must take, but it could assess whether that action had been adequate. Here it had not.

An aspect that must be noted is the use of Art 10. This is the article that provides:

> Member states shall take all appropriate measures, whether general or particular, to ensure fulfillment of the obligations arising out of this Treaty or resulting from action taken by the institutions of the Community. They shall facilitate the achievement of the Community's tasks. They shall abstain from any measure which could jeopardise the attainment of the objectives of the Community.

It is tempting to see this as a rather vague goodwill article that does not have much practical importance. *Commission v France* (and in fact many other cases in other areas of the law) shows that it has sharp teeth.

Therefore, it is also possible for an individual to take action against a member state in the national courts for failure to remove an obstacle to free movement created by another individual, and if the member state is found in violation of the Treaty, then the Community law principles of damages should apply. A member state could be held liable to pay for not protecting free movement from private obstructors.

Although the judgment concerned goods, the principles used seem general, suggesting that it could also apply to the other freedoms. Alternatively, this judgment could be seen as compensating for a lack of direct applicability of Art 28 to private actors. Then to use such an indirect approach in the area of workers, when post-*Angonese* it seems that a direct one is possible, might even be seen as abusive. It is suggested though, that the clear preference of the Court that private behaviour be constrained by Art 39 would also allow such indirect use, if it was necessary.

CHAPTER 13

INTELLECTUAL PROPERTY

The subject of this chapter is not the substantive law of intellectual property – what is a trademark, what is copyright, and so on – but the role of intellectual property as a possible obstacle to free movement, in particular of goods. In principle, the normal rules apply, and knowledge of Arts 28 and 30 remains the starting point. However, this is not enough. Intellectual property raises unique issues, and it is necessary to look at its particular nature and use in order to understand how the free movement rules apply.

13.1 WHAT IS INTELLECTUAL PROPERTY?

Intellectual property is non-physical property. This might be ideas, scientific processes, brands, trademarks, music, designs, computer programs, or the text of books, for example. These are all things of value, but they lack physical presence.

They should not be confused with their physical representations. A book can be physical, just as a trademark or brand logo can be printed on a physical packet, or a song or a computer program recorded on paper or CD. However, the book, the packet, and the CD are not the same thing as the text, the brand, the song or the program itself.

Intellectual property rights are rights to control these abstract things, comparable to ownership of normal goods. Typical IP rights are patents, copyright, and trademark rights. These give their owners the rights to control how the patented invention, or the copyrighted artistic creation, or the trademark, is used.

Therefore it is often said that IP rights confer a monopoly on their owner. Only she is allowed to use the intellectual property that the rights refer to. Other people may only use it with her permission, and if they break this rule, by selling pirated CDs or copied books, for example, she can ask a court to uphold her IP rights and stop them.

The creator of the property usually acquires the IP rights first. The author or inventor will therefore have the copyright or the patent. Some kinds of rights require registration or some other official process, such as a patent, which is only awarded after an application to a patent office.

Once the rights exist they can then be bought and sold, in part and in whole. A right to make a few copies of a product may be sold, or a right to make copies only within a certain country, or just in a particular format.

13.2 IP RIGHTS IN EUROPE

For historical reasons, IP rights are organised nationally. Intellectual property that is protected in one country, by a patent or design right, is not protected in others by that same patent or design right. An inventor has to acquire national patents for every country where he wishes to exercise his rights. These will not just be the countries where he wants to make or sell his product, but also those where he wishes to stop others making or selling his product.

It would seem an obvious step to have Europe-wide IP rights, and there are moves in this direction. It is possible to register trademarks and designs for the entire EU,[1] and it will, within the next few years, almost certainly be possible to register an EU patent. At the moment there is a European patent office, in Munich, to which a single application can be made for the whole Union, but the rights granted are not a single patent, but a bundle of national ones, each of which will have to be exercised according to the relevant national law.

However, for reasons which will become apparent in the next section, these European rights do not replace existing national IP rights, invalidating existing national trademarks or patents, but set up a parallel system alongside them, for new registrations. Holders of national rights, such as national trademarks, can prevent a Community right being created where this would be too similar to their own.

There is not yet a single Community copyright, but there are a number of directives partially harmonising national copyright laws, including Directive 93/98, which has standardised the length of copyright protection in the member states at 70 years. This is considered relatively long; previously many states had shorter periods.

13.3 IP RIGHTS AND FREE MOVEMENT

These national rights create problems for free movement. The most common situation is where the owner of an IP right in one country attempts to use that right to stop imports from another one. He says 'you may own the trademark in France, but I own it in the UK, so you may not sell these trademarked goods in the UK without my permission, which I refuse, because I want to sell them myself'.

Another situation is where the owner of the IP rights attempts to stop the supply of services, such as film or music broadcasts. Using a copyright, he may attempt to have a website, or TV channel, or radio broadcast blocked from the national territory. Only he has the right to use the copyrighted property in that country.

These actions might seem obviously illegal, contrary to Arts 28 and 49. Even if we are unhappy about applying those articles to private parties, the rights owners, we could say that the granting and protection of those nationalistic rights by the state is contrary to the Treaty, as is the refusal to recognise foreign rights. It should also be noted that this sort of behaviour will raise issues of competition law, and although that is not discussed here, most intellectual property issues are primarily decided using competition rules.

However, returning to free movement, there is in fact a complication. The Treaty allows these national rights. Article 295 says:

This Treaty shall in no way prejudice the rules in member states governing the system of property ownership.

---

1   Directive 89/104, Regulation 40/94 on trademarks, Regulation 6/2002 on a Community design.

Article 30 provides that Art 28 shall not preclude prohibitions or restrictions on imports justified on grounds of 'the protection of industrial and commercial property'. This phrase includes intellectual property, some examples of which are sometimes called industrial property. Therefore, neither the Court nor the Community institutions can do anything 'prejudicing' the national rules on IP rights, which are within the concept of 'property ownership'. Also, the member states can deny free movement of goods to protect IP rights.

Overall, it seems then that IP rights trump everything else. At first glance, free movement has a big hole in it. If we consider how many goods have some attached IP rights: a brand, a trademark, a patented component, a copyrighted content, it becomes clear how big this hole could be. None of these goods could be imported without permission from the national rights owner. In practice, markets would be entirely divided, and goods would remain national. This might make nice profits for the national rights holders, but it would deprive consumers of most of the benefits of the single market.

This would clearly be devastating for European integration, and we must ask why the Treaty includes these rules. One reason is no doubt because of member state sensitivities. They were open to the idea of free trade, but did not wish to threaten their property laws, which vary from state to state, and may have historical and cultural significance. Another reason may be practical. Many IP rights are owned by different people in different countries. The person who owns the trademark 'ABC' in Germany may not be the same person who owns it in Italy. There may be two businesses, one in each country, never coming into contact, that happen to use the same mark. If a European-wide right was created in place of the national ones, some kind of choice would have to be made: who would get the European right? This would clearly be an impossible task.

Hence the inability to simply replace national IP rights with Community ones, and their parallel existence.

13.4 EXISTENCE AND EXERCISE OF RIGHTS

Faced with the situation explained above, the Court has taken a purposive approach. Its purpose is to create a single undivided market, and to do that it is prepared to undermine individual Treaty articles. It has invented the idea that there is a difference between the existence and exercise of a right. The existence of an IP right means its possession by someone – the ownership of the patent, or the copyright, for example. Its exercise is the use of that right in a particular way – to demand royalties, or stop imports, for example.

The Court says that the existence of the national IP right is sacred. That is what Art 295 does. There is no Community jurisdiction to challenge or interfere with it. However, the Community can require that that right be exercised according to Community law, for example, in compliance with the free movement or competition provisions.

This is an empty distinction. To have an IP right means that one can control the use of that IP. If one has that right but cannot use it, it is no longer a meaningful right. To put it another way, the exercise of a right is part of its existence. The right is no more than a bundle of things one can do. If some of those things are taken away, of course the right itself is diminished. The real distinction that the Court is making is between certain core rights within the IP right, the most important things it enables one to do, and other things that it regards as less central. It simply cannot say this openly, because it would be admitting that it is defying Art 295.

In any case, the Court's distinction has been practically helpful. It means that although IP rights remain national, the way they are used is within Community law. The Court has then applied this principle to create a balance. On the one hand lies the protection of intellectual property and associated rights. On the other lie the demands of free movement and competition. In the free movement context, this means that sometimes an IP right can be used to prevent movement, but at other times it cannot. It is explained below when each situation applies.

13.5 USING IP RIGHTS

The major problem with IP rights arises from their use to divide member state markets from each other, as explained above. The holder of the rights in each country wants to keep the national market for himself. This is called territorial protection. The question can then become, when does the Court allow such protection?

The answer is when that particular use of the right is part of its 'essential subject-matter'. This will vary according to the type of right, but two well known cases make the general principle clear. In *Centrafarm v Sterling*,[2] Sterling Drug sold a medicine in the UK and the Netherlands at different prices. In the UK it was cheap, partly because of the bargaining power of the National Health Service, while in the Netherlands it was very expensive (this kind of differential pricing occurs a great deal with many goods types, and some of the reasons for it are discussed in the Note on Economics at the end of this chapter). Centrafarm bought the drug in the UK, and tried to import it to the Netherlands to undercut Sterling there. Sterling tried to use its patents in the drug to stop Centrafarm.

Dutch law said it could, and Sterling said that this law did not conflict with Art 28, because it came within the Art 30 exception for intellectual property. However, the second sentence of Art 30 says that these exceptions shall not be an excuse for disguised restrictions on trade or arbitrary discrimination. The Court considered this and said:

> Nevertheless, it is clear from this same article, in particular its second sentence, as well as from the context, that whilst the Treaty does not affect the existence of rights recognized by the legislation of a member state in matters of industrial and commercial property, yet the exercise of these rights may nevertheless, depending on the circumstances, be affected by the prohibitions in the Treaty.

This is a statement of the existence/exercise distinction, justified with reference to Art 30. The Court is saying that since Art 30 prohibits exceptions, including intellectual property exceptions, being used in discriminatory and arbitrary ways, that supports the view that using these rights is to some extent subject to the Treaty. It therefore went on to consider the particular situation. It said:

---

2   *Centrafarm v Sterling* Case 15/74.

In relation to patents, the specific subject matter of the industrial property is the guarantee that the patentee, to reward the creative effort of the inventor, has the exclusive right to use an invention with a view to manufacturing industrial products and putting them into circulation for the first time, either directly or by the grant of licences to third parties, as well as the right to oppose infringements.

Therefore the essential core of a patent, the specific subject matter, the thing that gave it existence, was the right to put the invention on the market for the first time, to stop other people making and selling your good. Therefore this right could not be interfered with. If Centrafarm had made the drugs itself, and tried to sell them in the Netherlands, Sterling could certainly stop it.

However, the implication here is that once you have sold your goods, stopping people buying those goods on the open market and reselling them is not part of the essence of a patent. Therefore, if you tried to use your patent rights in this way, and that created an obstacle to free movement, this would be an exercise of the right, which Community law could restrain.

It would restrain it, unless it could be justified so that it came within Art 30. In this case it could not, because:

In fact, if a patentee could prevent the import of protected products marketed by him or with his consent in another member state, he would be able to partition off national markets and thereby restrict trade between member states, in a situation where no such restriction was necessary to guarantee the essence of the exclusive rights flowing from the parallel patents.

In *Centrafarm v Winthrop*[3] an identical situation arose, but this time it was the trademark on the package that was used to try and keep the drugs out of the Netherlands. The Court took the same approach. It said that the essence of a trademark was the right to put trademarked goods on the market for the first time. Once they were sold, the right to stop resale was not part of the essence, and so could be restrained, and would be, because it was a major division of the internal market, which was not necessary to protect the essential right.

The important thing to know is, therefore, what is the 'essence' or 'specific subject matter' of an IP right? How can this be identified?

13.6 EXHAUSTION OF RIGHTS

The answer lies in the doctrine of exhaustion. When an IP right is exhausted, this means it is used up in Community law eyes, and a line is drawn around its essence. Any further attempts to use it, even though they may be permissible under national law, are just exercises of the right which are non-essential, and so in principle subject to Community law. If they result in market partitioning, or obstacles to free movement, they will not be allowed.

In general, an IP right is exhausted when the patented or copyrighted or trademarked product is put on the market in the EU for the first time. This first putting on the market is

---

3   *Centrafarm v Winthrop* Case 16/74.

the essential subject matter of the IP right. Thus, once Sterling had sold its drug in the UK it had exhausted its rights over those drugs. Other people could then buy them, and resell them, anywhere in the EU, and Sterling could not stop them.

This does not mean Sterling's patent is now useless; only the rights over the drugs it has already sold are exhausted. However, it still has the exclusive right to make new drugs and sell them for the first time, and to stop anyone else doing this.

The key to this is the idea of consent. Sterling consented to the drugs being sold. Therefore it has nothing more to say about what people do with them. This consent could be because it sold the drugs itself, or because they were sold by someone with its permission – a licensee. However, it made the choice to put them on the market, and thereby exhausted its rights over them. It can no longer restrain what people may do with them.

A number of notes now need to be made on this basic principle.

13.6.1 Consent

First, an absence of consent to the first marketing means there is no exhaustion. If Centrafarm had obtained stolen goods, for example, then, quite aside from the criminal law implications, Sterling would have been able to stop them selling.

A more likely scenario is the compulsory licence. Sometimes patent holders do not sell their drug in a particular country because they cannot get a high enough price, and they do not want to risk selling cheap in case those products are exported and undermine their high price markets. At other times they may sell, but at a price that the government finds too high. Alternatively, there may be strategic reasons why a government wants a drug produced nationally, but the patent holder prefers to import it.

In any of these cases the government, if its national law allows, may grant a compulsory licence to another manufacturer. This manufacturer then pays a fee to the patent holder, and produces and sells the drug. The government is happy because it gets the drug produced nationally at a reasonable price, but the patent holder is not because the fee is never as high as it thinks it deserves. If it has chosen not to supply that country at the price desired, there were certainly economic reasons for that. However, as the word 'compulsory' indicates, it does not get a choice in the matter. It can take or refuse the fee, but the drug will be made by someone else.

In *Pharmon v Hoechst*,[4] the UK government granted a compulsory licence to a company called DDSA, to produce a medicine for which Hoechst had the patent. The terms of the licence said that DDSA could not export these drugs – they were intended for the National Health Service. However, it did export them to Pharmon in the Netherlands, who then tried to sell them. In this case Hoechst was able to stop the sale, because there had been no exhaustion of rights because it had not consented to the first manufacture and sale – because the licence was a compulsory one.

Secondly, this emphasis on consent can put a company in a difficult position. Some countries do not allow medicines to be patented, believing this control of the sale of such goods to be wrong. Italy is one such. This means that in Italy anyone can produce a drug,

---

4   *Pharmon v Hoechst* Case 19/84.

and the creator of that drug cannot take out a patent to get himself exclusive rights. This tends to bring the price of the drugs down, and reduce the profits to be made from drugs sales in Italy – the point of the law, of course.

Merck had a patent for a drug in the Netherlands, but also sold in Italy, in competition with other sellers. However, the price was lower there, and when Stephar bought the drug in Italy, and tried to import it to the Netherlands, to undercut Merck in this very high price market, Merck tried to use its patent to stop this.[5] However, the Court said that because the drug had been sold in Italy by Merck, thus with its consent, its rights were exhausted, and it could not stop the import. This means that if Merck sells in Italy it risks bringing the price, and so its profits, down all over Europe. On the other hand, if it does not, it loses a large market to other manufacturers.

We may not wish to waste tears on drug companies, but it is worth noting that the function of a patent is to enable the holder to control sale of that product, and so get a particularly high price, and a high profit. This is called a monopoly profit. This can be seen as a reward for the costs that went into research and development, or a recoupment of them. Copycat manufacturers, such as in Italy, do not have to pay these research costs, and so they only have to recoup their manufacturing costs. If Merck is to compete with them it has to also sell at this price, and so it is essentially writing off its research costs. In other words, it makes a real loss on its Italian sales. If these threaten to undermine monopoly profit in other countries, through the activities of companies like Stephar – so called parallel importers – then it will recoup less and less of its research costs. If this goes too far it threatens the economics of drug development, and Merck will decide not to invest in research. This is good for nobody. Therefore an argument can be made that the decision in *Merck v Stephar* was an undermining of the essence of the patent, and wrong.

13.6.2 Changed products

Even where the goods were sold with consent, if they have been changed in some way the rights holder may be able to once again exert his rights against them. In *Hoffman-La Roche*[6] drugs were sold in packs of different quantities according to the country they were sold in, and whether they were for individuals or hospitals. Centrafarm (again!) bought big packs in the UK, at low prices, and planned to repackage them for the German market, but still under their original trademark. Hoffman tried to use its trademark rights to stop this.

The Court said that whether they could do this depended on the circumstances of each case. If it was clear that the repackaging could not affect the condition of the drugs, then the parallel imports could not be stopped. However, if the repackaging created the possibility that the drugs might be affected or interfered with, then the imports could be stopped. The trademark owner had the rights to protect its brand.

The Court gave some examples which indicate the general principles here. If little packages were just wrapped together, or if external wrapping – the big box – was removed but inner wrapping – a smaller sealed box or bag, say – remained, there was no

---

5   *Merck v Stephar* Case 187/80.
6   *Hoffman-La Roche* Case 102/77.

interference. However, if the drugs had been entirely removed from their packages and put into new ones, then even if tests showed them to be good, the parallel importer would not have the right to reattach the trademark and import them under it.

Sometimes there is no question about the integrity of the goods, but the repackaging may be seen as undermining the brand. Sometimes importers put pharmaceuticals into whole new boxes, or attach stickers covering up information on the original box. They usually do this for one of two reasons. It may be that national law in the destination state requires information in a certain form, or in the national language, to be visible on drug packages. If the original packaging does not comply with this, stickers or repackaging may be necessary to import. Alternatively, consumers may have a strong resistance to stickers covering the original label; they may not like having the original information covered up, or feeling they are reading safety advice not supplied by the original manufacturer. To overcome this consumer resistance, importers may prefer to entirely replace the outer package, re-affixing the trademark, but with new instructions and information conforming to national laws and tastes.

The original manufacturer then objects, partly to prevent the parallel imports of course, but also because he feels that his trademark rights are being interfered with, and the goods are not being presented in the way he chose. This may affect public perception of them, and so his, and his goods', reputation.

The Court's approach to this is to concede that the manufacturer has the primary right to determine packaging, and can use his IP rights to keep the goods out, unless the repackaging is objectively necessary to gain 'effective access' to the national market. This could be because of national law, or because consumer resistance to goods not presented in their language, or to stickered goods, is so strong that market access is effectively blocked without the repackaging.[7]

13.6.3 Different trademarks in different countries

Sometimes patent holders attempt to stop parallel importing by selling goods under different trademarks in each country. If the good is sold by the patent holder as 'X' in Portugal, then it may be imported to Spain by third parties. However, if in Spain the brand name is 'Y' no one will want to buy it. Therefore the market stays divided. Centrafarm, the Robin Hood of the drugs world, tried to get round this by repackaging drugs sold in the UK under the Dutch mark. They said that the goods had been sold with consent in the UK, so rights were exhausted, and American Home Products, the mark owner, could not stop them.[8]

However, the Court found this a quite different situation from mere importing. Centrafarm was actually attaching the Dutch trademark to these drugs for the first time. That was a right reserved to the trademark holder. It was part of the specific subject matter of the IP right.

The Court did add though, that where different trade marks were being used in different countries merely to divide the market, and not, for example, to appeal to

---

7   *Merck Sharp and Dohme v Paranova* Case C-443/99.
8   *American Home Products* Case 3/78.

different tastes or languages, this would be contrary to Art 28 and would not escape under Art 30, because it would be a disguised restriction on trade.

13.6.4 Imports from outside the EEA

Exhaustion only applies to sale within the European Economic Area (the EU plus a few other European countries). In *Silhouette*[9] the Court decided that it was acceptable to use IP rights to keep goods out of the EU, even if they had been sold in other countries with the consent of the rights holder. Thus a parallel importer cannot buy sunglasses cheap in Eastern Europe or Asia, where they have been sold by the brand owner at a low price, and then import them into the more expensive EU.

13.6.5 Copies or fakes

Obviously, if goods first put onto the market use IP in a way coming within the associated rights, but do not originate from the owner, or someone acting with his permission, then it will be possible to restrain sale. Such actions attack the essence of the rights. Examples would be products made according to a patent, or bearing a trademark and being a type of goods for which that trademark is registered.

It should be noted that it is not always as obvious as it might seem what exactly the scope of an IP right is, and so when it is infringed. For example, registering a trademark does not mean that no one can ever use that symbol without permission; the right is more narrowly and precisely defined than that. Details can be found in specialist books.

13.7 COPYRIGHT

A note should also be made on copyright. This is a little more complex than some rights, because often there is no tangible product to deal with, for example, rights over broadcasting of songs or images. Then it might seem that once a thing has been broadcast that would exhaust the rights, and it could be recorded and re-sold by someone else. The singing, or transmitting, or broadcasting, would be the first consensual putting on the market that exhausts the right.

However, this point of view would be wrong, which is just as well for copyright holders, since it would reduce their rights to almost nothing. In fact each new broadcast or use of the IP is treated as a new 'manufacture'. Therefore, if a song is recorded and re-broadcast, or burned onto a CD which is sold, these are each a new 'making and selling' of the song. The re-broadcast is analogous to an unlicensed company making a patented product. The essence of the IP right is infringed, and the violation may be stopped. This was summed up by the Court in *Coditel v Ciné Vog*,[10] which concerned broadcasting of a film without consent. It said:

---

9   *Silhouette* Case C-355/96.
10   *Coditel v Ciné Vog* Case 62/79.

> The right of a copyright owner ... to require fees for any showing of a film is part of the essential function of copyright in this type of literary and artistic work.

The same principle applies to music and static images. By contrast, if the film is released on video cassette, or the music on CD, then rights over the sale of those are exhausted. They are concrete products, like patented drugs, which may be bought and sold and exported. However, if someone began making copies of them, and marketing those, this would be a first manufacture and sale, and once again infringe rights.

Copyright is likely to become ever more important with the growth of the internet. E-services across frontiers will raise many copyright issues. This may raise some difficulties, since the services provisions do not contain an exception for intellectual property analogous to that in Art 30. Exceptions to the services provisions are confined to public policy, security and health. However, we can be fairly sure that the Court will somehow apply an analogous approach to goods, and will preserve the core of the copyright. Article 295 alone can justify this.

13.8 NOTE ON ECONOMICS

Some of the cases above become easier to understand if one knows how companies owning IP rights behave, and why. The key point is that they will attempt to get the highest price that the market can bear. Since the first time they put the product on the market they have no direct competition, there is no competitive downward pressure on price. The only question is how much the customers can afford, and how much they are prepared to pay. This will vary from country to country. Consumers in Europe and the US may be able to pay high prices for medicines and designer clothes, and may be prepared to do so. In other parts of the world people may only be able, or prepared, to pay less. However, even at the lower prices the company may be making a profit. Therefore it sells its goods at different prices all over the world. The risk is then that parallel importers undermine this, by buying cheap jeans or antibiotics or televisions in the lower-price markets, and selling them in the higher-price ones.

This is what producers want to stop, and what they use their IP rights for. They try to prevent the movement of goods between differently priced markets. Even within Europe this occurs. There are significant differences in wealth, and also in customer preference and market structure, so that goods may be sellable at a much higher price in Sweden than Greece.

The parallel importers are often seen as the heroes, and the producers as the greedy profiteers in this scenario. The profit maximising that they do is seen as somehow dishonest – why should I pay more than someone in another country? – and the parallel importers, who may be well known companies, perhaps major supermarkets, try to stop this unfairness and help the consumer.

However, there is another way of looking at it. Parallel importing will tend to lead to an equalisation of price, and this will occur at a price somewhere between the lowest and highest. This may be great for Northern Europeans, who will find that their products have come down in price, and who will feel that they are no longer being ripped off.

However, the poorer Southern Europeans will find that they are no longer able to afford as much of the good as they used to, or it will hurt them a lot more to pay for it.

Thus equalisation of price leads to the rich consuming more and the poor less, and represents a net transfer of wealth from poor to rich. By contrast, having different prices for different markets almost follows the Marxist principle of 'from each according to his abilities, to each according to his need'. Rather, it is here 'from each according to his means'. In any case, prices are adjusted according to wealth, arguably a very socially progressive policy. The rich are perhaps robbed, but to feed the poor. Centrafarm is no longer the Robin Hood, but rather Sterling is.

Whatever one's view on this, for the Court the issue of preserving the single market is more important. Division into nations is anathema to that, and the social aspects of pricing are not considerations that appear from the judgments to be relevant.

CHAPTER 14

SOCIAL ISSUES OF INTERNAL MARKET LAW

Although the internal market is built around economic law, it goes further than that. Opening markets to each other has meant opening countries, and so it has had effects on the way people live in Europe. The most obvious and positive effect may be increased prosperity; just what it was designed to achieve. However, there are also other issues that have been raised.

These are many and varied, from the occasional surges of far-right sentiment that may be connected with increasing movement of people, through to the changing nature of the workplace under the influence of European regulation that is partly aimed at ensuring free movement of workers, or from the effect on the consumer of deregulation of telecoms and utilities through to the increasing awareness of shared environmental and food safety issues that are also bound up with free movement of goods. It is outside the scope of this book to go too deeply into these social issues, but it is worthwhile to look at some, to give us an idea of the kind of society that Europe is becoming, and the role in that played by free movement. Three topics have been selected that have a strong and direct link with the law already discussed in previous chapters. Some of the consequences and implications of that law can then be seen.

First, human rights in the internal market are considered. Community law allows people to move from country to country, but does it help to ensure that their human rights are respected everywhere? The migrant can sometimes be very vulnerable, not familiar with the legal system and society he finds himself in. He may encounter xenophobia or racism or other forms of prejudice. Does freedom to move require that he be protected against this? This issue is particularly important in the light of enlargement.

The second issue explored is the position of third country nationals in the internal market. These may be family members of EU citizens, or immigrants, or asylum seekers. Can they benefit from freedom of movement, and do they acquire any rights to it? What role does the former Schengen Agreement play here? What is the future for non-EU citizens in Europe?

Thirdly, the effect of the internal market on the welfare state is examined. All over Europe there is now some kind of state provision of the basic health and educational needs of citizens. Traditionally this is organised nationally, and run by huge state organisations. How is this being changed by the requirements of free movement of services, and the liberalisation this involves? Does it threaten an American-style commercialisation of these things, or is there another way forward?

14.1 HUMAN RIGHTS IN THE INTERNAL MARKET

A question which has recurred throughout the history of the Union, most notably with the creation of the recent Charter of Fundamental Rights, is how much protection it gives to its citizens' human rights. Of particular interest here is whether Community law protects the human rights of migrant workers, self-employed people, or citizens. There are a number of reasons why one might think that it ought to, but the legal position remains unclear. Below, the arguments for and against such protection are explored, and then the relevant cases, in order to try and establish the current law. The discussion begins with a presentation of *Konstantinidis*,[1] a famous case in which the issue was first framed.

14.1.1 *Konstantinidis*

Mr Konstantinidis was of Greek nationality and lived and worked, as a self-employed masseur, in Germany. German officialdom required that his name be translated from the Cyrillic script used in Greece into the Roman script used in other member states. There was such a translation in his passport, but Germany was a party to a Convention on Translation, and that required a different method to be used. His name came out as Hrestos Konstantinides, rather than the 'Christos Konstantinidis' that he considered to be the correct spelling.

He claimed that the refusal to use what he – and his passport – considered to be his correct name was contrary to Community law. It risked confusion over identity, which could make it harder for him to do business, and so be an obstacle to establishment. Also, it was a violation of his fundamental rights: his 'right to a name'. He found the German version objectionable on both personal and religious grounds: it wasn't him, and the misspelling of 'Christos' offended his faith.

The Court decided the case entirely on the economic ground, finding that such a misspelling risked confusion, which could be an obstacle to movement. It did not address the issue of rights at all. It was able to avoid them because of the way the referring national court phrased its questions.

However, the Advocate General, in his opinion, did ask whether a violation of rights could be seen as an obstacle to movement. He found that where acts were likely to obstruct movement they came within Community law. Therefore they must comply with fundamental rights. He said:

> In my opinion, a Community national who goes to another member state as a worker or self-employed person under Arts 48 [now 39], 52 [now 43] or 59 [now 49] of the Treaty is entitled not just to pursue his trade or profession and to enjoy the same living and working conditions as nationals of the host state he is in addition entitled to assume that, wherever he goes to earn his living in the European Community, he will be treated in accordance with a common code of fundamental values, in particular those laid down in the European Convention on Human Rights. In other words, he is entitled to say *'civis europeus sum'* and to invoke that status in order to oppose any violation of his fundamental rights.

The Advocate General therefore said that migrants have Community rights against their host states. Since the Court did not address this point, it remains to ask if he was right; should such rights exist, and do they?

---

1   *Konstantinidis* Case C-168/91.

14.1.2 Why should there be migrants' rights?

Every member state of the EU provides some kind of protection of basic human rights in its domestic legal system. However, the methods of doing this vary widely.

The most common is the statement of basic rights in the constitution. Most EU member states have something like this. This does not mean that these rights can all be used in court to challenge offending acts or national laws though; that is quite another question, and something that also varies. In the Netherlands laws cannot be challenged on constitutional grounds, and the argument given for this is that laws are democratically made, and the Parliament should remain superior to the courts. In France, laws also cannot be overturned once they are passed, but this is because they are reviewed by the constitutional court for compatibility before they come into force.

The UK has no bill of rights. The traditional English lawyer's position was that rights are 'nonsense on stilts' (Jeremy Bentham) and that people were better protected by procedural safeguards. Better than a right to freedom of expression was a right to go to court and have your case heard by a fair judge. Decency would then be sure to prevail. This position has been modified with the recent Human Rights Act, which gives some domestic legal force to the European Convention on Human Rights (ECHR).

In any case, it is probably fair to say that many European lawyers regard their national systems of rights protection as logical, effective and fair, while those of other countries as incomprehensible, inadequate, or irrational (or vice versa!). From the non-lawyer's point of view, many people have some idea of how they should deal with oppressive government action at home, but no idea how to do it abroad. Not only are systems different, but what is considered oppressive varies. Were the UK government to introduce identity cards, and grant the police the right to check them at will, which is normal in some continental countries, there would be human rights challenges in a moment. Equally, if continental citizens were told that their criminal trials were to be heard by almost entirely untrained and unqualified judges – the position of the English magistrate – they would consider this a fundamental violation of their right to a fair trial. As to the possibility that their future might be decided by a random selection of totally unqualified people – the jury – they would no doubt imagine themselves transported to the dark ages.

Yet having some kind of sense of what one may and may not do, and what one's rights are, and what is considered acceptable, is important to a sense of safety and security. It makes one a lot more comfortable in society. For the economic migrant or the travelling citizen, a sense of vulnerability may accompany their movement abroad. This decreases the quality of their movement, and is a deterrent – a hindrance, as the Court puts it. That vulnerable feeling is probably increased by the fact that migrants lack the networks of social support that natives have. If they are faced with oppressive or difficult situations they are much less well placed to call upon the support of friends, family, the press, or politicians, than a local person would be.

For these reasons, one might think that migrants' rights would be a useful contribution to freedom of movement. The creation of some kind of standard level or form of protection across Europe, directly effective and accessible, would make people feel better about going abroad.

14.1.3 Is the European Convention on Human Rights enough?

All members of the EU are also members of the ECHR. This binds them to a common minimum standard of human rights. It could be seen as an embryonic European rights mechanism. However, there are a number of reasons why this does not remove the argument for Community rights.

First, the ECHR does not demand any particular method of enforcement. Somehow the rights must be respected, but this does not mean that they have to be written into domestic law as such. Thus they do not provide a European-wide concept of rights protection. By contrast, an individual can rely on directly effective Community law in any court in any member state and know that all contradictory national law will be set aside.

Moreover, the ECHR has a doctrine known as the 'margin of appreciation'. This allows member states to have a degree of national autonomy in interpreting rights. By contrast, Community law is uniform throughout the EU. If a common level of rights protection is to be created, it is therefore perhaps the better vehicle.

As well as this, the European Court of Human Rights can only be appealed to after the national appeals process has come to an end. In practice this takes years. Therefore, it is only really useful if national courts respect the Convention. They may do this, but in many cases they are not empowered to set aside conflicting national provisions or acts. For example, in the UK, a conflicting statute still overrides the ECHR. It is, therefore, not possible for the migrant to assume that the ECHR will protect his rights. By contrast, Community law always prevails, and if there is doubt over what it requires, a reference to the European Court of Justice is possible even from the lowest level of court.

But quite aside from these points, the presence of the ECHR is not a reason not to have Community law migrants' rights. National law may forbid discrimination on the grounds of nationality, but this does not mean that the Treaty prohibition on discrimination does not apply. It is possible to have parallel mechanisms of protection. One would expect Community law to be free standing, and to provide the rules necessary to ensure free movement, whatever other mechanisms might also be at work.

14.1.4 When does Community law enforce human rights?

The basic Community law position is that the Community itself is bound by human rights principles, as are the member states when they act within the scope of Community law.

A good statement of this is found in *Grogan*.[2] One of the issues in the case was whether an Irish restriction on advertising abortion was a violation of freedom of expression. Before that could be looked at it had to be decided whether the Court had jurisdiction to assess national rules for compatibility with human rights. The Court referred to one of the other leading cases, *ERT*,[3] and said:

---

2   *Grogan* Case C-159/90.
3   *ERT* Case C-260/89.

... where national legislation falls within the field of application of Community law the Court, when requested to give a preliminary ruling, must provide the national court with all the elements of interpretation which are necessary in order to enable it to assess the compatibility of that legislation with the fundamental rights – as laid down in particular in the European Convention on Human Rights – the observance of which the Court ensures. However, the Court has no such jurisdiction with regard to national legislation lying outside the scope of Community law.

In *Grogan* it was decided that the matter did not come within the services provisions, and so was outside Community law. However, the Court's position is clear: where national legislation, or action, is within the scope of Community law, Community law demands that it respect human rights.

14.1.5 Which human rights?

The rights that the Court protects are Community rights in that the final authority over their content and effect is the Court itself. However, they are inspired by and drawn from national constitutions and traditions, and international agreements, in particular the ECHR. Community rights are a kind of merger of all the statements of human rights found in the member states and the international bodies they are part of. This is now expressed in Art 6 of the Treaty on European Union.

This means that the precise scope of Community rights is not well defined. However, there is no doubt that all the basic and common rights are there: freedom of assembly, and expression, and religion, as well as some that not all member states formerly recognised. For example, the German 'right to trade' has been acknowledged by the Court, in *Hauer*.[4] The complainant said that a Community Directive infringed her right to freedom to pursue a trade, by preventing her using her land to grow grapes. She lost, but the Court accepted that the right was in principle enforceable in Community law.

In general, where the Court wishes to be restrictive of rights it does not do this by restricting the kind of rights it acknowledges, but by restricting the scope of those rights themselves. As in *Hauer* it will require them to be balanced against other considerations, and has been criticised for weighing the rights too lightly in the scales.

As well as these 'common law' Community rights, drawn from other documents, there is also now a Community Charter of Fundamental Rights. This contains a long list of what many would consider to be the most important basic rights.

However, the status of the Charter in law is very unclear. It will probably be binding on the Community institutions, but it is not clear whether it is legally enforceable against member states acting within the scope of Community law, although it is addressed to them. The doubt arises out of its unusual nature: it is a 'joint proclamation' of the Commission, Council, and Parliament. This is not a legal form acknowledged in the Treaty.

Many see the Charter as a first step. Ultimately they hope for a Community bill of rights which would be legally enforceable in all member states – a sort of partial common constitution. However, the political reality is that this is not an immediate prospect.

---

4   *Hauer* Case 44/79.

Because the Charter may progress in this way, a sort of ambiguity has been built into it. It includes rights such as the 'right to education', and not to be tortured, which are not obviously to do with the Community at all. This would suggest a broader role, a Charter binding the member states generally. Yet the Charter's preamble states that 'the Union recognises' the rights, rather than the member states as well. Or are they to be understood as included within 'the Union'?

The only thing that can be said with certainty is that the future role of the Charter is unclear. However, this is perhaps less of a problem than it seems. The wording of the preamble suggests that the role of the Charter is not to create new rights, but to clarify and reaffirm the existing ones. Thus, in itself it may not change the legal position; it just provides a convenient summary.

Therefore the migrant has to assume that the Charter does not provide rights for him at the moment, except against the Community institutions. If he is faced with human rights violations by a member state, the more likely situation, he will have to rely on the basic principles developed in the caselaw. Even if the Charter turns out to have legal force it will not change these principles.

The important question is then whether he can rely on these. Does Community law provide protection for migrants against human rights violations by host member states?

14.1.6 Community rights against member states

The cases mentioned above establish that Community law requires member states to respect the human rights of migrants in all their actions within the scope of Community law. Therefore, if member states implement directives or Community policies or requirements in a way that violates rights, this will be within that scope, and the migrant can protest.

There are also two new directives that prohibit discrimination, or harassment, on grounds of religion, belief, age, or sexual orientation (Directive 2000/78/EC) or race or ethnic origin (Directive 2000/43/EC). They also set out requirements for adequate enforcement of these rights, and are very powerful documents.

However, while the second applies to all matters to do with employment, social advantages, education, and public services, the scope of the first Directive is confined to employment and related matters (vocational training). Thus, although they are a step forward, they do not address all the rights problems and forms of discrimination that may occur in the life of a migrant.

For example, if member state security forces or officials act in an arbitrary or oppressive way, perhaps to the disadvantage of homosexuals, or those of a different religion, this might fall outside the Directives, and outside the Treaty prohibition on nationality discrimination, yet still be a powerful obstacle to migration. National law, or national authorities may not adequately solve the problem. In these circumstances, a ruling from the Court of Justice that Community law requires compliance with basic human rights could be of real assistance to migrants.

To obtain it the migrant would have to argue that the member state action was within the scope of Community law because it was an obstacle to movement. This would be analogous to *Cowan*[5] or *Bickel and Franz*,[6] or *Decker*.[7] The first two cases involved criminal law, and the third social security rules. All of these are, as such, outside the scope of the Treaty, but the Court said they came within it where they were applied in such a way that they caused an obstacle to movement.

However, in those cases, there was nationality discrimination present, which perhaps makes the situation a more obvious Community law matter. In the human rights situation this may not be so. Nationals may suffer as much as foreigners, or where there is discrimination it may be personal and non-rule based. The police or local officials may be prejudiced, but it may be difficult to find a legal basis for this to challenge it! On the other hand, *Bosman*[8] may suggest that discrimination should no longer be a crucial factor. The effect on movement should be defining.

The closest that the Court has come to answering this question directly is in *Kremzow*,[9] in which an Austrian judge wanted Community law to get him out of prison. His trial had already been found by the European Court of Human Rights to be unfair, and so he said he was held in violation of his rights. He said it was a Community law matter because he might want to go abroad to work.

The Court said that a hypothetical possibility of going abroad was not enough to establish a connection with Community law. However, this implies that if there had been a stronger connection he might have succeeded. If he had had a job offer in another member state, or if he was a national of another member state, perhaps his argument would have been good, and there would have been a connection with Community law. Then the situation would have been governed by Community rights.

Another situation may also occur. This is where people or groups who are not part of the state violate rights, and the state does not stop them. For example, groups of thugs may roam areas of town looking for foreigners to attack, and the local authorities may be ineffective in preventing this.

According to the European Court of Human Rights, the state has positive responsibilities to protect those in its territory.[10] If it does not fulfil these responsibilities it can be guilty of a rights violation itself. Thus if the local police ignored violence against foreigners, the state could be found in violation of the ECHR, although that violence was performed by private persons.

If the Community respects the ECHR this reasoning should translate. Then if the authorities do not act sufficiently to protect migrants from xenophobia, and that xenophobia was an obstacle to movement, then perhaps the state could be liable in Community law for that too.

---

5   *Cowan* Case 186/87 and see Chapter 5.

6   *Bickel and Franz* Case C-274/96.

7   *Decker* Case C-120/95.

8   *Bosman* Case C-415/93 and see Chapter 4.

9   *Kremzow* Case C-299/95 and see Chapter 11.

10   Eg, *X and Y v the Netherlands*, (1985) 8 EHRR 235.

14.1.7 Rights and enlargement

At the moment migrants' rights may seem rather academic. It can be argued that national law protects rights to a high standard throughout the Union. However, in 2004 the EU will expand to include a number of former Eastern Bloc countries, making it a much bigger, wider and more diverse body.

Before accession to the Treaties all those countries will have been thoroughly assessed on a number of grounds, of which one is their human rights protection. They all have constitutional structures and legal systems which aim to protect fundamental rights. However, there have still been a number of criticisms made of the situation in some of these countries, particularly the central and south-eastern European ones such as Poland, the Czech and Slovak Republics, Hungary, Bulgaria and Romania. The major one is that the position of Romanies, the people formerly known as gipsies, is not good, either legally or in fact. They suffer high levels of prejudice and persecution wherever they are found.

As well as this, it is claimed that high levels of racism, anti-semitism, and homophobia are found in the former Eastern Europe. Partly this is because non-majority identities were repressed during the 50 years under communism. There were few non-European immigrants, and neither religion nor sexuality were matters of public debate. As a result, people have not grown used to the presence of those that they may think of as not like themselves. Also, old prejudices, lingering from the first half of the 20th century and before, have not been swept away.

In any case, movement to and within the enlarged area of the EU may be considerably less attractive for members of the various kinds of minority than it is within the existing area. This is not to deny that problems exist everywhere, but to suggest that there may be a high level in the East, at least for the near future.

As well as these historical matters, it is also important to remember that the enlargement countries are taking a very big step. The current members of the Union integrated gradually, and free movement was a slowly growing process. Although it is likely that there will be some kind of staged accession for the new countries, they will still be going from relative closure to the West, to openness, at a higher speed than was experienced by the early members.

As well as this there may be problematic reactions to enlargement in the West. Just as hostility to immigrants may be found in the new EU states, so migrants to the West from these states may not always find a proper welcome, and the right-wing groups which lurk in the undergrowth of Western Europe may add Eastern Europeans to their list of targets.

Therefore, migrants' rights may become a considerably more important issue as enlargement occurs. Not only may claims of violations increase, but the help of the Court may be particularly useful. It can be difficult for a national court to go against the prevailing prejudices, and the legal systems of Eastern Europe have been through great change and upheaval in the last decade. Judges there particularly may welcome the support of the Court in defending foreigners' rights.

14.2 THIRD COUNTRY NATIONALS IN THE INTERNAL MARKET

There are many different reasons why someone with non-EU nationality may be living or working in the EU. Some just come to work, some immigrate for other reasons – if they can – some are applying for asylum, and others have come as the family members of EU nationals. The law covering all these people is vast, and includes provisions of national and international, as well as Community, law.

In particular, a number of nations, such as Turkey and some North African countries, have agreements with the EU under which their citizens acquire the possibility to live and work in the EU, under certain conditions.

However, whatever the basis of the residence here, all these people lack one thing that is very useful in the member states: EU citizenship. Here it is asked to what extent the internal market still applies to them. Can they rely on the free movement provisions? Can they rely on the principle of non-discrimination? And what is their position in the light of the Schengen Agreement, and the abolition of border controls?

14.2.1 Third country nationals and economic movement

For the third country national, the free movement of goods is the simplest of the economic articles to deal with. Article 28 applies to all goods moving between member states. It is irrelevant where they come from originally, or who owns them. Thus an American can rely on Art 28 to move goods he has bought from Italy to Sweden, even if they were imported to Italy from China. Once they are within the market, they are free to move.

Article 39 begins with a general statement that 'free movement of workers shall be secured'. This could also apply to third country workers. However, Art 39(2) provides that free movement shall entail the ending of discrimination between 'workers of the member states'. This seems to give a hint that perhaps the article is not so broad. This suggestion is reinforced by the wording of Regulation 1612/68, which speaks throughout as if free movement of workers only applied to nationals of member states.

In fact the caselaw has made it clear that this is the case. A third country national legally living and working in one member state has no Treaty right to move across the border to work in another. In *Caisse d'Allocations*,[11] the Court said:

> Article 48 [now 39] guarantees free movement of persons only to workers of the member states.

This is perhaps not surprising, but it can be harsh for non-EU family members, particularly in border areas. They may have the right to join their spouse in the EU, and to work in the member state where she lives and works, but if the nearest town, with the most jobs, is just across the border, they are excluded from that.

As far as the establishment provisions are concerned, there is no ambiguity. Article 43 requires the removal of restrictions on 'nationals of a member state'.

---

11   *Caisse d'Allocations* Case 238/83.

Article 49 is a little more subtle. It says that free movement of services only applies where the service provider is a member state national. However, the nationality of the recipient is not mentioned. Since the Court has now found that Art 49 contains a substantive right to receive services (see Chapter 5), this opens up the possibility that a third country national established in one member state could claim a Treaty right to travel to another member state as a service recipient. However, this is probably not the case. The cases, notably *Luisi and Carbone*[12] and *Cowan*, have all concerned recipients who are EU nationals. In *Bickel and Franz* the Court said:

> Article 59 [now 49] therefore covers all nationals of member states who, independently of other freedoms guaranteed by the Treaty, visit another member state where they intend or are likely to receive services.

This gives a strong suggestion that non-nationals are not covered.

Similarly, Directive 73/148 implements freedom of movement in the services context, and specifically refers in Art 1(b) to the abolition of restrictions on freedom of movement for recipients, but only for recipients who are nationals of member states. This deliberate narrowing of the Treaty article seems to make a fairly clear point. Non-EU citizens are not to be allowed to benefit from free movement of persons provisions.

The only way that this may be so is where one party to a service transaction is an EU citizen, and the other is not, but is within the EU. Then the EU citizen might still be able to rely on the article and Directive, even though the other party to the transaction is non-EU. However, the third country national will not himself be able to rely on the Treaty. Thus he gets only a sort of indirect benefit from it.

Therefore the overall position of the free movement articles is restrictive with respect to non-EU citizens. From an economic point of view this can be criticised. The free movement articles are deliberately confined to economic actors, because these benefit the member states, without being a drain on them. This is just as true of third country nationals who can work or provide services. To restrict their economic potential within the EU is to some extent contrary to the point of the internal market.

However, the political reality is that member states are not prepared to grant such rights to non-EU citizens. For one thing, the degree of economic activity required to come within the articles is slight; consider tourist 'service recipients' or 'work seekers'. Therefore the articles would be open to abuse by non-EU citizens wishing to move around the EU for non-work-related reasons, or not really intending to engage in meaningful economic activity. Of course this same abuse can occur from EU citizens, and does, but the politics of idle Europeans is less inflammatory than the politics of idle non-Europeans.

Indeed, member states would not even be prepared to allow free economic movement where genuine economic activity could be shown. The right to work in a member state is generally jealously guarded, and extending it to EU nationals has already caused a degree of national trauma. Extension to non-EU persons who are already based in another member state is not imminent.

---

12   *Luisi and Carbone* Case 286/82.

14.2.2 Third country nationals and non-discrimination

Despite the above, some third country nationals, notably family members, will come within the scope of the Treaty. An as yet unanswered question is whether they can rely on Art 12, the general prohibition on discrimination.

It will be remembered that Art 12 applies 'within the scope of this Treaty'. A notable feature of the article is that it refers to the prohibition of discrimination on grounds of nationality, but does not limit this to particular nationalities. Thus a Somali, an American or a Moroccan can rely on Art 12 to prevent discrimination against them based on their nationality, if they can show that they come within the scope of Community law. Therefore, one would think that for family members, for example, the situation would be clear. However, it has not yet been tested in Court, and so it cannot be confidently assumed. Moreover, Art 17 provides that citizens 'shall enjoy the rights conferred by this Treaty'. This seems to suggest that other people might not. On the other hand, many Treaty articles conferred directly effective rights before EU citizenship came into existence. Therefore Art 17 is clearly not the basis of citizens' rights.

If non-EU family members can, or could, rely on Art 12, this would be significant in a number of situations. There are many jobs advertised 'for EU citizens' that would have to be extended to 'EU citizens or their families'.

14.2.3 Schengen

The right to engage in economic activity is one thing. The right to move freely is another. One might think that the open borders resulting from the Schengen Agreement mean that, in reality, free movement is for everyone, whatever the Treaty says. This is not entirely true, although it is to a large extent. This becomes clear from looking at what Schengen did, and how it has been incorporated in the Treaty.

In 1985, in Schengen, in Luxembourg, France, Germany, and Benelux signed an agreement to gradually abolish border controls. This agreement was outside the framework of Community law, but undertook not to interfere with it. The agreement was implemented over the years so that travel within the EU area sometimes involved border checks, and sometimes not, depending whether it was between Schengen countries or others were involved. Other member states gradually joined Schengen, until only the UK and Ireland were left out. The UK did not wish to join, and Ireland felt unable to, since this would prejudice its open border with Northern Ireland (part of the UK).

The UK's reluctance was partly based on the fact that it felt abolishing border controls would expose it to uncontrolled immigration. This was particularly true of the UK, by contrast with other countries, for two reasons. First, as an island, the UK had a better chance of controlling its borders. Maintaining border controls on mainland Europe did not prevent illegal entry, since the long land borders were impossible to police effectively. Thus abolishing border controls was not a great security loss, and by freeing up movement of traffic was an economic gain. Secondly, the UK is unusual in Europe in not requiring its citizens to have identity cards. As a result, the police are unable to stop people and check their papers, as is normal in many member states. Therefore, while these member states retained the potential to control illegal immigration, by checking people's papers after entry, the UK would find this much harder. The loss of border control would be a much greater blow.

The Schengen Agreement was made because these member states were frustrated with the slow Community movement towards abolition of border controls. This was mainly as a result of the objections of the UK. However, it was also because Community law was unclear on the subject. It was not obvious how much openness the law actually required.

The legal position was based on Art 14, which calls for the creation of an internal market, which:

Shall comprise an area without internal frontiers in which the free movement of goods, persons, services, and capital is ensured in accordance with the provisions of this Treaty.

This seems to call for the abolition of frontiers, and so perhaps border controls, in the EU. However, it also says this is to be done 'in accordance' with the Treaty. Thus perhaps Art 14 is not intended to add to the other Treaty articles, but merely to summarise them. In that case it may be that there is not a requirement that border controls be abolished. Moreover, there was always debate about whether this article applied to third country nationals as well as EU citizens.

Therefore, as debate continued, and Community law failed to deliver the free movement of persons, Schengen took over the task. However, although Schengen achieved a great deal, it was subject to criticisms. The rules made under the agreement were extremely complex, and were made in a very secretive way. Moreover, they did not provide rights to individuals, and member states were still able to impose border controls under certain conditions. This, of course, was part of the attraction for some member states, who preferred to keep these matters outside of Community hands.

As well as this, Schengen did not succeed in harmonising the related areas of visas and external border control. This meant that although in many cases it was possible to move freely over the physical frontier, a third country national was still subject to legal obligations that varied from country to country. Papers could still be checked internally, and not complying with national entry requirements could result in fines or expulsion or problems with other matters, such as residence. Therefore, movement was not truly free. The Schengen countries were not so open as to resemble one nation for the purposes of movement.

Thus, both practically and ideologically, Schengen was imperfect. It lacked democracy and accountability to the law, and it had not fully removed frontiers.

Moreover, Community law had been developing. In particular, two things ensured that it reclaimed from Schengen the task of creating a borderless Europe. First, the Treaty of Amsterdam, which came into force in 1999, incorporated the Schengen Agreement within the EC Treaty, and set out a timetable and a method for finishing the task of abolishing internal obstacles to movement. Schengen is therefore now obsolete, although one still sees the name. Secondly, the case of *Wijsenbeek*[13] removed any lingering doubts about Art 14, and made clear that the direction of the law was towards complete abolition of border controls.

---

13   *Wijsenbeek* Case C-378/97.

The Schengen *acquis* was incorporated into Community law via a protocol to the EC Treaty, signed in Amsterdam. The same states are bound to the same extent, but now as a matter of Community law. Moreover, the Treaty adds to the *acquis*. Title IV, called 'Visas, Asylum, Immigration and other Policies related to the Free Movement of Persons', sets out a plan to harmonise these matters, so that free movement of third country nationals can also be assured within the EU.

The provisions in Title IV need to be read with Title VI of the Treaty on European Union, on police and judicial co-operation in criminal matters. The movement of criminals was another factor delaying the complete removal of border controls. Together, the aim is to fill the gaps in Schengen, which had not fully completed its development, and extend Community co-operation to cover a broader area – visas and crime and so on – so that full free movement can be accepted. This aim is summarised in Art 62 EC:

> The Council, acting in accordance with the procedure in Art 67, shall, within a period of five years after the entry into force of the Treaty of Amsterdam, adopt
>
> (1) measures with a view to ensuring, in compliance with Art 14, the absence of any controls on persons, be they citizens of the Union or nationals of third countries, when crossing internal borders …

However, the path towards this is complex. Rather than immediately binding provisions, the Treaties empower the Council to take steps to achieve the ends. For example, Art 63(4) provides that the Council may pass measures defining the:

> Rights and conditions under which nationals of third countries who are legally resident in a member state may reside in other member states.

Very many measures have been taken, and many more are in the pipeline. However, there is as yet no complete body of law, and so no clear overall picture. It seems likely that in the longer term, the rights of third country nationals who are long-term residents will be made as close as possible to those of EU citizens. However this leaves open the conditions of legality of such long-term residence, and also the rights of other third country groups.

One problem is that dealing with matters in an incremental way, producing secondary legislation addressing technical issues such as the rights of third country workers resident in one member state but then posted to another, though without a clear umbrella principle such as Arts 12 and 18 provide for citizens, leaves third country nationals occupying an ill-defined and uncertain space. If they change their activities or residence just a little, they may find they have fallen outside the law. This uncertainty is increased by the fact that the Court's jurisdiction is limited in this area. It has always been limited over the EU Treaty, but now it is also excluded from aspects of Title IV EC.

Moreover, three nations have only limited involvement. The UK, Ireland and Denmark all have opt-outs in various forms from the development of the Schengen *acquis*, and from the abolition of border controls. While they may co-operate in selected areas, they are not obliged to. Thus the UK is joining the co-operation on cross-border police matters, of which it approves, but not joining in the removal of passport checks.

Therefore, for the third country national an area of true free movement may be opening up, but it may not be an area covering the entire EU.

Moreover, there may be a price to be paid for it. When borders are removed, and visas and immigration harmonised, entry to one country is potentially entry to all countries. This means member states have an interest in rates of immigration from outside the EU to other member states. The Albanian coming to Italy is potentially an immigrant to Germany too. In particular, some of the richer states are worried that they will become the destination for a disproportionate number of the immigrants to the EU, be they legal or illegal economic migrants or asylum seekers.

Therefore, in harmonising immigration the tendency is towards increasingly restrictive policies. A strong external frontier, that is difficult to cross, is the price for openness within. This is the so called fortress Europe tendency: internally open, closed to the outside.

Wijsenbeek came shortly after Amsterdam, and provided a useful interpretation of its significance. The case concerned a Dutch citizen, who refused to show his passport when returning to the Netherlands from another member state. He said this was contrary to both Art 14, and Art 18, the citizen's right to move. This second point has been discussed in Chapter 4.

The Court found that he was wrong: Art 14 did not forbid a member state from maintaining border controls. However, this was only at the present stage of Community law. The reason was that at this moment, the rules on visas for third country nationals, and on entering member states from outside the EU, were not harmonised. A third country national might require a visa for one state, but not for another. Therefore it followed that these people could not have free movement between member states, but could be subject to border control, to make sure they had the right visas. EU citizens, by contrast, did have a free movement right, but member states were still entitled to check their passports, in order to establish that they were indeed EU citizens. The point of the border checks was not to hinder their free movement, but to establish that they did have a right to it. As the Dutch and UK governments argued, 'it is impossible to carry out border controls on a single category of persons'. Since third country nationals could be checked, everyone could be.

The implication of this judgment is that if visas and external border controls were harmonised, as they ultimately will be, then there would be no remaining justification for internal checks. The goal of Art 14 is indeed a borderless EU.

14.3 THE INTERNAL MARKET AND THE WELFARE STATE

This section looks at the tensions between the internal market and the welfare state. These are both legal and economic, and may result in a new approach to welfare provision.

14.3.1 The tension between internal market and welfare state

It is generally a source of pride to Europeans that their nations provide for the basic needs of their citizens. Everyone is normally entitled to education to the highest level they can achieve without high fees, and everyone will receive the health care they need, irrespective of their wealth. Those who are unemployed, or ill, will receive financial help from the state to prevent complete destitution. Even transport is often subsidised so that people can afford to travel, who otherwise would not. These kinds of activities of the state could be broadly summarised as the welfare state. They represent a model of society in which part of the obligation of the government is to look after the most vulnerable members.

In some ways the internal market fits with this philosophy. It should lead to an overall increase in prosperity, and in particular it leads to a reduction in the wealth differences within Europe. The poorer areas of the EU have caught up with the richer ones in recent decades, partly thanks to subsidy, but mainly thanks to free movement between the countries, to the benefits of free trade. Moreover, just as welfare provision is sometimes justified economically, by saying that in fact good education and health care and social insurance makes economic sense – it provides healthy, well-trained workers, for example – the increase in the relative wealth of the poorer European countries is also thought to be good for the others. It provides trading partners and customers, and it increases the stability of Europe. The wealth of all is in the interest of all.

Therefore the broad idea of wealth sharing, and of community solidarity, is not alien to the internal market at all. However, in the internal market it is on a European basis. By contrast welfare states remain national. Responsibility for the welfare safety net remains firmly with the member states, and not the Community. This creates a tension between welfare state and internal market. One is built around national borders, while the other aims to remove them. The economic free movement articles of the Treaty sit very uncomfortably with national provision of care.

As well as this legal tension, there is also an economic one. Although the internal market can be seen as a form of inter-state solidarity, and even of mutual assistance, it does not aim to achieve this through state-to-state action, but through the market. It is free trade which brings the benefits.

This promotes a deregulatory approach to the economy, which has led in recent years to smaller, less economically powerful governments. Vast areas of the economy which used to be state controlled are now privatised, because private companies fit better in a market place, where they can buy and sell each other, and move across borders, in a way that state enterprises cannot. Telecoms, energy and transport are notable examples of this kind of change.

The welfare state begins to look like an anomaly in this context. As the orthodox point of view becomes that private companies do things better, it seems strange that vast areas of economic activity – health and education are the obvious examples – are dominated by the state. The mentality of the internal market can therefore be said to be, to some extent, in tension with the welfare state.

As well as this, the requirements of EMU, although not strictly part of the internal market, are relevant. As discussed in Chapter 6, euro member states are required to limit their financial excesses. This means that the possibility of spending on welfare beyond what 'sound finance' allows is no longer open, or at least is incompatible with the Treaty. This may seem like common sense to some, but to others it is an unjustified subrogation of compassion to accounting.

All of these tensions are real, and their impact can already be seen. Even left-wing governments find it increasingly acceptable to limit welfare and public spending on budgetary grounds, and to involve private organisations in formerly key state activities. There are moves towards less generous provision, or provision under stricter conditions, in many member states, particularly in the areas of social insurance, such as unemployment payments. There can also be said to be a move away from the direct providing state, which achieves its ends through spending its own money, to the regulatory state, which achieves its ends through telling private actors what to do.

However, the tension between the free movement articles and the welfare state is the one which is most based around the law, and which will be expanded upon below.

14.3.2 Free movement law and the welfare state

The most relevant of the economic articles to the welfare state is Art 49, on the free movement of services. Most of what is involved in state care can be seen as service provision of some kind: health services, educational services, even re-training or unemployment or sickness insurance services. One might think that these fall outside the article, as not being economic. However, as was discussed in Chapter 5, at least to some extent this is not true. There is simply too much money involved in welfare for an economic aspect to be excluded. For example, while governments may not aim to make money out of health care provision, the pharmaceutical companies, doctors' surgeries, dental practices, nursing agencies, opticians, and many other organisations that may be relevant to the state health systems do.

Indeed, in some countries, the basic health system is largely operated by private organisations. Hospitals may be private foundations or even companies, and patient costs may be met through private health insurance. What makes this part of a welfare state, rather than a free health care market, is that these organisations will be very tightly regulated, and bound into a national system. However, they remain profit-making organisations. That is enough to ensure that their relations with even non-profit public bodies may be governed by Art 49 – as in Kohll,[14] where the rules of state health insurance were concerned.

In higher education the situation is slightly different. The major organisations, the universities, tend to be public. However, they increasingly behave in a profit-making manner, and as the Court made clear in Wirth,[15] when they do this, they will be subject to Art 49.

The result is that much of what comprises national health and education systems could now be described as economic services. It is important to remember that not all of it can, but the amount of health and education provision subject to Art 49 is probably significant, and also increasing. This would result from the general trend of increased involvement of private organisations with the state, and increasingly commercial behaviour of public organisations. In the following discussion, it is assumed, for ease of discussion, that most health and education does comprise economic services. In the individual case, it would be necessary to examine if this is true.

14   *Kohll* Case C-158/96.
15   *Wirth* Case C-109/92.

In any case, where it is true, this means that restrictions to the entry of foreign providers must be removed. The foreign health insurance company or hospital must be able to offer its services on the same terms as a domestic one, and patients and students must be able to go abroad for care or education on the same terms as they could stay at home. Then rules such as in *Decker*[16] or *Kohll*, where health insurance only refunded dental and opticians' costs if they were from domestic dentists or opticians, become illegal, as would grants for students that were only applicable if they studied at home. The UK student must be able to take her grant to Majorca or Athens, provided she studies there.

In one way this can be seen as a very positive development. The consumer gets more choice, and the mechanism of the market should ensure increasing quality. Perhaps I will go, and take my fees, where the hospitals are cleanest or the universities have the best libraries. It is already the case that the universities across Europe are competing with each other for students and for research funds, and may be becoming more disciplined, and giving students and research consumers a better deal as a result.

One may hope, and free market enthusiasts would believe, that the same will occur in the area of health. However, at least three clear problems can be identified.

One is that the national structures are detailed and complex and not at all created with a view to openness. Indeed, the opposite is true. They have largely been created with a view to ensuring that the entire health or education sector is regulated and controlled and no 'free' activity within it allowed. Tinkering with these structures is difficult. For example, the UK National Health Service is simply not organised in a way that would make it easy for UK patients to be funded to receive treatment abroad. There is no mechanism for this kind of payment.

Also, it is difficult for national systems to monitor foreign providers for fraud or cost-effectiveness. A national health insurance fund, or educational grant-giving body, may not be very happy about paying for treatment or education anywhere in Europe, at the choice of the patient or student. The principles of mutual recognition and mutual trust should deal with this; we have to accept other member state providers. However, the reality is not always as simple as the theory.

Allowing free movement may also undermine domestic relationships. What about the national hospitals or opticians or colleges? Their relationship with the national funding organisations will change, if they can no longer assume an adequate supply of clients. This may mean new contracts, or contracts where they were not previously necessary, but it also may involve new attitudes. It was acknowledged in *Geraets-Smits*[17] that this need for stability could be a legitimate reason for limiting patients to a confined list of service providers, but any principle that these be national would be unacceptable.

As well as the domestic institutions, there is also the problem of the regulatory structure surrounding them. Such is the importance of the services in question, that they will always have to be highly regulated. If this is done nationally, it will inevitably lead to divided markets, as has been the case with financial services. A simple *Cassis* 'strike it down' approach will almost never be possible in such sensitive fields.

---

16   *Decker*, see note 7 above.
17   *Geraets-Smits* Case C-157/99. See also *Müller-Fauré* Case C-385/99.

Therefore there are clear structural and regulatory problems with creating free movement of services. These may not seem significant, but large organisations are notoriously difficult to change, and this is particularly true where they are politically sensitive.

Another kind of problem is essentially economic. The funding of public services is greatly affected by the fact that the money that goes into the services remains within the domestic economy. It pays domestic doctors or teachers or builders, and so benefits the national economy directly. Payments to foreign service providers do not do this. Thus it was argued in *Decker* and *Kohll* that the ability to use medical insurance abroad would undermine the social security system. Its economic basis would be turned upside down. In those cases the Court rejected this argument, but remained open to the possibility that at some point it might become true.

In particular, some member states may be losers, and others winners. Some will be destinations, because of their high quality services, while natives of other countries will go abroad wherever they can. These loser countries will have a very good motivation to restrict their public funding, or to move the arrangements of their services more into private hands, to prevent this draining of government funds abroad. Even the 'winner' countries may have problems. Services are often highly subsidised from taxes. Thus compulsory health insurance may not actually meet the full cost of medical care. If these high quality, high cost, countries receive large numbers of welfare immigrants, then they will be subsidising not just their own poor – the point of the welfare system – but the poor of other countries. There may be a moral argument that they should do this, but it could certainly represent a political problem.

Again, one solution is privatisation, and reduced subsidy. Private companies will calculate the real costs of welfare, and pass this on to the individual customer. Then everyone pays their own costs, and the subsidy problem is solved. However, this creates inequality in the system, and reduces the help given to the poor. This makes it politically difficult for governments to remove subsidy while welfare is still provided by state institutions, and gives them a motive to privatise first. Insisting that private companies must be self-supporting, even if they provide welfare, is much easier than insisting that a state system should not be given extra cash.

Therefore, from every perspective, complying with free movement creates pressures on governments to reduce funding and to privatise.

The third problem arises out of the very idea of economic services. Can a system based on compassion survive a philosophy based on economics? If commercial principles, such as free movement of services, are to lead the restructuring of the welfare state, will this not inevitably lead to a change in its character, and an emphasis on profit above care?

In particular, can private organisations ever provide the same kind of unconditional, non-cost minded assistance as the state can? Don't they simply lack the idealism? Moreover, as deregulation allows them to become less national in character, does this not risk also releasing them from a sense of responsibility to the public?

One possible, if partial, answer to all these fears lies in Art 16, which reaffirms the place in the Community of services of 'general economic interest'. Given 'their place ... in the shared values of the Union as well as their role in promoting social and territorial cohesion' they are to be allowed to operate on 'the basis of principles and conditions which enable them to fulfil their mission'. This is expanded upon in Art 86, which says that undertakings entrusted with such services shall be subject to the Treaty only insofar as that does not obstruct their performance of the tasks.

At first glance this seems to be a protection of welfare, an affirmation that economic law is not to be used to undermine important social functions. It seems to suggest that if free movement were to threaten the national organisation of these, it would cease to apply. However, there are two reasons for doubting whether this is correct.

First, these articles seem to offer a derogation from the Treaty, and while their interpretation is a topic outside of this book, it may be commented that the Court does not seem to be abandoning its usual approach to derogations: it is very slow to use them. Thus it may be that the articles do not add anything to the public policy and health exceptions which have already been considered in *Kohll*. If there was a threat of breakdown, the Court might allow a derogation. A mere nibbling away at the structure would not suffice (see Chapter 5).

Secondly, it is far from clear that welfare services would come within the concept of 'services of general economic interest'. The phrase is usually applied to services such as water, electricity and telecoms, which have been recently privatised. The aim of the article is to ensure that member states can still require the private suppliers to act in the public interest, for example by providing universal telephone connection at a fixed price, which might otherwise be seen as an abuse of a dominant position contrary to Art 82.

However, these services are clearly of general importance to the economy. Business relies upon them. In a long-term sense this is true of health, education and welfare as well, but the link is less direct. They are primarily social services. Thus even though they may be run for profit, they are better described as 'economic services of general interest' rather than 'services of general economic interest'. Articles 16 and 86 may not apply to them.

Another answer to the fear of privatisation may be that the state is not the idealist it once was. Under the sway of current economic and budgetary constraints it can seem as money-minded as an insurance company. However, there is still an understandable reluctance to take welfare provision out of its hands.

14.3.3 The future possibilities

Welfare states are about countries caring for their own people. In the end, there is no place for this in a borderless Europe. Not only does it exclude vast areas of the economy from the internal market, it preserves the political and social divisions between nations. If there is to be the 'ever-closer union' of the peoples of Europe that is called for in the preambles to the Treaties, then compassion has to be on a less nationalistic basis. This means inevitably that it cannot be the monopoly of the state, since states remain fixedly national. Yet private organisations just don't care. They will not on their own provide the level of security and equality Europeans expect. They have to be managed.

The only answer to this seems to be a Community-wide framework, creating a Community-wide market for services such as health and education. The regulation would have to address the same basic issues of burden sharing as does national organisation, in order to preserve the social values that Europeans appear to cherish. However, it would also allow free movement of people and services to continue.

The problem with this is that politically it is not even on the horizon. No member state wishes to begin harmonising health or education. As well as that, it can be argued that the creation of ever larger regulatory structures will result in ever greater bureaucracy, and therefore ever greater inefficiency, and thus perpetuate the worst of national systems, without increasing quality for the consumer.

Reality is likely to fall somewhere in between the extremes. At the moment most of what is proposed in this section is speculative; national welfare states are largely intact. However, the first signs of attack upon them are present, and the history of the Community, from war-ravaged Europe, filled with rubble and hatred, to today, shows that one should not underestimate how much can change, and how quickly.

FURTHER READING AND BIBLIOGRAPHY

Below is a selection of articles in journals, and a few books, which go into more depth, or breadth, on the subjects covered in this book. Sources are generally given in the order the topics appear in the chapter.

Free movement of goods: taxes and duties

Danusso and Denton, 'Does the European Court look for a protectionist motive under Article 95?' (1990) 1 Legal Issues of European Integration 67

Easson, 'Fiscal discrimination: new perspectives on Article 95 of the EC Treaty' (1981) 5 EL Rev 318

Free movement of goods: quantitative restrictions

Gormley, 'Actually or potentially, directly or indirectly? Obstacles to the free movement of goods' (1989) 9 YBEL 197

Heydebrand ud Lasa, 'Free movement of foodstuffs' (1991) 16 EL Rev 391

Reich, 'The November revolution' (1994) 31 CML Rev 459

Gormley, 'Reasoning renounced? The remarkable judgment in *Keck* and *Mithouard*' (1994) European Business Law Rev 63

Oliver, 'Some further reflections on the scope of Articles 28–30' (1999) 36 CML Rev 783

Koutrakos, 'On groceries, alcohol and olive oil: more on free movement of goods' (2001) 26 EL Rev 391

Free movement of persons

Marenco, 'The notion of a restriction on the freedom of establishment and the provision of services in the caselaw of the Court' (1991) 11 YBEL 111

O'Leary, 'Flesh on the bones of EU citizenship' (1999) 24 EL Rev 68

O'Keeffe, 'Union citizenship', in O'Keeffe and Twomey (eds), *Legal Issues of the Maastricht Treaty*, 1994, London: Wiley

Reich and Harbacevica, 'Citizenship on trial: a fairly optimistic overview of recent Court practice with regard to free movement of persons' (2003) 40 CML Rev 615

Free movement of services

Hatzopoulos, 'Recent developments of the caselaw of the ECJ in the field of services' (2000) 37 CML Rev 43

Free movement of capital

Sideek, 'A critical assessment of the ECJ judgment in *Trummer and Mayer*' (1999) 14 Butterworths International Banking and Financial Law 396

Exceptions to free movement

Martin and O'Leary, 'Judicial exceptions to the free provision of services' (1995) 1 European LJ 308

Common principles

Hilson, 'Discrimination in Community free movement law' (1999) 24 EL Rev 445

Johnson and O'Keeffe, 'From discrimination to obstacles to free movement. Recent developments concerning the free movement of workers' (1994) 31 CML Rev 1313

Barnard, 'Fitting the remaining pieces into the goods and persons jigsaw' (2001) 26 EL Rev 35

Davies, *Nationality Discrimination in the European Internal Market*, 2003, Dordrecht: Kluwer Law International

Competition and the internal market

Bork, *The Antitrust Paradox: A Policy at War with Itself*, 1987, London: Basic

Barnard, 'Social dumping and the race to the bottom; some lessons for the EU from Delaware' (2000) 25 EL Rev 57

Ogus, 'Competition between national legal systems; a contribution of economic analysis to comparative law' (1999) 48 ICLQ

Barnard and Deakin, 'Market access and regulatory competition', in Barnard and Scott (eds), *The Law of the European Single Market*, 2002, Oxford: Hart

Harmonisation

McGee and Weatherill, 'The evolution of the single market; harmonisation or liberalisation?' (1990) 53 MLR 578

Weatherill, 'The role of the informed consumer in EC law and policy' [1994] CLJ 49

Dougan, 'Minimum harmonisation and the internal market' (2000) 37 CML Rev 853

The wholly internal situation

Bernard, 'Discrimination and free movement' (1996) 45 ICLQ 82

Nic Shuibne, 'Free movement of persons and the wholly internal rule: time to move on?' (2002) 39 CML Rev 731

Private actors

Baquero Cruz, 'Free movement and private autonomy' (1999) 24 EL Rev 603

Davies, 'Restrictions on private actors', in Davies, *Nationality Discrimination in the European Internal Market*, 2003, Dordrecht: Kluwer Law International

Intellectual property

Marenco and Banks, 'Intellectual property and the Community rules of free movement; discrimination unearthed' (1990) 15 EL Rev 224

Vinje, 'Harmonising intellectual property law in the European Union: past, present and future' (1995) European Intellectual Property Rev 361

Urlesberger, 'Legitimate reasons for the proprietor of a trademark registered in the EU to oppose further dealings in the goods after they have been put on the market for the first time' (1999) 36 CML Rev 1195

Social issues

De Burca, 'Fundamental human rights and the reach of EC law' (1993) 13 OJLS 283

Cremona, 'Citizens of third countries: movement and the employment of migrant workers within the European Union' (1995) 2 Legal Issues of European Integration 87

Barrett 'Family matters: European Community law and third-country family members' (2003) 40 CML Rev 369

Guild, 'How can social protection survive EMU? A UK perspective' (1999) 24 EL Rev 22

Ball, 'The making of a transnational capitalist society' (1996) 37 Harvard International Law Rev 307

Davies, 'Welfare as a service' (2002) 29 Legal Issues of Economic Integration 27

Hatzopoulos, 'Killing national health and insurance systems but healing patients?' (2002) 39 CML Rev 683

INDEX

Art, works of
   customs duties 5–6

Capital
   free movement of
   see **Free movement of capital**

Citizens
   Art 18
   direct effect of 70–71
   free movement of person
     subject to 72–73
   free movement of 2, 66–73
   identifying EU citizens 66–68
   new directive 70
   non-discrimination principle 118–19
   residence right 69–70, 71
   rights of 68–69
   secondary legislation 69–70

Competition
   free movement law and
     differences between 137
     overlap between 138
     relationship between 136–37
   Title VI 135–36
   generally 135
   harmonisation and 139–43
   influence of competition ideas 138–43
   Title VI 135–36

Copyright **186, 193–94**
   see also **Intellectual property rights**

Customs duties
   charges having equivalent
     effect 5
   definition 5
   exceptions 7
   fiscal duties 12
   generally 5
   goods
     exceptions 6
     meaning of 5–6
     money 6
     works of art 5–6
   inspections, compulsory 7–8
   internal taxation appearing
     as charge 8–9
   levy on domestic producers 9–10

   meaning 5
   no equivalent domestic goods
     produced, where 10–11
   payment for service 7–8
   purpose of charge 6
   refunds of taxes 11
   works of art 5–6

Discrimination
   Article 12 . . . . 118–19, 120
   Articles 17 and 18 120–22
   caselaw 119–22
   citizenship 118–19
   defining 122–26
   direct discrimination 123–24
   economic articles and 118, 120–22
   effects 122–23
   equal treatment 123
   generally 117
   indirect discrimination 17, 124–26
   intention 122–23
   principle of non-
     discrimination 117
   reverse discrimination 163, 169–72
   social advantages 120–21
   students 66
   third country nationals and 207

Discriminatory taxation
   alcohol 17–18
   cars 16–17
   consumer preference 14
   direct imposition 13
   equal treatment 12–15
   generally 12
   globalisation 16–18
   indirect discrimination 17
   indirect imposition 13
   internal taxation, meaning of 13
   justification 18
   other products, protection of 15–16
   product, meaning of 12
   progressive tax 16–17
   refunds of taxes 11
   similar domestic products 13–15
   third country imports via other
     member states 12–13

E-commerce
 Directive 2000/31 158–62
 harmonisation 158–62
 meaning 158

Economic and monetary Union (EMU) . . . 94

Economic policy
 of European Community 94–95

Enlargement of Community
 human rights and 204

Equal treatment 123
 see also Discrimination

**Establishment,
 freedom of**
 see **Freedom of establishment**

Euro, the **94, 95–97**

European Central Bank (ECB) 94, 97–98

**European System of Central
 Banks (ESCB)** **94, 97**

Export restrictions
 see **Quantitative restrictions**

Families
 established people, of 59, 60
 gay marriages 50–51
 self-employed persons, of 59
 workers, of 48, 49–50

Fiscal duties **12**

Football transfers **55–57, 127**

Free movement
 capital
  see Free movement of capital
 competition and 135–38
  differences between 137
  overlap between 138
  relationship between 136–37
  Title VI 135–36
 convergence 130–33
 exceptions
  acceptability of measures 113–14
  articles 99–101
  capital 101

Community concept 102
Directive 64/221 100
domestic action 106–08
economic factors 109–10
environmental
 considerations 110–12
establishment 100
generally 99
goods 99–100
half measures 108–09
human rights 114
intellectual property 99
interpretation of 102–14
judging the threat 105–13
member states acting
 honestly 103–04
mutual recognition 114
objective justifications
 distinguished 101–02
personal conduct 112–13
persons 100
presence of Community
 measures 105–06
proportionality 47, 113–14
public service 115–16
restrictive interpretation 103
seriousness of threat 104–05
services 100
workers 100
generally 1
goods
 see Customs duties; Discriminatory
 taxation; Quantitative restrictions
human rights 114
intellectual property rights 186–87
persons
 see Free movement of persons
private actors and
 see Private actors
services
 see Free movement of services
welfare state and 212–15

Free movement of capital
 development of 89–92
 economic policy 94–95
 exceptions 101
 future of 92–94
 generally 58, 89

monetary policy 94, 95–98
property ownership 91
public policy exceptions 101
security exceptions 101
shareholding cases 92

Free movement of goods
  see **Customs duties; Discriminatory
  taxation; Quantitative restrictions**

Free movement of persons
  citizens
    direct effect of Art 18 70–71
    free movement of person
      subject to Art 18 72–73
    generally 2
    identifying EU citizens 66–68
    new directive 70
    non-discrimination principle 118–19
    residence right 69–70, 71
    rights of 68–69
    secondary legislation 69–70
  establishment
    see Freedom of establishment
  exceptions 100
  generally 2, 41
  students 65–66
    Directive 93/96 65–66
    non-discrimination 66
    vocational training courses 65–66
  workers 41–58
    exceptions 100
    see also Workers

Free movement of services
  administrative or bureaucratic
    requirements 80
  cold-calling 84
  exceptions 100
  freedom of establishment
    distinguished 75–76
  generally 75
  immoral activities 78–79
  meaning of services
    generally 75
    non-economic things
      distinguished 77–79
    other economic factors
      distinguished 75–76
    medical services 78

moving provider 79–81
moving recipient 81–83
moving service 83–84
problems of services 84–87
proportionality 80
public service exceptions 77, 115–16
registration requirements 80
social advantages 81
university education 77–78

Freedom of establishment
  companies 58
  exceptions 100
  free movement of services
    distinguished 75–76
  generally 58
  meaning of 'establishment' 58
  rights of established people
    families 59, 60
    generally 58–59
    qualifications 61
    regulatory requirements 63–65
    secondary legislation 59
    social advantages 59–60
  self-employed persons 58, 59

Gay marriage **50–51**
Globalisation
  discriminatory taxation 16–18

Goods, free movement of
  see **Customs duties; Discriminatory
  taxation; Quantitative restrictions**

Harmonisation
  arguments against 140–41
  arguments for 141–42
  competition and 139–43
  e-commerce 158–62
  effect of 153
  examples 155–62
  framework harmonisation 142–43
  generally 2, 145
  informal harmonisation 145
  judicial harmonisation 145–46, 154–55
  legal base 150–53
  legislative harmonisation 146, 154–55

meaning 145–47
minimum harmonisation 142–43, 146
negative harmonisation. 145–46
new approach 147–49
    criticisms of 149–50
old approach 147–49
optional harmonisation 146
partial harmonisation 146
qualifications, recognition
    of 61–62, 155–57
tax harmonisation. 140

Homosexual marriage **50–51**

Human rights
    Community Charter of
        Fundamental Rights 201–02
    Community law on 200–01
    Community rights against
        member states 202–03
    enlargement of Community and 204
    European Convention 200
    free movement. 114
    generally. 197–98
    migrants' rights. 199, 203
        Konstantinidis 198
    protected rights. 201–02

Import restrictions
    see **Quantitative restrictions**

Intellectual property rights
    acquisition of 185
    changed products. 191–92
    consent 190–91
    copies 193
    copyright 186, 193–94
    different trade marks in different
        countries 192–93
    economic considerations. 194–95
    in Europe 185–86
    exceptions to free movement 99
    exercise of. 187–88
    exhaustion of. 189–93
    existence of 187–88
    fakes 193
    free movement 186–87
    generally. 185
    imports from outside EEA 193

meaning of 'intellectual property' 185
using 188–89

Internal market
    meaning 1

***Lex specialis* rule** **41**

Market access
    caselaw 128–30
    open markets in internal
        market 127–28

Monetary policy
    of European Community 94, 95–98

Part-time workers **43–44**

Patents
    see **Intellectual property rights**

Persons
    free movement of
        see Free movement of persons

Private actors
    binding of. 175–76
    free movement law,
        application of 176–84
    generally. 175
    indirect control of 182–84
    mixed public/private bodies 177–78
    ordinary 180–82
    private rule-making bodies 178–80

Qualifications
    recognition of 61–62, 155–57

Quantitative restrictions
    Article 28 20–37
    Article 29 37–39
    Cassis de Dijon. 26–27, 28,
                                        29, 31, 32, 33, 35
    Danish Recycling 31
    Dassonville 21–22, 28, 32, 33
    definition 19
    discriminatory measures. 23–25

export restrictions. 37–39
generally. 19, 117
German Beer 30
import restrictions 20–37
indistinctly applicable
    measures. 25–26
Keck 32–34, 35–37
measure, meaning of 19–20
measures having
    equivalent effect 20–21, 23–24
objective justification 26–27, 28–31
private measures. 20
public measures 20
rule of reason. 22–23, 28
selling arrangements 31–37
    meaning 34–35
socio-economic rules 31–32, 34
Sunday trading. 31–32

Residence permits **46, 47–48**

Residence, right of **68–69, 71**

Reverse discrimination **163, 169–72**

Schengen Agreement
third country nationals and 207–10

Self-employed persons
freedom of establishment 58, 59
human rights. 198

Selling arrangements
meaning 34–35
quantitative restrictions. 31–37

Semi-workers
rights of 54–55

Services
free movement of
    see Free movement of services

Social advantages
economic migrants. 72–73
established people, for. 59–60
non-discrimination principle 120–21
service providers, for 81
workers, for 52–54

Social issues

see **Human rights; Third country
nationals; Welfare state**

Students
Directive 93/96 65–66
free movement of 65–66
non-discrimination. 66
vocational training courses. 65–66

Sunday trading **31–32**

Third country imports
discriminatory taxation. 12–13

Third country nationals
economic movement 205–06
generally. 205
non-discrimination principle 207
Schengen Agreement. 207–10

Trademarks
see **Intellectual property rights**

Welfare state
free movement law and. 212–15
tension between internal
    market and 210–12

Wholly internal situation
abstract questions. 172–73
facts within scope of
    Community law 164–69
generally. 163
meaning 163
reverse discrimination. 163, 169–72

Workers
amount of earnings 43–44
collective agreements. 48–49
families of. 48, 49–50
    divorce and. 49–50
football transfers. 55–57, 127
free movement of 41–58
    exceptions. 100
    gay marriage 50–51
job seekers 45, 54
language requirements 52
meaning 42–45
no employment contract, where 44–45
part-time work 43–44

residence permits 46, 47–48
rights
  collective agreements 48–49
  Directive 68/360 . . . . 45, 46–48
  families 48, 49–50
  football transfers 55–57
  gay marriage 50–51
  generally 45
  language requirements. 52
  practices excluding
    foreigners. 51–52
  Regulation 1612/68 48–49,
                                              51–54, 55
  semi-workers 54–55
  social advantages 52–54

social security and benefits
  systems. 44
tax advantages. 52–54
semi-workers. 54–55
trainees 43
unpaid workers. 44–45
work
  amount of 43–44
  earnings. 43–44
  formalities. 44–45
  meaning 42–43
work seekers 45, 54

Works of art
  customs duties 5–6